TRIBAL COHESION IN A MONEY ECONOMY

TRIBAL COHESION
IN A MONEY ECONOMY

A STUDY OF THE MAMBWE PEOPLE
OF NORTHERN RHODESIA

by

WILLIAM WATSON

Lecturer in Sociology in the University of Manchester
Sometime Research Officer of the Rhodes-Livingstone Institute

Published on behalf of

THE RHODES-LIVINGSTONE INSTITUTE

NORTHERN RHODESIA *by*

MANCHESTER UNIVERSITY PRESS

© 1958   C.1

Published by the University of Manchester
at THE UNIVERSITY PRESS
316–324, Oxford Road, Manchester, 13

U.S.A.
The Humanities Press, Inc.
303, Fourth Avenue, New York 10, N.Y.

Reprinted 1964

Printed in Great Britain by Butler & Tanner Ltd., Frome and London

FOREWORD

MANY social scientists and many Government commissions have discussed the problems created in Africa by labour migration; and Dr. Watson has been able to base his analysis of how Mambwe tribal cohesion has persisted through large-scale migration on excellent earlier work. He refers to this other work in his text. Most of my references are to works listed in his bibliography. Yet I, as an anthropologist who has spent many years studying the process of labour migration both in the field and in the library, consider that Dr. Watson tells us something substantially new about it. This is perhaps the best overall analysis I know of the political and economic reaction of a single tribe to the constant temporary migration of its able-bodied men to distant labour centres.

Watson has asked me to put his book into perspective against previous studies in the region. Briefly, then, from its early years on, the Administration in Central Africa encouraged the flow of labour from tribes to farms and mines and towns, as in the best interests of the tribes as well as of the settlers and Government. But this flow of labour grew, and soon the Administration became concerned about the effect of the absence of the men on tribal life. Their problem was difficult: the tribesmen could only earn money to raise their standard of living and to pay taxes by going out to work, and yet clearly their absence was likely to have deleterious effects on home production and on domestic and political relations. This Government concern reached its climax in the alarming *Report on Emigrant Labour* (1935) in Nyasaland.

The first substantial work by a social scientist in Central Africa was Dr. Audrey I. Richards' study of the Bemba of North-Eastern Rhodesia (made from 1932 to 1934); and her major analysis, *Land, Labour and Diet in Northern Rhodesia* (1940), stressed the same points as the Nyasaland Report. She described the general impoverishment of Bemba nutrition and of their social life because of the absence of able-bodied men, and the listlessness and general malaise, which I have myself seen in Barotseland, that strikes villages denuded of their men. For among many other important points, she showed that an overall tribal male absentee-rate of

v

50 per cent could be misleading; it suggested that half the men were absent from each village, while she found that in fact some villages might at one time retain most of their men, and other villages have nearly all of their men away and be bound to break up. This picture of the Bemba country was confirmed by a short visit which the late Mr. Godfrey Wilson, first Director of the Rhodes-Livingstone Institute, made to Bembaland to learn Bemba before beginning on a study of the other end of the flow of labour, the mining town of Broken Hill (*An Essay on the Economics of Detribalization in Northern Rhodesia*, in two parts, 1941 and 1942). Wilson took up Richards's theme of, as he called them, 'hungry, manless areas', which 'bought clothes with hunger'. From this he developed the thesis that Central Africa required stabilization of labour in the mining towns, with settled urban populations to provide markets for agricultural development in the tribal areas. Here he drew also on research done with his wife, Professor Monica Wilson, among the Nyakyusa of South-East Tanganyika, and on published work on South Africa. Later the Wilsons expanded this account of unequal urban and rural development into a general theory of unequal change in various social and cultural elements (*The Analysis of Social Change*, 1945). This view of deteriorating tribal social systems was also held by Professor Margaret Read (articles published in 1938 and 1942).

I was the next Rhodesian anthropologist to examine the process, in Barotseland, from 1940 to 1947; and I came with experience in South Africa to support the idea that labour migration impoverished tribal life. Over the years during which I worked in Barotseland, I observed a rapid decline in home production of food as the labour-migration rate rose under demands for more workers during the War. I was less struck by a *general* accompanying decline in political life; and domestic arrangements had persisted substantially though an already high divorce-rate increased as the tribal authorities reduced the period allowed to a man to be away before his wife could sue for divorce. I was impressed, however, by the strong persistence of tribal systems of land tenure: and a general survey showed that as these systems entered the modern economy, the right most emphasized in all Southern and Central African tribes was the right of every man to some arable land, as shown in the way chiefs, when land became short, first took over unused allocated land for the landless, then cut the period of allowed fallows, and then limited the acreage any one man could work. I suggested that chiefs and elders were holding land against the money which the younger men earned away from home, and that the younger men wanted this land against their ultimate retirement from labour migration (*Essays on Lozi Land and Royal Property*, 1943). Watson develops this thesis with greater cogency than it has previously attracted, together with two other theses which I shall shortly discuss.

Nevertheless, when Watson went to study the Mambwe in 1952, the general picture of labour migration which we held was of an impoverishment of tribal life, accompanying hunger and deterioration of tribal production. Watson found the opposite situation among the Mambwe: most of them, both as individuals and in villages and groups of kindred, had profited from labour migration and their standard of living was rising still. His book therefore is the first study which analyses this situation for a British Central African tribe, under labour migration; we have had studies of tribal enrichment from cash-cropping and fishing (e.g. Allan and others, *Land Holding and Land Usage among the Plateau Tonga of Mazabuka District*, 1949). In itself, this detailed interconnected analysis of how the Mambwe have profited from new economic opportunities by deploying their labour on two fronts, and of how their tribal organization enabled them to do this and was affected by the new situation, is excellent; the merit of the book is enhanced by Watson's comparative study and isolation of the various factors which go into producing the total reaction of a tribe to labour migration and new economic goods.

Firstly, the Bemba, the Ngoni and the Barotse, who were studied by Richards, Read and myself respectively, were all powerful raiding tribes, battening on their neighbours, and clearly *pax britannica* would involve them in relative loss. The maize-growing Plateau Tonga (Allan and others, op. cit.) had clearly grown richer under British protection; and this applied also to the Mambwe, who had been raided by the Bemba and by Arab slavers.

The second important set of factors lay in the nature of the tribal system of agriculture/fishing/animal-husbandry. The Bemba lopped trees to provide brushwood for burning to an ash seed-bed for finger-millet, with limited subsequent use of the garden. The presence of men to lop the trees was essential for this system, and it collapsed under their withdrawal. The Lozi of Barotseland were hit in a contrasting way. Where the Bemba productive system was simple, but based on an operation demanding men's labour, the Lozi system was a highly complex one. It involved the use of a dozen different kinds of garden, planted in different places at the same and different times, of fishing-sites exploited simultaneously far apart, of herding cattle yet elsewhere, and so forth. Again, obviously, it is difficult for people to re-deploy their labour in this sort of complex economy when a large number of men begin to go away; and Loziland, which David Livingstone had described as 'a land of milk and honey', and which was still this when I first visited it in 1940, was almost a 'famine area' by 1947. Indeed, it was striking that where the Lozi, in their formerly productive flood-valley,[1] were short of food, the tribes further up the Zambezi had been able to expand the acreages under their relatively simple methods to produce a surplus for export to Loziland, though many of their men were also out at work.[2] On the other hand, in one of the two Mambwe systems of agriculture —an elaborate system of grassland green-manuring—major operations occur simultaneously, and men and women are largely interchangeable, so that if only a limited number of men leave a village it can still maintain its output. Here Watson also emphasizes that men were not leaving full-time agricultural work: he assesses the demands on their labour in the past, in terms of their having been a raided tribe, and shows that before *pax britannica* they had to guard against raiders, herd against carnivores, etc. Now they go out to work; and provided that sufficient men remain to work with the women, the subsistence system keeps the village going in food, and earnings out of wages can be expended on clothes and other modern goods, and on better housing.

But a second set of Mambwe, practising agriculture like that of the Bemba, have also 'done well' out of labour migration. This draws attention to a third set of factors, those involved in the organization of domestic life: the village must consist of a group

---

[1] The late Mr. D U. Peters, Agricultural Officer, in an unpublished study' stressed the very low proportion of cultivable soil in the valley, but the worth of fishing and grazing did not come into his survey.

[2] Dr. V. W. Turner tells me the same expansion has occurred among tribes yet further north.

of men who will co-operate sufficiently for them consciously to
plan their departures to work at labour-centres so that they deploy
their labour successfully on two fronts: that of subsistence agriculture and that of cash-earning. This is an arrangement which
the Bemba could not achieve, so that, as I have quoted Richards,
some villages were denuded of men, others were full of men—
though these were often not working at agriculture but 'resting'.
Watson argues that the Mambwe can handle this situation, even
the ash-planters among them, because their villages have as their
cores groups of men related to one another in the patrilineal line;
and he refers to earlier statements by Richards and Read that a
patrilineal society may be able to organize their absences from
home better thus than a matrilineal one (Richards, *Bemba Marriage
and Present Economic Conditions*, 1940; also Gluckman, *Analysis of
a Social Situation in Modern Zululand*, to be republished in Rhodes-
Livingstone Papers, 1958). Villages in matrilineal societies tend
to have a more diverse group of men, brought together in co-
residence by their marriages to a set of kinswomen, and it seems
more difficult for them to co-operate. This is a gross statement
of the variables, which Watson treats meticulously; for here we
are dealing with a very complex problem. In particular, it seems
that societies with matrilineal descent groups and either uxorilocal
or virilocal marriages will vary considerably in their reaction.
Thus Marwick describes Cewa matrilineages as less seriously disrupted by labour migration than the conjugal family, but it is
a very bare statement.[1] Watson opens the way to a better analytic
treatment of these variables.

Watson's analysis is based not on gross qualitative assessments
but on a steady deployment of various factors, numerically stated,
as they affected a series of village groups. He describes the local
employment available in Mambweland, the two main centres of
distant employment in Tanganyika and the Copper belt, the way
these are exploited by different villages and men of different ages,
and many other geographical/historical/social factors. He even
gives us, for the Mambwe, a numerical measure of the proportion
of men whose absence a village can tolerate without breaking
up: it is roughly that there must not be more than two women

---

[1]'The Kinship Basis of Cewa Social Structure', *South African Journal of Science*,
xlviii, 8 (1958), pp. 258–62.

per man in a village. He first describes the background situation carefully, with analysis reduced while he puts us in possession of his facts; then he moves to careful analysis which explicates the complex reaction of tribal systems to labour migration. The analysis itself is pulled together towards the middle of the book, when he comes to consider the significance of land and the tribal political system in modern Mambwe life. It is here that I consider Watson has lifted his analysis above the level reached by earlier students.

Watson stresses that though the Mambwe have profited materially from entry into a cash-economy, this economy is hazardous for them. They remember loss of work in the great depression; they know that sickness, or old age, will throw them back on the land, and have among them living examples to prove this; the labour-centres do not provide places where they can rear their families satisfactorily; wages are not high and must be backed by subsistence agriculture. Hence they remain, as he puts it, peasants raiding the cash-economy for goods. They see their security in the land, and in doing so they accept with the land the whole tribal system of political and domestic arrangements in which they hold and work the land. This basic point has nowhere been as well demonstrated as in this book, for here we learn more sharply than before, how tribal cohesion survives into a cash-economy. Watson shows us that tribal cohesion survives not despite labour migration, but because of the conditions in which the Mambwe participate in the cash-economy as labour migrants. Powers of chiefs may have changed, and domestic arrangements have altered, but the tribal social system endures on the land which is the Mambwe's main security. And we can assume that unless there are radical changes in the industrial sector, or the land becomes grievously over-populated, the tribal system can continue to endure.

Watson stresses that here, in Mambweland, 'tribalism' survives as a whole system of political and domestic relations. Government policy has supported the chiefs. In addition membership of the tribe and allegiance to the chief give a man a right in land as a Mambwe, as against Africans of other tribes. This basic point has been demonstrated by Dr. E. Colson in her *The Makah Indians* (Manchester University Press, 1954). With allegiance to the chief goes acceptance of a whole range of political relations with associated customs and beliefs. But land is held in the Mambwe system through subordinate political groups, and ultimately through a place in kinship relations. And as we have seen, the kinship group alone enables a Mambwe to earn his living on two widely separated fronts. Hence also the system of kinship and family culture survives. Indeed, as Watson shows in a brilliant analysis paralleling that by Professor Mitchell of *The Yao Village* (1956), even where a village breaks up because it has too few men, or because as an abode of Jehovah's Witnesses it is suppressed by the authorities, the old agnatic structure of the central core reasserts itself.

Tribalism thus survives in the rural areas as a working system of political and domestic relations based on the land. He contrasts this situation with the persistence of tribalism in the urban areas, as analysed by Mitchell (*The Kalela Dance*, 1957) and A. L. Epstein (*Politics in an Urban African Community*, 1958). They have shown that tribalism in urban areas is something quite different from tribalism in the rural areas: in urban areas, tribal ties link people in many forms of association, but are not an organized system of relations involved in the bases of production or in political authority. Tribal affiliation is a first category for defining people in the heterogeneous populations of the towns, and Mitchell has shown that special links, often of a joking kind, develop between various tribes. Thus Watson's work in the rural areas, and his colleagues' work in the urban areas, complement one another.

The basis of the continuing tribal system is the land; and land is the ultimate security for the Mambwe in so far as they participate in the modern economy. This general process, Watson points out, also occurred during the industrial revolution in Britain.[1] Hence the land has nowadays high political as well as economic value. Watson suggests that this is why the Mambwe, like other Africans in Central Africa, were so afraid that the establishment of Central African Federation threatened their security on the land. Any political change might strike at the central core of their lives; for even while young men and women desire to go to the towns to earn a living, they feel that in the end they will spend their middle years and their old age in the tradi-

---

[1]Dr. J. van Velsen has stressed the same point in a study of modern life among the Lakeside Tonga of Nyasaland (unpublished doctorate thesis at Manchester University, in press).

tional tribal system. He shows that, as Professor Schapera found
in Bechuanaland, it is important in assessing changes in allegiance
due to labour migration, to look at these at the different stages
of an individual's life. And in the end attachment to the tribal
land remains. The chief therefore, as trustee for the land, was
thrust into the position of opposing Central African Federation;
and the principal Mambwe chief was deposed for his resistance
to agricultural measures affecting the land.

Watson has described these events in some detail, though they
raise matters which were highly controversial during the Central
African Federation debates. This is necessary for his analysis, since
the crisis exhibited sharply the political conflicts and interlinkages
with which his analysis is concerned. And the exhibition of this
detail of actual political crises fits in with one important trend
in modern anthropology, against the earlier tendency of anthropologists to content themselves with general statements on political relations.[1] Here, in describing the Mambwe opposition to
Central African Federation, Watson is moving on delicate ground,
since there was considerable debate at the time about the extent
and basis of this opposition. Watson is himself aware that one
person cannot observe everything, and cautiously states on the
basis of his own data that the 'majority of the Mambwe appeared
to be opposed' to the proposals for the Federation. But he shows
how this opposition, and its expression in worry about the
security of their land, are related to persisting tribalism in the
modern industrial situation.

This, then, is a first-class account of the reaction of the Mambwe
to their new economic situation, and an excellent analysis of how
far and in what manner their traditional social system has persisted
and changed, and of what new forms of social relations have
emerged. Beyond that, I add for my own colleagues, it is a study
which presents new and illuminating material on the more
'orthodox' problems of traditional anthropology. I have space to
mention only a few. Watson's analysis of the tribal structure, as
a system of organized relations between groups on the land, feeds
into our main stream of thought and helps it flow more strongly.

---

[1]Contrast among modern studies, L. Fallers, *A Bantu Bureaucracy* (Soga of
Uganda), and A. W. Southall, *Alur Society* (also Uganda): both publications
are undated, but appeared in 1956-7.

He shows how, as among Tallensi and Barotse, the spirits of dead rulers operate at several levels of political organization: each royal cenotaph has power to affect not only its local area, but also the whole country. For (as Professor Fortes showed for the Tallensi) among the Mambwe the land is divided among different groups, but The Land is also the basis for the existence of all men and specifically of the Mambwe tribe. Watson also shows in a series of detailed studies of particular villages how these may pass through a cycle of development and dismemberment, with the constant reassertion of the patrilineal principle, so that old villages continue, or new villages are founded, around a core of agnates. These developments, based in the continuing and expanding need for a co-operative group of kin, have to be understood by examining the age-cycle of villages and the points attained in their life-cycle by important men in the groups concerned. The young man interested in the new things that the British sector of life offers, passes the age when he can go out to work, and his ambitions perforce turn back to the good things of the tribal system, in which he lives his middle and old age. Since the study was made in 1952, Watson cannot help but stress how modern variables affect these processes of village development: how the situation of villages varies according to the schooling, skill, local employment, or religious affiliation of its men, as well as by the royal or commoner attachment of their headmen.

Of outstanding interest is his analysis of the genealogies of the royal clan in relation to political authority over land and people. One of my Manchester colleagues, learned in another sphere, has told me that the Greeks deliberately altered their genealogies to accommodate extant political alignments. This point was important in Professor Evans-Pritchard's study of *The Nuer* (Clarendon Press, 1940), which deals with a system of genealogies approximately 11–12 generations deep—a figure recorded also for the Bedouin of Cyrenaica by Evans-Pritchard, the patrilineal Tallensi and the matrilineal Ashanti of the Gold Coast by Professor Fortes, the Barotse of Northern Rhodesia and the Zulu of Natal by myself, the Polynesian Tikopia by Professor Firth, and for other societies. A depth of 11–12 generations, since it occurs so frequently, is unlikely to be historically valid, and it cannot be mere chance. It must correspond to some persistent features in particular types of social system, such as those elucidated by

Evans-Pritchard for the Nuer. He stressed that there is some foreshortening of the genealogies, in a stabilized system of relations
between territorial groups, though he also suggests that genealogies
are kept constant in depth by tribal splits.[1] 'Nuer-type' systems
are not found in Central Africa, where genealogical foreshortening
takes place by different processes. Dr. Cunnison particularly has
made a series of analyses of these processes among the Lunda
of the Luapula valley.[2] He shows that the shapes of genealogies
vary in different parts of the population, and that some genealogies are persistently foreshortened through the institutions of
positional succession and perpetual kinship, and by certain modes
of grouping kin together in terminology. Under positional succession an heir replaces and becomes his dead predecessor (as in
the Roman *universal succession*, whose importance Sir Henry
Maine emphasized so strongly). That is, the heir becomes a social
position; and this position, if it is politically important, may be
linked to other important positions by kinship ties which persist
independently of who are the incumbents of the positions. These
ties Cunnison called 'perpetual kinship', a usage followed by
Mitchell in his study of a similar situation among the Yao. In
this way, a series of positions which are at the head of kinship
groups are permanently linked as kin or in-laws; and these links
are part of the enduring structure of the tribe. This type of kinship, 'political kinship', is quite different from kinship links in
domestic and personal life—and the advance of work here has
made it confusing to speak any longer of 'kinship systems'.
There are political and domestic and other relations, affected by
different types of kinship. It also seems to suggest that we must
approach the study of kinship terminologies, abstractly, with
great caution. These terminologies may not be consistent in terms
of domestic arrangements—marriage, personal links, affiliation of
children; on the contrary, kinship systems may contain incon-
sistencies and anomalies because they deal with different types of
social process. Evans-Pritchard saw that the changing network of
extant relations, which are affected by demographic biological
and social chance, are in time among the Nuer stabilized in

---

[1] Dr. E. Peters has developed this analysis considerably in an as yet unpublished
work on the Bedouin, and a Lebanon village, as well as on the general problem.
[2] See Watson's bibliography.

permanence as a political structure on the land. I indeed suggest
—though he did not—that the Nuer institution by which a
woman can marry another woman, acting as a man and becoming
a *pater* to children fathered on her wife by some kinsman, has
an importance far out of proportion to its actual numerical
occurrence. It may enable groups related to local aristocrats
through uterine descent from a woman to assert that the woman
'fathered' and did not 'give birth' to them; and thus to change
their allegiance from a maternal link to an agnatic one in terms of
the dominant ideology of Nuer society. This seems to have
happened among the Zulu.

In Cunnison's system, the stabilization of kinship relations takes
place through the identification of a man's brothers with his
sisters' daughters' sons. Both these relatives are called *wesu*: it is
not that a 'sister's daughter's son' is called by the same term as
'a brother'; there is only one term by which these kinsmen two
generations apart refer to one another. Positional inheritance
among the Lunda is to uterine brother, or to sister's son, or to
sister's daughter's son—preferably to the first and third. But this
means that all males in a matrilineal lineage can only address and
refer to one another by terms spread over two generations, and
heirs can only be distinguished in those generations. When a
section of a lineage breaks away from its parent group, its leader
must therefore have stood as *wesu* (brother or sister's daughter's
son), or as sister's son, to the leader of the parent group; and the
new group's leader's successors are therefore fixed by positional
succession and perpetual kinship within these two possible relations to the original leader. Hence as new lineages form there
develops an expanding, fixed band of positions within two generations; and Cunnison has cogent evidence to show that the founders
of some of these positions must have lived many decades apart.
The fruitfulness of their distant ancestresses, of which Lunda boast,
as against the comparative sterility—and hence immorality—of
their living kinswomen, which they berate, must be fictitious:
Cunnison shows that old positions, descended from a distant
ancestress, must be accumulating *wesu*'s and sisters giving birth
to sisters' sons, through history. *Sisters and brothers* 'move up' the
genealogy, for they are sisters and brothers to a position. Below
this fixed band of two generations come the living members of
the various lineages, up to five generations of living people, so

that Lunda genealogies of this type tend to be about seven generations deep.

Watson develops this analysis for the patrilineal Mambwe,
where on top of the living five generations comes a fixed band of
three generations of inheritable positions linked by perpetual
kinship as father and sons, brothers and brothers, grandfather and
grandsons. (Is the three against two generations here a reflex of
patriliny as against matriliny?) These positions are those of the
paramount chief, chiefs under him, and royal headmen under
them. New positions are formed here under the rule that only
sons born in the purple, and therefore often only younger sons,
can succeed their fathers. Powerful fathers therefore create new
sub-positions for their elder sons: but the sub-position, established
for a son descended from a wife separate from the wife who will
bear the main heir, is created when the father holds a chieftainship, not before. Hence the new post is always 'son' to a chieftainship; and the fixed band at the top of the royal genealogy does
not increase in depth. *Wives* giving birth to sons holding new
positions are wives of the position which made the post, and they
'move up' the genealogy. Ancient chiefs may not have been as
many-wived as tradition makes them out to be. Here the significant point in the kinship terminology is that an elder brother (for
there is fraternal as well as filial succession) is addressed as *tata*,
'father', so that all successors in time appear as 'sons'. Here then
is a big further advance in our understanding of genealogical
manipulation, and of systems in which political links are always
stated in terms of kinship.

With all these contributions to our knowledge, I can commend
this book to anthropologists, economists and political scientists;
to the officials, politicians, and peoples of Central Africa; to everyone interested in Africa and in human society.

MAX GLUCKMAN

Department of Social Anthropology,
The Victoria University of Manchester.
December, 1957.

CONTENTS

LIST OF TABLES

LIST OF FIGURES

LIST OF PLATES

PREFACE

EVERY year in Northern Rhodesia thousands of African tribesmen put aside their hoes and migrate to the copper-mining towns in search of work and wages. After a year or two at work they return to their tribal lands and resume their cultivation. The ceaseless movement of these Africans in search of work is an important part of the economic and social life of the country, and has had a profound effect on both African and European communities. The Mambwe people who are the subject of this book are involved in this system of migrant labour, and at any one time more than half of all the active men between the ages of twenty and forty are absent from their villages earning wages in the towns. I have tried here to describe and analyse some of the effects of this exodus on Mambwe life and politics.

I shall try to show that the industrialization of Central Africa, which has brought about so many cultural changes, has not yet destroyed the cohesion of Mambwe society. Although the Mambwe are now accustomed to work in mines and factories, they still depend on the land for the greater part of their living, and Mambwe tribal cohesion is related to traditional Mambwe rights to the use of land for specific methods of subsistence cultivation. This type of cultivation is an integral part of the past and present Mambwe social organization, and Mambwe institutions cannot be fully understood without a description of their environment and mode of life. Accordingly, I have given a general account of the country and the people, their motives in seeking work, and the labour markets to which they apply. The Mambwe village is a basic residential and political unit of their society, and I have endeavoured to trace the changes that have taken place in the structure of the village during the last sixty years—that is, since the British came—together with the effects of wage-labour on the present-day village. I use the term 'wage-labour' throughout to distinguish the labour that the Mambwe expend on earning money from the labour they expend on cultivating their fields. I have described the larger territorial groupings into which villages are organized, and examined the clan and lineage system in relation both to these groups and to the internal political system.

Finally, I have attempted to analyse the effects of wage-labour on the political structure (particularly the position of the chief), and the entry of the Mambwe on to a wider political stage involving many other groups, both African and European.

The fieldwork was carried out when I was an officer of the Rhodes-Livingstone Institute, between July 1952 and October 1953. I again visited the Mambwe between June 1954 and September 1955, but have relied almost entirely on the material gained during my first visit.

When I arrived among the Mambwe in 1952, they were much disturbed by the proposed incorporation of Northern Rhodesia within the new Federation of Central Africa. They feared that they might lose their land when Federation was implemented, and were in a suspicious and unco-operative mood. These circumstances were unfavourable for sociological research, for the Mambwe suspected all Europeans, and distrusted my motives in asking questions. On the other hand, the critical political situation helped to clarify the division of interests between Africans and Europeans, and the strains that wage-labour had thrust on the Mambwe social system. I am glad to say that the Mambwe lost their distrust of my motives, and I render my warmest thanks to the many Mambwe, both chiefs and commoners, who gave me their confidence and befriended me at a time when the relations between Africans and Europeans were not altogether happy. The sturdy independence and robust humour of the Mambwe made living among them a pleasure.

My colleagues at the Rhodes-Livingstone Institute have been an unfailing source of encouragement and inspiration, and I owe them a debt of gratitude for their advice and criticism, particularly at the two conferences in Lusaka during my period of research. Dr. A. L. Epstein visited me in the field, and has allowed me to refer to his unpublished research work among the Bemba. Dr. V. W. Turner corresponded with me on the subject of labour migration. Miss E. M. Richardson also visited the Mambwe while I was with them, and helped me also with Bemba material. Dr. J. Van Velsen has discussed the problems of migrant labour at great length, both in Africa and England. Miss M. McCulloch lightened the burden of administrative work by her efficiency and commented on my work. I am grateful to them all for the interest they have shown.

My fieldwork would have been impossible without the advice and stimulation of Professor J. C. Mitchell, who was then Director of the Institute. He has discussed my ideas with me and made many constructive suggestions and criticisms. He visited me in the field at a time when matters were not going well, and his support then, and his confidence in the outcome of my research, were invaluable. He read and annotated the manuscript; if it is deficient, the fault is entirely my own. My association with him has been most fruitful and happy.

I wish to express my especial appreciation of Professor Max Gluckman for his support and encouragement. His knowledge of Central African peoples was made freely available to me, and his insight into social life and sociological problems has illuminated for me much that was dark and obscure. Both in preparing the field trip and supervising my writing, his generous help has been of the utmost value.

I must acknowledge particularly the assistance of my clerk, Mr. W. M. Pearson Mwanza, a Mambwe of ability and experience. His travels have taken him to many parts of Africa and even to England, and he took a personal interest in the research.

My wife was a constant support in the trying conditions of the field. Her friendship with Mambwe women and her shrewd observations on their lives were of primary assistance to my enquiry.

For statistical and other data, and for practical assistance in the field, I am indebted to various officers of the Northern Rhodesia Government.

The pronunciation of Mambwe words is quite straightforward: as spelled here they should be pronounced as though written in Italian. I have used only a few Mambwe words and phrases, where they are necessary, and after the first translation have used the English equivalent.

W. WATSON

CHAPTER I

INTRODUCTORY

THE process of industrialization now taking place in Northern
Rhodesia is in some ways similar to the industrial revolution
in Europe. Between 1780 and 1850 English manufacturing towns
expanded rapidly in size, and this expansion was accompanied by
an equally rapid increase in population. The great development of
copper-mining in Northern Rhodesia during the last twenty-five
years has produced similar phenomena. But there are many differences in the process of industrialization in England then and
in Africa now. In Africa industrial operations are organized by
large companies with international connections and enormous
capital, the end-product of 150 years of technological and financial development. The main mining companies are large imper-
sonal organizations, with complicated systems of management
and labour control. This has brought about the apparently para-
doxical situation that the most advanced forms of European
industry exist simultaneously with age-old methods of subsistence cultivation, and that modern urban communities are
arising in the midst of simple tribal groups. The maintenance of
the complex industrial system depends on a constant flow of the
unskilled labour of illiterates.[1] But the new industrial towns
developing round the copper mines are not the antagonists of the
tribal groups; on the contrary, the tribal groups are the very
foundations of the new towns, for the tribal Africans are also the
miners and labourers of the new industries. The new industrialism
perforce brought with it from Europe its own skilled workers,
for the Africans, with their simple technology, could offer only
unskilled labour.

In England the peasants were forced into the towns by poverty,

---

[1] Cf. R. L. Prain, Chairman of the Rhodesian Selection Trust, who states
in 'The Stabilization of Labour in the Rhodesian Copper Belt' that: 'Before
posing the problems created by the industrialization of the Northern
African, we must accept two postulates in order to prevent our considerations
ranging over too wide a field; first, that the mining industry is a necessary
element in Northern Rhodesian life; second, that African labour is necessary
to that industry.'

famine, and land enclosure, but many also went voluntarily, to better their conditions. They came from smallholdings or rented land, and shared a common Christian culture with the industrialists. Master and man spoke the same language, and shared a common system of values. There were exceptions to this, of course, where immigrants had to acquire new languages and beliefs. But in Africa, the cultural gulf between employer and employed was far greater than in Europe, because of the Africans' unfamiliar and misunderstood background. The African labourers came from small self-sufficient communities, with pagan beliefs and uncomplicated technologies. They were suddenly thrust into a world-wide economic system and confronted with a complex technology. Naturally they were inefficient workers at first, but they have shown considerable powers of adaptation and today they are striving to acquire both the skills and standards of behaviour of the Europeans.

Thus the situation of the Mambwe who seeks work in a copper-mining town such as Mufulira has many points in common with, for example, that of the Irish peasant who sought temporary work in Manchester in the 1800s. The Irish too were subject to racial discrimination and on the whole could find only unskilled work. English workers were hostile to Irish immigrants and fought pitched battles with them when they were employed to build the railways. The Mambwe today receive much the same sums in wages as the Irish did then. Redford quotes a contemporary as writing: 'Perhaps half-a-crown a day would be too liberal an estimate of their earnings', and the labourers took back to Ireland sums of £5 to £7, and thought £12 a large sum to save. In Manchester in 1835 a bricklayer's labourer earned from 10s. to 18s. a week.[1] Although in Northern Rhodesia today the Mambwe labourers earn and save similar amounts, their real wages are in fact much less, owing to the decline in the value of money.

In Europe a great part of the countrymen who migrated in search of industrial work settled permanently in the towns. The 'labour question', in England at least, concerned such problems as unemployment, housing, schemes of social insurance, industrial organization, and political representation. In Africa, the labour

---

[1] Redford, *Labour Migration in England, 1800–1850*, pp. 128, 139 et passim.

question turned on the problem of migrant labour. 'The migration of large numbers of the male population from their homes to
distant places of work is one of the characteristic features of the
labour question in Africa.' [1] The industrial centres in fact offer
only casual employment for African unskilled labour. The Africans are segregated within Native Reserves, in which the unemployed grow their own food and look after themselves. The
reserve is used, Lord Hailey states, 'as a "shock absorber" in the
sense that it provides for the unemployed, the infirm, and the
aged without any charges on the state'.[2] A permanent labour
force, settled in the towns nearby the mines and factories, without land to cultivate, needs higher wages, adequate housing,
schools, amusements, and social insurance. Read says: 'White
employers on the whole are ready to put up with migrant labour
provided the supply is constant, for the important reason that
migrant labour is likely to be cheaper in the long run than
permanent labour.' [3] But another price must be paid for cheap
labour. Low wages and inadequate housing and lack of social
amenities breed disease and crime. Many Whites express the
fear that town life demoralizes the Africans; they lose all respect
for their own tribal institutions, and do not seem to acquire any
for those of the Whites. This subject has been widely discussed
in South Africa, where the policy of migrant labour has been
longest applied. De Kiewiet[4] says of the result of migration there:

> From the time that the young men could leave the tribe and take
> service with Europeans the ties that bound them to chief and tribe
> slackened. Their former dependence upon the chief and their elders
> for counsel and aid in marriage and every emergency went the way of
> respect and deference. Because they were no longer dependent, they
> lost their old respect for their chiefs.

This is an authoritative statement of an assumption commonly
held. While it may be true of South Africa, and is the subject of
anxious speculation by both Government officials and employers
in Northern Rhodesia, I believe that this problem of 'detribalization', as it is usually called, has been misunderstood and

---

[1] Lord Hailey, *An African Survey*, p. 605.
[2] Op. cit., p. 804.
[3] Read, 'Migrant Labour in Africa and Its Effects on Tribal Life', p. 608.
[4] De Kiewiet, 'South Africa, Rhodesia, and the Protectorates', p. 827.

exaggerated. It is contradicted by other social phenomena, such as the rise of tribal nationalisms that tend to reject European culture and resurrect for admiration the old values of tribal life. Fortes has condemned the use of the word 'detribalization' in socio-logical analysis, and pointed out that it is usually used evaluatively, as a synonym for such words as 'pathological', 'disintegrated', 'demoralized', in a pejorative or deprecatory sense. According to Fortes, the concept of 'detribalization' arises from a false com-parison between the condition of Africans living in locations in the towns and a hypothetical, uncontaminated tribal life in the past.[1] The tribes were never isolated from outside influence in the past, and like many others, Mambwe tribal unity survived wars, famines, and pestilence.[2] The advent of the Europeans did not destroy tribal institutions. Even in South Africa, where both European rule and industry have been longest established, the tribal systems survived. Kuper reports that migrant labour among the Swazi is not necessarily a sign of tribal decay, in spite of the great pressure on the land.[3] Schapera states that 'it is not correct to assume that all the people who go to the Union from Bechu-analand tend to become "detribalized"'. While abroad, the Bechuana tribesmen associate mainly with members of their own tribe, and the common tie between them is sometimes given concrete expression, through the formation of mutual aid societies, etc.[4] Indeed, the impact of Europeans seems to have tended to strengthen tribal institutions, and Gluckman says of the Zulu of Natal: 'Increasing opposition [of Black and White] has height-ened resistance to White innovations and revived old customs'. This development is not peculiar to the Zulu, for he adds that similar developments have occurred in other parts of South Africa; there has been a spontaneous movement among Ciskeian Africans to restore chiefs where these had already lost their power to the Whites.[5] Hellmann found that 'the process of detribaliza-tion has been exaggerated' among the urban African population, although 'the average European would unhesitatingly classify

---

[1] 'Culture Contact as a Dynamic Process', p. 61.
[2] A few tribes did collapse, e.g. the Marawi and Bisa.
[3] *The Uniform of Colour*, p. 24.
[4] *Migrant Labour and Tribal Life*, p. 24.
[5] 'Analysis of a Social Situation in Modern Zululand', p. 167.

these Natives as detribalized'.[1] Under urban conditions, the
Africans rapidly assimilate European dress, material culture, and
outward forms of behaviour, but this assimilation does not
necessarily imply 'detribalization'. On the contrary, many attempts to organize African industrial workers on a common basis
of economic interest have encountered great difficulties because
of African tribal solidarities and inter-tribal hostilities. In South
Africa, 'tribal cleavages and differences' are said to account for the
backwardness of the Non-European Co-operative Movement,[2]
and the African National Congress included in its original pro-
gramme the aim 'to discourage and contend against . . . tribal
feuds and to secure the elimination of tribal feuds, jealousy, and
petty quarrels'.[3] Thus, even after the arrival of the Europeans,
the Africans appear to have retained a sufficient identity with
their tribal groups to be willing to fight for these, in spite of their
common economic interests as labourers.

In Central Africa the chief has retained his authority, with which
the solidarity of the tribe is intimately bound up, throughout
the whole period of direct and indirect rule and the development of industry. Read states that among the Ngoni of Nyasaland, who have a high rate of labour migration, there is an
'admittedly strong tribal organization',[4] an observation confirmed
by Barnes for the Northern Rhodesian Ngoni.[5] Richards says of
the Bemba: '. . . the institution of chieftainship, far from being
moribund, is very much alive, even after years of direct administration. The authority of the [Paramount Chief] Citimukulu has
never been questioned'.[6] Similarly, we shall see that the Mambwe
chief is still the focal point of tribal loyalties, and that his identification with his people's interests led him into such strong
opposition to the Government that he was deposed.

Thus some historians, Government officials, and European
employers view the general effects of industrial labour on Africans
in a way quite different from most sociologists. These opposing
views are, briefly, that:

---

[1] *Rooiyard*, pp. 110 and 116.
[2] *Handbook on Race Relations in South Africa*, p. 471.
[3] Ibid., p. 518.
[4] *Native Standards of Living and African Culture Change*, p. 56.
[5] *Politics in a Changing Society*, p. 135.
[6] 'Tribal Government in Transition', p. 21.

(*a*) industrial employment breaks up African tribal society so that Africans lose their respect for their chiefs;

(*b*) industrial employment does not seem to affect the retention by Africans of their tribal identity, nor their adherence to their chiefs.

The latter view is true of the Mambwe; and I would even add that industrial employment has enhanced the value of tribal ties and loyalty to the chiefs.

The first view arises, I believe, from a misapprehension of the nature of social relations. Any field of observation open to a sociological observer is only part of a greater whole: and the whole is present in every social situation within the part observed. Events in another sector of the social field undoubtedly affect events in the sector under observation. But it may only affect and modify them; it need not necessarily destroy them. The concept of 'detribalization' implies that an African must choose between two systems of social relations and values, one based on modern industrial production, the other on traditional subsistence production: if he is absorbed into industry, this necessarily dissolves his tribal social relations and the moral values implicit in them. But a man can participate in two different spheres of social relations and keep them distinct and separate. He need not transfer the behavioural patterns of one sphere to another. An African may move from his tribal area to a town, engage in paid labour, and take part in social and economic organizations there. But these organizations are relevant only to his status as an industrial worker, and have no place in the system of subsistence production, which is controlled by traditional tribal social relations. The two economic and social spheres are spatially and socially distinct, and although men undoubtedly carry ideas from one to the other, the spheres exist conjointly. The returned worker quickly resumes the tribal ways on his return to the reserve, for the good reason that his claims to the use of land are bound up with the whole nexus of social relationships that form tribal society. The returned wage-earner does not try to introduce a new system of political organization within the reserve: he does not demand that there should be a democratic representative political system with elected leaders and a secret ballot. He is content to recognize the authority of his traditional rulers, and if he is ambitious of political power, he seeks this within the traditional system. Nor does he attempt to apply European concepts of individual property to the land that he cultivates, and rarely does he change his system of cultivation, and then only under considerable pressure from without. As Fortes remarks of the techniques acquired by West Africans while working for Europeans: '. . . these skills and ideas cannot function independently of the proper material apparatus, the relevant social context, and the recurrent situations in which they are appropriate. All these are lacking in the tribal community, hence there can be no "transfer of training".' All the skill and behaviour learned in the towns 'drops off like an old coat' when the labour migrant returns home.[1] Schapera notes the same loss of acquired urban forms of behaviour and says that the returned workers settle down quietly to the routine of tribal life. He observes that many of the headmen and other tribal leaders of today have had considerable experience of industrial employment, and yet they are now among the more conservative elements of the population.[2] This was also my observation among the Mambwe, where all the traditional chiefs, except one, had had experience of industrial labour before they succeeded to chieftainships. They are now the main upholders of tribal tradition.

The dual nature of African interests in the total economic system that comprises both reserves and towns necessitates the adoption of different patterns of behaviour appropriate to each situation. Certainly these patterns are mingled, and affect each other, and many cultural changes are taking place in Mambwe life, such as the change from wattle-and-daub huts to brick houses. But the tribal bonds persist. Tribal membership guarantees the rights of men to the use of land, for land rights are an inalienable part of an African's status as a member of a tribe; these rights are embedded in the matrix of social obligations that makes up tribal

---

[1] Op. cit., p. 87. This generalization was made in 1938 and must be qualified in the light of the changes that have since taken place. Some of the ' proper material apparatus' now exists in the Mambwe tribal community—for example, brick houses and European furniture. There is therefore an opportunity for exercising some acquired skills, such as carpentry, brick-making and -laying, tailoring, etc.

[2] Op. cit., p. 171.

society. Thus the African secures himself against the vagaries of industrial employment, and the uncertainty of its continuance. The industrial complex is a new thing, and for all they know may disappear as quickly as it came; or, what is more likely, jobs may be denied to Africans and given only to immigrant Whites. The copper mines may suffer from a slump, as they did once before in 1930. The industrial situation is insecure in African eyes, whereas tribal life represents a coherent and understood social order.

CHAPTER II

THE LAND AND THE PEOPLE

THE LAND

THE Mambwe live on the great plateau of Northern Rhodesia, immediately to the south of Lake Tanganyika. This elevated plateau, a series of rolling ridges covered with low forest bush, has a general altitude of about 4,500 feet, but here and there peaks stand out, the most notable being Mount Sunzu, about 6,000 feet high. On the north the plateau falls precipitously to the shores of Lake Tanganyika, itself 2,539 feet above sea-level.

To the north-east of Mambwe country the thick forest gives way to open grassland interspersed with clumps of trees. In this open grassland the valleys between the ridges form grassy plains (*dambos*) which are often waterlogged in the rainy season. The whole of this open area is drained by the Saisi river and its tributaries, and the Saisi river itself forms an approximate boundary between the grasslands and the forest. This variation in type of vegetation affects Mambwe agricultural practices, for they have two distinct types of cultivation to correspond with the two distinct ecological areas. The Mambwe distinguish the two types of cultivators, calling the grassland-people, Aisa Mambwe, and the forest-people, Maswepa Mambwe.

The scenery is magnificent. Every European traveller has commented with enthusiasm on the natural beauty and grandeur of the country, and Sir Harry Johnston was moved to describe it as a 'veritable paradise'. The climate is delightful, almost Mediterranean, for owing to the elevation of the plateau the temperature seldom exceeds ninety degrees, and even in the cold season falls only to provide brisk, sparkling mornings, although occasional ground-frosts are not unknown at night. The rainfall is confined to the six months from October to April, the larger part from January onwards, and is in the region of 42 inches a year. This rainy season is the spring and summer, the season of cultivation. After the rains, between May and July, the weather gradually becomes cool and dry, and the temperature falls to its lowest, so that this period is counted as winter, although this is an inappropriate word to describe the most invigorating time of the year. From July to October the temperature begins to rise once more, and the country gradually becomes dry and dusty. However, it is very well watered, and most of the streams are perennial. The many rivers, of which the largest are the Chambezi, the Kalungu, and the Saisi, have no considerable seasonal variation in volume.

This country has always been a natural highway between East and Central Africa. Long before Europeans discovered it, the Arab slave-traders approached the interior along this route, and the Ngoni twice passed through on their travels—harsh visitations which are still remembered by the Mambwe. Livingstone used this route on his journey to Lake Tanganyika, and other European explorers followed him. Joseph Thomson passed through Mambwe country to Lake Tanganyika in 1879, and two years later the devoted Dr. Stewart began the construction of a through road, from Karonga on Lake Nyasa to Kasikalawe on Lake Tanganyika, to open up the country permanently to European enterprise.[1] Both Stewart and his successor William McEwan died while building this road, but others finished it, and for long it was the main route between the two great lakes. This Stevenson road, as it was called,[2] was carried over the Saisi river in Mambwe country on a bridge built specially for it, and at this bridge the German troops from Tanganyika under von Lettow fired their first shots against the British in Central Africa in the 1914–18 war.

The Stevenson road is no longer used, and long stretches have disappeared, for it was superseded by a soft unmetalled road which passes through the European township of Abercorn,[3] in the heart of Mambwe country, on its way into Tanganyika Territory. This route too has now been superseded by a new metalled road further to the south, which runs through Mpika and Tunduma to the town of Mbeya in Tanganyika.

---

[1] Stewart, 'Lake Nyasa and the Water Route to the Lake Region of Africa', pp. 257–277.

[2] After John Stevenson, Chairman of the Livingstonia Central Africa Company, a missionary enterprise that hoped to open up the area surveyed by Livingstone.

[3] In 1952 Abercorn had a White population of about 180 persons, men, women, and children.

The Great Lakes themselves have always been used as highways, and the missionaries operated a steamship on Lake Tanganyika as early as 1884, while the Arabs had always used it. Today a number of steamers link the Kigoma railhead in Tanganyika with the port of Mpulungu in Northern Rhodesia, twenty-six miles from Abercorn, and provide a regular service every three weeks which now brings in much of the district's heavy freight.

The central position of the country, and its salubrious climate, at one time held out the promise of considerable European development: but that promise has not been fulfilled, owing to certain important drawbacks. The poor and shallow soils, which need fertilizers to give really good crops, are not suited to present European farming methods. The rainfall, although moderate and dependable, comes in sudden and violent storms. The threat of erosion is therefore constant, and can be warded off only by extensive preventive measures. The whole area lies between two great breeding-grounds of the red locust, Lake Rukwa in Tanganyika and the Mweru Marshes in Northern Rhodesia, and has suffered constantly from their depredations. Locusts destroyed one-quarter of the crops in 1931, and another invasion in 1933 caused further damage.[1] Above all, the isolation of the district puts many obstacles in the way of development. Distances are very great, for Abercorn is 650 miles from Lusaka, the capital of Northern Rhodesia, and even further from Dar-es-Salaam, the capital of Tanganyika. Communications are still poor by modern standards, and in the rainy season the unmetalled roads are a hindrance to regular motor traffic. There is no railway. These distances and the poor roads have gravely handicapped economic development and kept the European population at a low level. The early settlers grew such crops as coffee, pineapples, strawberries, and fruit and vegetables of all kinds.[2] Among these, coffee was the important cash crop, and the Blue Mountain variety sold well on European markets. The amount grown was never very great, only 627 cwt. in 1935, of which 474 cwt. was exported. A co-operative society was formed by the European

---

[1] This pest is now controlled by the International Red Locust Control, which set up its permanent field headquarters in Abercorn in 1948. The employees of this organization form the bulk of the present European population of Abercorn.

[2] Three tenancy agreements between White farmers and Africans were signed in the year 1914 alone (District Commissioner's records, Abercorn).

farmers to deal with the marketing of the entire crop, but the
high cost of transporting it to markets led to a decline in the
number of European farmers, and today only a few are left.
Central African Airways maintain an aerodrome at Abercorn at
which aircraft call regularly, almost daily, and one European
farmer has had the enterprise to send out meat by air; but the full
possibilities of air freight still lie in the future. A certain amount
of freight now comes in and out by air, but most of the traffic
consists of passengers in transit. Any considerable economic
development of the area in the future is therefore likely to depend
on a major improvement of communications.

THE PEOPLE

The Mambwe therefore live directly on a junction of routes
between East and Central Africa, and have long been subject to
influences from without. In the past not all of the travellers who
used these routes brought benefits to the Mambwe, and they tend
to regard strangers with suspicion, an attitude justified by their
past experiences. They are a small people, and though insular,
are hardy and resilient, and cherish the independence that has
been assailed so often in the past.[1] They have occupied their
present territory for at least 200 years, for according to Coxhead
their Bemba neighbours found them already in possession, when
the Bemba themselves arrived from the Congo in the eighteenth
century. The Bemba claim to have pushed the Mambwe back
towards the north and forced them to pay tribute.[2] This may be
so, although the Mambwe deny that they ever paid tribute to the
Bemba, who lie on the southern boundary of their country. The
Bemba are the largest tribe on the plateau, and before the Europeans arrived dominated the whole area. The Mambwe regarded
the Bemba as their traditional enemies, and the Lungu, who

---

[1] The first Europeans to live in the district explained Mambwe truculence on
the grounds that they were not a 'true' people, but the descendants of a heterogeneous collection of runaway slaves. This explanation is still current. A senior
Government official told me that the Mambwe were far more difficult to
administer than the Bemba, because their chiefs had no power and the people
were by nature rebellious and unruly. This natural disability they inherited
from their forefathers, who were those slaves so troublesome to the Arab
traders that they were either discarded or allowed to escape.

[2] Coxhead, *The Native Tribes of Northern Rhodesia: Their Laws and Customs.*

occupy the lake shore and also have a western boundary with the Mambwe, the Inamwanga, and the Iwa to the east, as their allies. It is certain that throughout the nineteenth century the Bemba raided the Mambwe.

There is no reliable historical evidence concerning the origins and previous movements of the Mambwe. Their own accounts distinguish between the origin of commoners and chiefs. The chiefs say that Changala, the founder of the royal clan, was a Mulua[1] from Kola (Angola) in the west, and that when he came to the present Mambwe country to hunt, he found several groups of people already living and cultivating there. These people asked Changala to become their chief, and he agreed. All members of the present royal clan, including the line of royal chiefs which rules today, claim descent from Changala.

The first indigenous group that Changala encountered was composed of the members of the Simwinga clan, at that time said to be under the rule of the senior clansman (*cikolwe*), a man called Chindo. Changala had with him two 'hunting leopards',[2] animals which Chindo had never seen. Chindo was so much impressed that he asked Changala to stay with him for ever and provide meat for his people. In return, Chindo offered to marry his daughter to Changala, and to recognize him as chief. Changala accepted this offer and agreed to settle there as chief of the people. Thus Changala, the first royal chief, became Chindo's son-in-law. This marriage is said by the Mambwe to explain why the holder of the commoner title, Chindo, always addresses the holder of the senior royal title, Nsokolo, as son-in-law. The clan name Simwinga is derived from the root word for marriage; *simwinga* is the common word for a bridegroom, and *namwinga* for a bride.

Another story suggests that their first relations were not quite

---

[1] This word also means a stranger. Johnston writes: 'The remarkable Luba peoples [of the Kasai] who were no doubt fundamentally connected in history with the Lua (Rua) and Lunda tribes . . . seem to have founded the empire of Lunda . . . and to have created powerful monarchies here and there between the Kasai, Ankuru, and Lake Mweru; in the valley of the Lulua river they are usually known as the Bena Lulua; in the east they are the Barua. . . . The Barua . . . of the south-west coast of Tanganyika and the regions between that lake and the upper Lomani are connected, linguistically at any rate, with the Luba congeries of people.' Johnston, *George Grenfell and the Congo*, p. 143.

[2] These animals may have been cheetahs.

so cordial. Changala is said to have asked Chindo for seed, because he knew only how to hunt, and did not know how to cultivate millet. Chindo agreed to give him seed, but cunningly boiled them first, so that when Changala planted them, they failed to sprout. Changala revenged himself by playing on Chindo's cupidity and ignorance concerning his hunting leopards. Chindo asked Changala whether these useful animals could cross with goats, and when Changala assured him they could, allowed them to be put overnight into his goat pen. In the morning Chindo found that the leopards had killed his entire flock of goats. After Chindo's duplicity with the seeds, Changala went to the Sichilima people, who lived in another part of the country, and asked them to give him some. This they did, and Changala was so pleased with his crops that he married one of the Sichilima women. The clan name Sichilima is derived from the verb *ukulima*, to cultivate, and thus may be translated as 'the cultivators'.

Finally, Changala settled permanently as chief near a prominent landmark called Tembo Hill, near which Chief Nsokolo's village is still sited. Changala found the Simpemba people living there, and married one of their women. The clan name Simpemba is derived from the word *mpemba*, a kind of white clay used extensively for ritual purposes by the Mambwe. Today these three clans all have a joking relationship with the royal clan, and claim that they 'gave the chiefs to the country', for they say that it was from the women of their clans whom Changala married that the present Mambwe chiefs are descended.

The tradition of the commoners is that 'long ago' they came from the north-east and lived in the country without chiefs until Changala arrived among them and introduced them to chieftaincy. There is no inherent improbability in this. The commoners may originally have formed part of the southwards drift of patrilineal Bantu peoples, for their country is the natural highway from east into central Africa. The Mambwe differ greatly from the matrilineal peoples on the plateau to the south, such as the Bemba, who claim that they originated in the Congo, and Mambwe institutions are more akin to those of Tanganyikan tribes, to whom they say they are related. The Mambwe language has affinities with those spoken by Tanganyikan peoples; Guthrie groups Mambwe directly with the languages spoken by the Pimbwe, Rungwa, Fipa, and Lungu, who all live to the south-east of Lake Tanganyika.[1] Mambwe accounts seem to support the familiar picture of autochthonous 'owners of the land' and immigrant rulers. However, other interpretations are possible, and in the light of present knowledge, only conjectural answers can be given to questions on their origin and previous history.

The Administration Census of 1952 estimated the Mambwe population to be 22,692, of whom 13,221 were forest cultivators and 9,471 grassland cultivators.[2] The Mambwe occupy a territory of approximately 3,000 square miles, at an overall density of 7·56 persons per square mile. In 1933 Moffat Thomson estimated the Mambwe population at 14,686;[3] if this figure is correct, the population seems to have shown an annual rate of increase of 2·32 per cent during this period of nineteen years. The actual rate of increase may not be in fact so great, for the census methods are not sufficiently stringent, and there is no compulsory registration of births and deaths. But even although the figures are estimates, it is nevertheless quite clear that the Mambwe have continued to grow considerably in number under British rule, and that this growth is continuing.

The principal cause of this increase is probably a sharp fall in the death-rate. In the past the Mambwe suffered periodically from famine and pestilence, and these are now virtually eliminated. Food is brought in during famine years, and such natural pests as the red locust are controlled. Smallpox, malaria, yellow

---

[1] *The Classification of the Bantu Languages*, p. 56 f. Guthrie puts Bemba within the same general zone, and indicates that Mambwe is in some measure related to Bemba. Doke, *Bantu, Modern Grammatical, Phonetical, and Lexicographical Studies since 1860*, p. 37, classifies the Mambwe language as one of the Central Zone group, of which Bemba is the most prominent. However, the two languages are not mutually intelligible, although most Mambwe men speak some Bemba. Few Mambwe women understand Bemba, except in the forested area adjoining a Bemba chieftaincy. Doke bases his classification on a small grammar by D. Picton Jones, *Outline of Ki-Mambwe Grammar*, first published in 1893 but now out of print. This is the sole publication on the language. Jones was a missionary at the London Missionary Society Station established on the shores of Lake Tanganyika, and evidently compiled his grammar from Lungu informants, using a Swahili interpreter, for it contains many foreign words, and uses throughout the Lungu pronunciation. Lungu and Mambwe are closely related.

[2] Northern Rhodesia Mambwe only. About 4,000 Mambwe live in Tanganyika Territory.

[3] *Memorandum on the Native Tribes and Tribal Areas of Northern Rhodesia.*

fever, leprosy, and tuberculosis still exist, but medical treatment is widespread; yellow fever, for example, is now practically non-existent. Some public health measures, such as the building and use of village latrines, and inoculations against smallpox, have been made compulsory. There is also an African hospital in Abercorn, as well as dispensaries throughout the reserves.[1]

If the Mambwe population continues to grow at the current rate there is bound to be pressure on the land in the near future, unless the present methods of cultivation are radically altered. In the grassland area, land is not yet in short supply; but in the forests, the Mambwe had to be given additional land in 1937 to enable the Citemene Control Scheme to function properly, and thus to preserve the forests.[2]

An ordinary Mambwe village (*muzi*) generally consists of a group of huts, between thirty and fifty in number, with grain-bins (*intanta*) and kitchens. The chiefs' villages are larger, and Chief Nsokolo's the largest of all, with about 150 huts. The buildings are made of wattle-and-daub, and are rectangular in plan, although there are a few round huts. The verandah is enclosed round three sides of the hut. This enclosure forms an extra room which can be used either as a pen for small stock or as a kitchen. Houses of sun-dried brick are now being built.[3] The huts are laid out in rows, with the doors facing one another, to form rudimentary streets. The grain-bins, kitchen huts, and latrines are sited behind the living huts. The grain-bins are of two kinds, one much larger than the other. They are cylindrical in shape, and raised from the ground on platforms. They are all

---

[1] There may have been a small improvement in the food supply, which would help to increase the population. The peaceful conditions that followed British rule and the improvements brought about by European supervision of Mambwe agriculture, mainly to prevent soil erosion, may have improved production sufficiently to allow for an increase in population, taken together with the improvement in medical services and sanitation. Chambers states that in England 'among the sources of the demographic revolution of the eighteenth century was the slow-moving but immensely powerful tide of agricultural change'. See 'Enclosure and Labour Supply in the Industrial Revolution', p. 341 et passim.

[2] See p. 28 below.

[3] Brick houses are rapidly replacing the wattle-and-daub huts. If present trends continue, all Mambwe will be living in brick houses within a generation.

thatched. The women use a ladder to gain access to the taller bins, which are about twelve feet high. The smaller bins are about three to four feet high, and grouped in batteries of three. This type of bin is said to have come into use only since the Europeans came. The whole village is surrounded by banana trees, and mango trees are planted in the open spaces between the huts. Each village has one or more open-sided shelters where the men gather twice a day to eat their food.

The cattle kraal is always sited outside the village boundary. All the beasts belonging to a village are kept in the common kraal; there are no individual kraals. The kraals are not substantial structures, but simple square palisades of long poles, projecting outwards at the top. The Mambwe say, paradoxically, that stouter kraals would offer less protection to the cattle.[1] For they claim that when a lion jumps into the present type of kraal, the terrified cattle can burst out of the rather meagre fence and scatter, and this keeps down the losses. If the kraals were made stronger, the lions would kill all the cattle at their ease, for the cattle would be unable to escape. A more robust roofed enclosure is sometimes built in which to keep newborn calves, although some villagers prefer to bring calves into the village at night and keep them in the enclosed verandahs of their huts.

The village has no obvious centre. The open shelters are used as meeting places, and visitors are welcomed there. Some men have private shelters. The headman's hut is not noticeably larger than the others. However, many headmen now have brick houses, and these are immediately distinguishable.

A village is known by the name of the specific area of cultivation which surrounds it. From time to time the huts are rebuilt on another site, when the old site is dirty or the huts dilapidated, but a village usually stands on the same site from about eight to ten years, and occasionally longer. The new site is always within the recognized area which the village may use for cultivation. This permanence of site is related to the methods of cultivation.

Each village has a shrine (*kavua*) dedicated to the ancestors of

---

[1] Lions and leopards take an annual toll of hundreds of Mambwe cattle, and lions attack cattle kraals. Elephants are seldom troublesome, for there are no longer such large herds as those which hunted Livingstone on the night of his arrival at the shores of Lake Tanganyika. See Waller, *The Last Journals of David Livingstone*, i, p. 206.

the headman, where the headman prays for the well-being of the village. It is a small square structure with a thatched roof and open sides, and is usually to be found on a former village site. Pieces of calico are put on this shrine as an offering to the spirits (*imipasi*) of the ancestors. There is also a shrine in each hut, in the shape of a small clay pot (*katindya*) marked with whitewash. When beer is brewed, a little is always poured into this pot.

The core of a Mambwe village is the segment of an agnatic lineage of which the headman is usually the senior member. Round this core of agnatic kin are grouped a number of men of other clans linked to the core by various ties of kinship and marriage. Approximately half the present headmen are members of one or another lineage of the royal clan, and thus claim agnatic kinship with the chiefs. The commoner headmen are almost invariably linked to the royal clan by cognatic or affinal ties. Of the fifty-four commoner clans, none has more than four headmanships. The royal clan therefore dominates politically in the control of villages.

Villages are grouped together within chieftaincies, and villages within the same chieftaincy are usually linked to one another and to the chief through the headmen. There are sixteen traditional chieftaincies, thirteen of whom have chiefs of the royal clan, but the British recognize only three chiefs, all of them royal. One of these, Chief Nsokolo, is the senior, and his court a court of appeal from the other two. Chief Nsokolo is the traditional head (*cikolwe*) of the royal clan, and is recognized as such by the other administrative chiefs, Mpande and Mwamba. These three administrative chieftaincies correspond approximately with the division between grassland and woodland cultivation. Chief Mpande rules over an entirely woodland area, and Chief Mwamba over an entirely grassland area. Chief Nsokolo has both types of land under his control, as a number of the traditional chieftaincies which are no longer recognized by the British now come under his authority.[1]

The area of the plateau occupied by the Mambwe people[2] is

---

[1] The Mambwe under Chief Muti in Tanganyika are grassland cultivators, but his chieftaincy does not come within the administrative sphere of the Northern Rhodesia Government. Muti recognizes the traditional superiority of Nsokolo.

[2] Between 8′ 30″ and 10′ south latitude, and longitudes 30′ 30″ and 32′ 15″.

divided into two Native Reserves demarcated in 1928, together
with some Native Trust Land.[1] All Native Reserves in Northern
Rhodesia are vested in the Secretary of State for the Colonies,
and are set apart in perpetuity for the exclusive use and occupation
of the natives. No person, other than a native, is allowed to
occupy any portion of a Native Reserve except for the following
purposes:

(a) Government Stations and sites for other public purposes;
(b) Trading sites of not more than five acres, and on leases
  not longer than five years, and not within twenty miles of
  each other. The chief or headman concerned must recom-
  mend the site for such use;
(c) Missionary stations;
(d) Hotel sites, where the Government considers these necessary.

The two Mambwe Native Reserves lie entirely within the
Administrative District of Abercorn, in the Northern Province.
The District Commissioner's office is in Abercorn, the main
centre of European settlement.

The chief nominally 'owns' all of the land in his chieftaincy, and
in return for giving it to his subjects to cultivate, they return him
obedience and respect. In Gluckman's term, these subjects have
'estates of holding'.[2] The chief grants rights to each village headman, who in turn grants his villagers rights in village land. Each
person granted such rights in the hierarchy has duties and obligations of a similar kind to the holder from whom he obtained his
particular rights to the use of land. A Mambwe who is dissatisfied
with the rule of one chief is at liberty to move to another chieftaincy, and provided he can find a headman who will take him
into his village, will be granted rights to the use of land by the
chief and headman in return for obedience and recognition.
These rules apply to strangers, who are welcomed and encouraged
to settle on the land.

The Mambwe village is the traditional unit for residence and
production, and therefore the basis of the polity. Here a man can
claim rights to the use of land and to the assistance of kin and

---

[1] The Northern Rhodesia (Crown Lands and Native Reserves) Order in
Council, 1928.
[2] 'Lozi Land Tenure', p. 29.

friends. [When he goes off to work for wages, he can confidently expect that his wife and family will be cared for while he is away, and that his rights to the use of land will be recognized as long as he is a village member. He can retire to the village when he is too old or ill to work for wages. In return, while he is living in the village, he will care for the interests of his own absent kin and their dependants.]

THE SYSTEM OF CULTIVATION

The staple of Mambwe diet is a porridge (*insima*) made from finger millet (*eleusine coracana*). The millet is prepared by the women who grind it into flour, and the porridge is generally eaten hot, with other foodstuffs as a relish. They also grow cassava, a crop introduced by the Administration as a standby against failure of the millet, as well as pumpkins, several types of beans, sorghum, maize, groundnuts, sweet potatoes, and bananas. Various wild fruits are collected from the forest. The Mambwe who live near the Saisi river obtain a certain amount of fish, but the Saisi is so blocked with immense reeds for most of its way through their country that fishing is an extremely difficult and tiring process and they usually fish only once a year. On the whole they prefer to buy dried fish from peddlers who fetch it from the Lungu fishermen on Lake Tanganyika and bring it round the villages. Game formerly abounded, but the great rinderpest outbreak of the 1890s and the acquisition of firearms by the Africans have almost exterminated the herds. The villagers rarely have fresh game meat other than reedbuck and duiker. They very seldom kill their own cattle for meat, as they prefer to sell any available mature stock. They must have permission from the Administration to slaughter beasts, as killing is controlled in the interests of the immature and breeding stock.[1] Occasionally, wild pig is killed and the meat eaten. They also buy tinned food from the stores.

The Mambwe do not have a cash crop, although in good years the Administration buys their surplus to store against the bad years. The subsistence economy cannot consistently show the profit needed to meet taxes and all the new wants that sixty years of European rule has created: clothes, tools, bicycles, furniture,

---

[1] Cattle (Slaughter) Control Ordinance, 1949.

pots and pans, school fees, and many other items they now consider to be necessities. The many stores in the area, both in the
reserves and the European township, continually tempt them to
earn money. Apart from their inadequate cattle and crops, the
Mambwe have only their labour to sell for money to pay taxes
and to buy these imported goods.

Thus the Mambwe are no longer simple subsistence cultivators.
All of the men, at some period of their lives, work for wages both
at home and abroad, and these earnings have become essential
to them. For most Mambwe men, life is an alternation between
work in the fields and work in the enterprises established by the
Europeans. This alternation is now fully established, and the
present standard of living of the Mambwe depends very largely
on their ability to earn wages. Their subsistence production allows
them to exploit the labour markets as far as they can; dependants
can be left in the village to live off the land, while the man saves
as much as possible of his wages, or invests the money in goods
to bring home. The proportion of men of working age (from
eighteen to forty-five) absent from their villages at any one time
seldom falls below 50 per cent of the total male population of this
age-group. The profit that these men can make from wage-
earning is directly dependent on the capacity of the subsistence
economy to release them from the fields and still maintain a
sufficient production to feed those left at home, and even, in
favourable circumstances, to send food to the wage-earners.

Although finger millet is the main crop grown in both the
grasslands and the forest, the preparation of the fields is quite
different in the two areas. In the open grasslands the main rock
formation is sandstone with outcrops of dolerite.[1] The principal
soil types are a light sandy soil which turns dark when damp and
full of humus, and in the valleys an even more productive but
heavier sandy soil, which has a fairly high silt content. On these
soils the Mambwe practise a fallow system of cultivation, marked
by a distinctive method of green manuring and crop rotation
that enables them to use the same land for periods up to ten years
in succession, although usually they cultivate one field for between five and seven years before resting it. They also keep cattle
on the grassy plains.

---

[1] Round such outcrops the soil is reddish in colour and it is not popular with
the Mambwe for cultivation.

In the forests, which are dominated by *Brachystegia spp.*, the sandy soil is mostly grey or yellowish-red and there are also ridges of red and red-chocolate doleritic soils. Here the Mambwe use a variation of the ash-planting (*citemene*) system,[1] based on the preparation of a seed-bed from wood ash.[2] The forest Mambwe cultivate one field for between three and five years, and then cut trees to make a fresh field. These forest Mambwe do not keep cattle in any numbers, owing to the scarcity of suitable pasturage in the forest. I shall describe the fallow method first.

In the grasslands a man takes virgin soil (*insinde*) under cultivation for a new garden in March, towards the end of the rainy season. The grass is long at this time, anything from three to five feet high, and sometimes higher. The Mambwe use hoes to work the soil into mounds, varying from three to eight feet in diameter, turning the long grass into the centre of each mound. This method prevents the grass from seeding, which reduces weeding to a minimum. The grass at this time is at the succulent stage and rots quickly. When the grass is very high, the Mambwe first cut it with a scythe, and pile it together with any bushes and small trees on the site into small circles of brushwood. When these piles are dry, the Mambwe set fire to them and plant pumpkins in the ash. These burnt patches seldom exceed twenty-five feet in diameter.

Some people plant beans when they first prepare the mounds and are able to gather a crop in May, at the end of the rainy season. This is a subsidiary crop.

This mounded garden is called *ntumba*. The Mambwe leave these mounds fallow for the remainder of the dry season (from May to September) and through the early rains (October to December). When the heavy rains begin in January, they begin to cultivate in earnest. They first cut the weeds, then break them up and spread them between the mounds. After this they turn over the whole garden with hoes, to flatten the mounds and bring the dark humus soil from their centres to the surface. This is arduous work, for the soil is wet and heavy, but Moffat states that 'on account of the sandy nature of the soil and because of its high

---

[1] I have adopted the useful term 'ash-planting' to describe *citemene* systems from Gluckman, who first used it in 'Anthropology in Central Africa', p. 647.

[2] Ash-planting is practised by many tribes throughout the whole plateau, from Abercorn right down to the railway line some 600 miles away.

(a) A VILLAGE SHRINE

This shrine is situated on a former site of the village, marked by the trees. Logs are placed on the thatch to prevent it from being blown away.

(b) WOMEN HOEING

A section of a women's work-party breaking up mounds and spreading the dark humus soil to make a flat field (*mpepe*).

PLATE I

humus content, it can be worked even when wet without spoiling its texture'. This operation leaves the garden quite flat and smooth, and covered with about six to eight inches of excellent soil in good condition, which can easily be worked into a fine seed-bed. The necessity of having a very fine and even seed-bed is one of the chief difficulties in the cultivation of finger millet, according to Moffat.[1] The garden in this level state is called *mpepe*.

~~In January, as soon as they have prepared the seed-bed, the Mambwe sow the millet, and usually they plant some sorghum with it. Formerly the women used small hoes to cover the seeds with soil, but nowadays many grassland Mambwe drive the village cattle over each man's gardens in turn. This mode of covering the seeds and harrowing the garden simultaneously is much less laborious.

The millet germinates in six to ten days. When the plants are about four inches high, the women begin to weed, a task almost entirely left to them. At this stage the allied weed, *Eleusine indica*, can be distinguished from the millet.[2] A garden made from virgin soil needs little weeding, but each year it remains in use the weeds grow thicker and the work more arduous. The Mambwe often abandon a garden on which a further crop could be raised because weeding requires an excessive amount of labour.

In June the millet heads turn brown and hard, and the women harvest the crop. They spread the heads on drying platforms near the fields and leave them there in the sun for three or four weeks. The crop is then carried to the village and stored in wattle-and-daub containers. Some people thrash the crop and store it as grain. The Mambwe say that millet in this form keeps for long periods as neither weevils nor moths damage it.

The garden is level when the crop is reaped. The Mambwe leave it like this throughout the dry season. In November, when the first early rains have fallen, they again throw it up into mounds, in which state it is now called *icitikula*. At this time they plant groundnuts, beans or groundbeans (*inzu*), and leave them to

---

[1] 'Native Agriculture in the Abercorn District', p. 55.

[2] Moffat experimented with the use of kraal manure and found it had a selective influence on the weed *indica* and depressed the yield of the millet, *coracana*. He stated that the use of kraal manure is quite impracticable, unless some method of clamping to destroy weed seeds is introduced. Op. cit., p. 62. The Mambwe are aware of this.

ripen, occasionally weeding the garden during the rest of the season before harvest.

Throughout the next dry season they leave the field mounded until in the following November they level it once more. Again they plant millet and sorghum. At this stage the garden is called *mpepe* once more. They continue this process until the field is worked out, or weeding becomes too laborious, when the land is rested. They call fallow *icisampa*, and leave it fallow for five or six years at least before beginning once more to cultivate, when they treat it like virgin soil.

There are a number of variations in this cycle of planting and fallow, but all follow a more or less definite system of rotation. This of course retards the process of soil exhaustion, and the crops are generally very good, although the soil is not rich and could not stand a continuous cereal crop. The Mambwe do not suffer from the hunger months that the Bemba accept so fatalistically.[1]

The woodland Mambwe use a form of ash-planting cultivation (*citemene*) common to all the tribes who inhabit the forested areas of the plateau: Bemba, Lungu, Inamwanga, Iwa, Lala, etc. Methods vary from tribe to tribe, and many of the systems have been described.[2] Trapnell classifies the Mambwe method among the Northern Citemene Systems, in which a single large circular garden is prepared from a surrounding clearing in the forest. He calls the woodland Mambwe method the Developed System, because it is marked by the practice of spreading mounds in the main gardens during the latter part of the cultivation sequence, as the grassland Mambwe do in their gardens. By contrast, the Lungu and Bemba variation is more primitive.[3] The Inamwanga

---

[1] See Richards, *Land, Labour, and Diet in Northern Rhodesia*, pp. 35 ff.

[2] See Trapnell, *The Soils, Vegetation, and Agriculture of North-Eastern Rhodesia*. This report of an Ecological Survey gives an exhaustive account of the different methods of cultivation in the area. Allan, *Studies in African Land Usage in Northern Rhodesia*, deals with the carrying capacity of land in relation to particular agricultural systems, and contains a note on ash-planting control. Richards, *Land, Labour, and Diet*, describes Bemba cultivation and social organization. Peters, *Land Usage in Serenje District*, describes the small circle methods used by the Lala.

[3] Trapnell considers that the Bemba adapted their simple system from the more progressive agricultural method of the Mambwe, which is of a consider-

and Iwa, who both speak a dialect of Cimambwe, also use a variation of this Developed System.

In July, August, and September, before the trees begin to lose their leaves, the woodland Mambwe start to lop the branches. They lop only the branches when the forest is abundant, but cut down the whole tree about four feet from the ground in thinly-wooded regions or in places where the trees are not large. They then chop the loppings into lengths suitable for handling, and arrange them in a circular pile, with their points towards the centre where the garden is to be made. The pile is usually about two feet high, but on sandy soils such a thick pile is not considered necessary. The Mambwe say that the heat enters sandy soil more readily and so the garden does not need so much fire. They choose the area of garden with great care, and often include the base of an ant hill, on which to plant castor-oil seeds. The men cut the branches from the trees and pile them in parallel heaps of about half a dozen boughs. These little piles are called *ivizaka*. Women then collect the branches and carry them to the garden site, taking care not to drag them along the ground, lest the leaves be lost. The area of piled wood is called *icitambi*. The whole is left to dry for firing just before the rains begin. Certain protective measures are necessary to keep the early grass fires, which start spontaneously in the bush, from reaching the prepared gardens before all the wood has been collected.[1] The men fire the piled wood about the end of October when the windy weather is over, and immediately before the rains begin, so that the rain will settle the ash before it is blown off the garden. After burning, the garden is ready to be sown.

The Mambwe plant pumpkins and squashes round the edge of the garden and sometimes stick in cassava cuttings at very wide intervals, although most people also have separate cassava gardens. They sow the millet about the end of December or

---

ably more advanced type. He states that the Bemba have a tradition that they were hoe-cultivators in Lubaland [from whence they came in the eighteenth century] and learned ash-planting cultivation from the peoples they found already living in this area when they arrived. Op. cit., p. 25.

[1] Formerly the chief determined the day when fires would be lit, and fired his own gardens first as a signal for others; but now the whole system is under European control, through the Citemene Control Scheme. A man can be fined for firing his gardens before a prescribed date. To set fire carelessly to grass in the neighbourhood of gardens was and is a serious offence.

D

during the first weeks in January. Everyone recognizes the importance of having suitably wet weather for sowing, and at this time, as soon as they think that a wet spell is due, they rush to begin sowing. Usually a few sorghum seeds are also planted. Both men and women sow, and women and boys follow and scratch in the seed with a small hoe. In this prepared and seeded state the garden is known as *ipia*.

The next operation is fencing. When they lop the trees, the Mambwe lay aside for fences any pieces of wood over four inches in diameter. Most men encircle the garden with a double line of upright stakes about nine inches apart. Each pair of stakes is some four to six feet from the next pair. The spaces between this double line of stakes is filled with thick poles, piled one on top of the other, and then tied together with bark rope. These fences, about four to five feet high, are quite stout, and are effective against all game except elephants. The task of making these fences is laborious; each year a fence must be strengthened, and every third year remade. Sometimes bush fires destroy fencing, and then a man will usually prefer to make a new garden rather than rebuild a fence round an old one, for he feels that the poorer crop from the old garden does not justify the labour of re-fencing.[1]

Harvesting begins earlier in the woodland gardens than in the grassland gardens, and in normal years the women are well on with the harvest by the end of May. They dry and store the millet on platforms at the gardens until it is ready to be carried to the village storage-bins.

The ash-planting system has some advantages over the fallow system in Mambwe eyes. The labour of weeding is eliminated, and cultivation is far less laborious, for after the intense activity of tree-cutting and preparing the bed for seed, little other work is needed.[2] Ash-planting may also produce larger crops. In 1930–1, Mr. U. J. Moffat, then a Government Agricultural Officer, carried out some experiments at Lunzuwa, near Abercorn, to test the two

---

[1] The grassland Mambwe do not fence gardens, owing to the scarcity of wood in their area. Instead they dig deep surrounding pits or trenches, to keep out wild pig.

[2] For these reasons the grassland Mambwe describe the woodland Mambwe as a lazy lot.

methods.[1] He prepared two lots of gardens on the same soil, one by the fallow method, the other by the ash-planting. The yields were as follows:

Yields in lbs. per acre

Fallow method

After sweet potatoes 1,200
After beans and sweet potatoes 1,270
After groundnuts 1,370
Ash-planting method 1,800

Others continued the experiments over a period of years, and the results are shown in Table I.[2]

TABLE I

Difference in yield between plots cultivated by the *citemene* [ash-planting] and fallow methods on the same soil

Year of harvest	Millet yields in lbs. per acre	
	Citemene	Fallow
Block A—Three years of cropping completed		
1936	1,616	Failure
1937	beans and groundnuts	
1938 (after beans)	1,824	640
(after nuts)	1,128	352
Block B—Two years of cropping completed		
1937	2,552	1,168
1938	beans and groundnuts	
Block C—One year of cropping completed		
1938 C1	2,944	1,526
C2	2,800	1,424
	2,624	1,144

These experiments do not conclusively prove the superiority of the ash-planting system. The grassland soils are thought to be

---

[1] Op. cit., p. 61.
[2] Compiled from reports in the *Annual Report, Department of Agriculture, Northern Rhodesia*, 1938, pp. 10 ff.

superior on the whole to the woodland, and Moffat considers
that by means of a proper rotation of crops, and by improvements
in the methods of cultivation, the yield of the fallow method
might be considerably increased, even on the poor soil on which
he conducted his experiments. Moffat states that the ash-planting
system is undoubtedly suited to the production of millet on the
very sandy ridges which form the larger part of the plateau in this
area.[1] Where the forest is thick, only the branches of the trees
are lopped, and the trees quickly recover. The timber is of no value
for any other purpose, and the forest regenerates completely in a
period of between twelve and twenty years, when the fact that
the trees have ever been cut is scarcely noticeable. But the system
demands that a large area of forest should always lie fallow, and
the increase of population in this century has brought about the
danger of deforestation. Clearing and burning large areas of forest
each year can cause serious deforestation, which in some parts of
the plateau has already threatened the tribes with famine.[2] The
onslaught of the deforestation process can be traced in Mambwe
country to the south of the Saisi river. First there is an almost
treeless area, which is succeeded by thin scrub consisting mainly of
seedlings. Next comes a belt where all the trees have been cut out
at about four feet. Further on is an area where many trees are
lopped and others cut low down. Finally there is a thickly-
timbered area where branches only are lopped, and only here is it
doubtful whether the ash-planting system has caused any damage.

The Mambwe lost some of their land through alienation to
Europeans and through the creation of Crown Lands. Their
numbers are also increasing, according to the Administration.
Pressure on the available land is therefore increasing, with the
consequent possibility of serious deforestation. These reasons
caused the introduction of the Citemene Control Scheme in
1937.[3] The Administration purchased land adjoining the wood-

---

[1] Op. cit., p. 60.

[2] Peters, op. cit., describes the Serenje Lala system which is already in an
advanced state of degradation and is rapidly causing deterioration of the land.
He considers that in the Serenje area the carrying capacity of land under unaided
ash-planting cultivation is in the neighbourhood of four persons per square
mile, and that this capacity could be raised to about six per square mile if cutting
was controlled as in the Abercorn District.

[3] *Annual Report, Department of Agriculture*, 1938, p. 10.

land Mambwe reserve from the British South Africa Company to extend the area available for cultivation by the Mambwe. Blocks of land for cutting and for regeneration were allocated to each village.[1] In addition, villagers were ordered to cultivate 200 mounds per hut by hoe cultivation. This scheme is still in force, and has successfully halted the erosion that had already begun through cutting trees along the streams and on the steeper slopes.[2]

In addition to these main gardens, both sections of the Mambwe cultivate kitchen-gardens (*ivizule*), using strips of land in the immediate vicinity of the village. The kitchen-gardens are much smaller than the main gardens, and may be mounded or flat, according to the quality of the soil, for some soils do not give a good yield when mounded. Maize, beans, and pumpkins are planted on the kitchen-gardens year after year, in spite of falling yields during the whole time that the village remains on a particular site, and they are top-dressed daily with the kitchen refuse and sweepings from around the huts. The people plant these gardens during the early rains in October, and thus get a harvest before the crop is due from the main gardens in May or June.

The grassland Mambwe sometimes cultivate riverside gardens (*mianda*) on the sides of dambos, near the perennial streams. There are few suitable sites for these, and they did not appear to be a significant element in the Mambwe economy.[3]

Old cattle-kraal sites (*lua*) are used to grow tobacco. During the rainy season the men move the palisades that surround the cattle-kraal a few yards to one side whenever it becomes choked with manure. This leaves an extensive area of manure round the

---

[1] The nature of the soil and top cover determines the extent of the blocks. The Agricultural Officer at the Experimental Station, Lunzuwa, informed me that the area to be cut for one garden was roughly determined as follows: good country, 6 to 8 acres of forest to one garden; medium country, 8 to 10 acres; bad country, 10 to 15 acres. In 1931/1932 the average area of forest cut per garden for 1,346 Bemba gardens in the Kasama District was 6½ acres (Moffat, op. cit., p. 58).

[2] Cf. *Annual Reports, Department of Agriculture*, from 1939 to 1942.

[3] I saw only two of these gardens among the grassland Mambwe, and they scarcely existed in the forest. One man grew European potatoes and other vegetables on such a garden to sell in Abercorn. Trapnell notes their scarcity. Op. cit., p. 43.

actual enclosure in which the animals are kept. During the dry season this dries off, and at the beginning of the next rainy season, in October, tobacco may be planted. Many Mambwe villagers plant maize on these sites, and they give a heavy yield. Other villagers, because of the scarcity of wood, use the manure to fire clay pots.[1]

The Mambwe do not give that attentive care to cattle which marks the true pastoralist. Cattle in the kraal generally stand knee-deep in manure before the palisade is moved.[2] Cattle are allowed to lie in the open in all weathers at all times of the year. In the past the Mambwe seem to have been an agricultural people with flocks of sheep and goats and only a few cattle. They themselves say that formerly only the chiefs had cattle, which they got by raiding the Fipa, a cattle-keeping people in Tanganyika. The Mambwe do not esteem milk as an article of diet, and use it as a relish only as a last resort, when nothing better can be found, although it is largely used in medicines. Since the

TABLE II

Number of cattle and small stock owned by Mambwe in 1952

| | Chieftaincy | | |
	Nsokolo	Mpande	Mwamba
Bulls	131	27	361
Cows	2,246	339	2,594
Oxen	287	25	89
Calves	919	205	1,374
Total:	3,583	596	4,418
Sheep	30	3	42
Goats	250	189	173

Condensed from Annual Stock Register

[1] Only men who have cattle in the village herd may use these sites for gardens.
[2] The Bemba say that lions never attack Mambwe kraals, for when they leap in they find themselves engulfed in the morass. The Administration is trying to encourage the use of roofed kraals.

1914–18 war, the flocks of sheep and goats have practically disappeared, and the cattle herds have increased. The number of
cattle and small animals in the possession of the Mambwe in
1952 is shown in Table II.

The village herd uses a common kraal, and individual owners
do not keep separate kraals. The largest herd owned by any one
village in 1952 was 244 cattle. One other village had more than
200, and most villages had less than half that number. The herds
in grassland villages are much larger than those in woodland
villages, but this does not necessarily mean that individual grassland Mambwe own more cattle than individual woodland
Mambwe. A recognized system exists for sending cattle to a
friend to be herded and cared for in return for a fee (*lusoso*).
Thus a Mambwe living in the forest, where there is little pasturage,
can own cattle herded in a village on the plains. The distribution
of herds of different sizes in grassland and woodland villages is
shown in Table III.

TABLE III

Number of cattle in grassland and woodland villages with herds, 1952

Number of cattle in herd	Number of villages with herds		
	Grassland Mambwe	Woodland Mambwe	Total
1– 9	2	12	14
10– 49	13	49	62
50– 99	25	5	30
100–149	20	1	21
150–199	12	—	12
200 up	2	—	2
Total:	74	67	141

Cattle are milked once a day, in the morning, except during the
short season of abundant pasturage, when they may be milked
in the evening as well. The boys take the cattle to the pasture
about seven o'clock in the morning and bring them back a little
before sunset, about half-past five.[1] Each man who has cattle in

---

[1] The Principal Veterinary Officer, Northern Province, informed me that a
longer period at grazing would improve their condition.

the herd is responsible in turn for two successive days' herding. The men themselves do not herd cattle nowadays, except when two villages are using the same pasture: then a man must be in charge to control the bulls. The men delegate the task of herding to their sons, boys between the ages of eight and fourteen. If a man has no sons of the proper age to do his share of herding, he engages the sons of other men. The father of these borrowed boys is given a herding fee in return for their services, usually the first female calf born after the arrangement begins. The boys do not give the cattle much care. I watched boys from two villages setting their bulls to fight, while both groups of herders applauded.

Bulls are allowed to run with the herd. Bull calves are not usually castrated, although some of the more progressive Mambwe have begun to use oxen to pull ploughs. This arrangement is not yet common. If a village has no full-grown bull of its own, it borrows a bull from another village and sets it to run with the herd. No charge is made for this.[1]

Cattle are now a valuable economic asset, as there is a growing demand for meat in the Northern Province that can be met only from among the cattle in the Mambwe area.[2] This has affected the Mambwe evaluation of their beasts. In the past the usual rate of exchange for cattle was two bulls for one cow. The price of a full-grown bull in Abercorn is now £15, while a cow fetches only £7–£8. Nowadays, if a Mambwe wants oxen for his plough, he can exchange a female calf for a full-grown ox. The Mambwe do not like to kill their cattle, and prefer to see their herds increase, if they can manage it. Cattle are used as part of marriage payments; to tie friends together through the herding system; and to pay fines. A Mambwe will rarely state how many cattle are in his possession, and the mutual herding arrangements effectively conceal the actual number in which a man may have rights. Nevertheless, the money to be gained from selling cattle

---

[1] This is what the Mambwe tell me. I did not observe any instance of a bull being borrowed, nor hear of any disputes concerning such a transaction. When a bull is borrowed, some fee may be charged.

[2] The cost of meat as sold in the butcher's shop reflects the increase in the value of cattle. In 1953 meat was one shilling a pound in Abercorn, an increase of 600 per cent on the 1935 price of twopence per pound. The price has gone up again since 1953.

See Macdonald, *Memorandum on the Economics of the Cattle Industry in Northern Rhodesia with Special Reference to the Native Cattle Industry*, p. 9.

to butchers is a constant temptation. In 1952, 798 African-owned cattle from the Mambwe area were sold to butchers or slaughtered for meat. Lions and other vermin killed another 498. A further 370 died from disease or other natural causes. In spite of these losses the cattle population remained stable.

The Mambwe are primarily cultivators. Cattle, although important to them, and significant in their social transactions, are not essential to their subsistence. Millet is the staple of their diet, and they consume it in large quantities, both as food and beer. Nevertheless, they grow only enough food to provide a bare subsistence, and even in good years the millet surplus is too small for its sale to satisfy their new wants. The grain-bins begin to run low in April and May, in the period before the harvest, but they do not suffer from 'hunger months', for they are able to eke out their supply of millet with such subsidiary crops as maize and cassava. Village social life declines before the harvest, for the beer-pot is the centre of many social activities,[1] and when it is empty the men tend to become restless. The fields no longer require their labour, so that at this time most men leave for work abroad.

The members of a village have common economic interests, and this emphasizes their interdependence, and encourages them to co-operate. The division of labour between men and women is defined, and is part of the general social relationships of the sexes. Among the grassland Mambwe both sexes have an equal share in the work of hoeing the fields, and men and women are therefore interchangeable units in this fundamental activity. In the woodlands, the men specialize in the task of lopping the trees, but share all the subsequent cultivation with the women. Weeding is a specialized task confined to women.[2] Fishing, hunting, and herding cattle are all collective enterprises, in which villagers co-operate.

Their rights to the use of land and their co-operative activities

---

[1] All important ceremonies, such as marriage, take place in the months immediately after the harvest, when the Mambwe have plenty of food and beer and are temporarily freed from toil in the fields. After the harvest they have both the supplies and time to expend on entertaining and visiting each other.

[2] Three women in Chief Mpande's court were fined 5s. each for failing to weed their gardens. Their husbands, though present, were not charged: weeding is women's work.

give economic independence to the members of each Mambwe village; they do not have to depend on neighbouring villages for economic assistance. Within any village each household has its own fields, and its own grain, and cooks for itself. But the men of a village usually eat as well as work together, and share any dish that is put before a man in company. They drink beer in each other's huts. The women and children eat apart from the men, but they too share meals with other women and children. Hospitality is enjoined, and there is wide sharing of food. Although the principles of individual ownership are quite clear, villagers draw from a common store of food.

This co-operation in production and consumption within Mambwe villages is a fundamental prerequisite of the system of migrant labour. The simple family can be described as an independent economic unit only in a limited sense, for in fact it is not self-sufficient and depends on co-operation with other groups. The withdrawal of a man's labour from the community therefore does not seriously hinder food production, for, although his labour is lost, he no longer consumes food from the common stock. His wife can take her place in the co-operative work-parties and ensure the cultivation of her absent husband's fields, as others will work for her in return for her assistance in their fields. If production depended entirely on the labour of the members of a simple family, the husband would be obliged to take his wife and children with him when he went off to work. But in the Mambwe system of cultivation, a man may leave his wife and family at home. They do not remain there passively, demanding care and upkeep from the absent husband; they can take their places in the co-operative tasks of cultivation and thus feed themselves. The specialized tasks which are the province of men can be left to the co-operative labour of men still resident in the village. Only when the disparity between the number of men and women resident in the village is too great does production break down, and then the village tends to break up as well. This critical point is reached when there are more than two women to each man in the village: anything higher than this disrupts both the economy and social life, as I shall show. The family of an absent wage-earner is therefore neither a burden to the resident villagers nor a drain on his wages. The profit of wage-labour to the Mambwe is underwritten by the subsistence economy.

Mambwe agriculture, whether in grassland or forest, is relatively complex when compared with that of neighbouring peoples. The cycle of cultivation through mounded and flat gardens, and the rotation of crops, demand regular and persistent co-operative labour. A man may have two or three gardens in different stages of the productive cycle, and must bring a new field into cultivation as an old one works out. He must use foresight and skill to balance gardens in different stages of the productive cycle. This stable form of cultivation demands residential stability of the productive group and the attachment of the group to a specific area of land for a considerable time. The people invest their labour in land that will continue to bear for many years. Thus the Mambwe are conditioned by their indigenous productive system to work regularly, to co-operate in production, to appreciate residential stability, and to value present investment for future benefits. These values are not dissimilar to those current among Europeans in the industrial sector of the economy, and may help the Mambwe wage-earner to benefit from the industrial labour markets in a way quite different from other shifting cultivators on the plateau.

CHAPTER III

THE QUEST FOR WAGES

PRESSURES TO WORK

UNLIKE some African peoples, such as the Masai who have turned their backs on Europeans and their goods and have refused to take part in their economy, at least as workers,[1] the Mambwe apparently accepted the opportunity to earn money with alacrity. The labour histories of older informants show that within ten years of the arrival of the British, Mambwe were already travelling far afield in the search for work and experience. The main reasons why the Mambwe accepted a cash economy with such ease, and were prepared to work for wages, lie in their economic system and their history.

The Mambwe were accustomed in the past to exchange goods, and bartered among themselves and with neighbouring peoples. There are rich deposits of iron ore in Mambwe country, which a guild of iron-workers (*yamusyanyi*) had the skill to smelt and work. These blacksmiths smelted the ore in kilns (*malungu*) about nine to twelve feet high, using charcoal, and from the raw iron (*imbulo*) they worked up a variety of artefacts: spears, axes, hoes, arrow-heads, knives, scythes. The blacksmiths paid tribute of these articles to the chief for the right to mine and use the ore. The manufactured items were exchanged with other Mambwe for grain and stock. The unworked ingots were themselves used as a medium of exchange. Many of these kilns are still standing, although no longer used, and in the past there was at least one in the bush near each village.[2] Decle stated that the Mambwe were 'famous for their skill in working iron',[3] and the Mambwe claim that they exchanged both tools and raw ingots with other tribes, and with the Arab slave caravans.

The ivory-hunters (*mwami*) were another group of specialists. They had to give the ivory to the chief, who rewarded them with

---

[1] Lord Hailey, op. cit., p. 694.
[2] Stewart described the many kilns he saw in one small area and the method of smelting. Op. cit., p. 267.
[3] Decle, *Three Years in Savage Africa*, p. 297.

calico or lengths of copper wire (*nsambo*), and they wore anklets of this wire as the badge of their speciality. They were entitled to keep a portion of the meat from the animals they killed, which they exchanged for grain. These men did not work in the fields and had considerable prestige.

Thus the Mambwe have never been entirely isolated. Besides this trade and barter with neighbouring peoples, they traded with the Arab caravans which followed the natural highway on which the Mambwe live. The Mambwe chief sold slaves[1] and ivory to the Arabs in exchange for trade goods such as calico, copper wire, beads, and guns. In 1880 Stewart found Chief Nsokolo wearing Arab dress, and at first mistook him for an Arab.[2] A former official in the village state of Chief Fwambo stated that the chief's great wife was distinguished from the other wives by wearing a cloth with distinctive spots and a necklace of large beads, both obtained from the Arabs. The chief had a monopoly of this trade, and through him goods from without were brought into the economy and distributed to the people. The chief rewarded his subjects with beer and presents in return for tribute labour.[3] He also gave presents of calico and copper wire to those who rendered him special services, for instance, the blacksmiths and ivory-hunters, and the young men who acted as his bodyguard and police. Lengths of calico, together with iron objects, cattle, and small stock, were used as marriage payments, which circulated them among the people.

It is clear, then, that before the British arrived, the Mambwe already had a range of goods obtained from outside their own subsistence economy, that they were accustomed to barter, and that they valued the goods brought from without. They were prepared for the introduction of a cash-economy, and for labour that would earn material rewards.

The British South Africa Company began to rule the area in

---

[1] The Mambwe enslaved prisoners-of-war, but the chiefs could also enslave their own subjects for certain offences. If one man killed another, the killer could claim sanctuary in the chief's palace. The chief could then pay the relatives of the dead man an indemnity, and impound the property of the killer. When the killer had no property, the chief enslaved him.

[2] Op. cit., p. 268. The Mambwe chiefs today wear a cloth headdress.

[3] Each man was expected to work in the chief's garden for a few days each year.

1893. The first representative was a Mr. Marshall, accompanied by a force of six armed Sikh soldiers and some Tonga from Nyasaland.[1] Marshall was commissioned by Sir H. H. Johnston, H.M. Commissioner and Consul-General, who was then at The Residence in Zomba, Nyasaland. Marshall set up his headquarters at a place he called Zombe, after the title of the Lungu chief within whose area it lay, but since changed to Abercorn, to prevent confusion with Zomba.[2] Marshall's title was prophetic: Collector of Revenue and Postmaster. He began to collect the revenue and the Mambwe had to pay tax. This tax was their first compulsion to work outside their own economy. They were put to work making roads and buildings for the Administration, and are still able to earn their tax in this way, although today the task of keeping the roads in order within the reserves is the responsibility of the Native Authority. Many Mambwe were employed in various jobs within the Administration. Gouldsbury described them as possessing considerable intelligence, and said that they made good station workers.[3]

But even before the imposition of tax the Mambwe were eager to work. Travellers and missionaries were in the area prior to the administrators, and explorers like Livingstone and Thomson found them willing to act as carriers. In 1883 the African Lakes Company transported a steamer in sections ready for assembly from the north end of Lake Nyasa over the plateau to Lake Tanganyika. This steamer, the *Habari Ngama* (Good News), was for the use of the London Missionary Society who had set up a mission station on the shores of Lake Tanganyika, at Kasakalawe, near the present port of Mpulungu. The Stevenson road was not yet completed, and a bridge of tree stems from six to eight feet long was built to carry the parts across the Saisi river. This was the first time that European endeavour had provided work for the Mambwe, for they were employed both to carry the steamer parts and to build the bridge.[4]

In 1890 the missionaries moved up on to the plateau from the lake shore, which they found unhealthy, and settled at Kawimbe,

---

[1] Gouldsbury and Sheane, *The Great Plateau of Northern Rhodesia*, p. 40.

[2] After the Duke of Abercorn, then President of the British South Africa Company.

[3] Op. cit., p. 11.

[4] It is still standing, in good repair.

where the London Missionary Society still has a station. They bought six thousand acres of land from Chief Fwambo, a royal Mambwe chief, and began their work. This mission was at once flooded with refugees from the war then proceeding with the Bemba, and the Mambwe were introduced to a stable and permanent European society. Two great themes of Mambwe life for the next fifty years were established: peace and work. The missionaries supervised the agriculture of the people in the Fwambo area, besides employing them to build a church, school, hospital, and other mission buildings. Thus, before the imposition of tax, some Mambwe were already engaged in paid labour.

The new religion brought by the missionaries had a profound effect on the Mambwe, but the impact of the missionaries' material possessions was perhaps equally important.

The buildings that the missionaries put up, their clothes, their food, the multitudinous manufactured articles they brought with them, set before the Mambwe new standards of material possessions. The schools opened a new world of reading and ideas. Missionary teaching brought the Mambwe to despise 'naked savages', and to look upon European clothes and other articles as essentials of progressiveness.[1] The missionaries acted on the assumption that Mambwe life was barbarous; they made the people conscious of their own backwardness.

The missionaries trained some of their new proselytes as evangelists, and paid them a salary to live in the villages and help convert the heathen. These men wore European clothes, had cash incomes, could read and write, and were the precursors of the class of educated clerks and officials of the future.[2] They spread the gospel, not only of Christianity, but also of the material benefits of work for Europeans.

Today, after more than sixty years of European contact, the

---

[1] An assessor at Chief Mwamba's court showed me a photograph of his father and mother taken by a missionary in the 1890s, just after they were married in church. Bride and groom are both dressed in the florid Victorian style familiar to us from countless such photographs in our own society. The bride sits in a rustic chair wearing a long frock with leg-of-mutton sleeves, and the bridegroom stands erect behind her, negligently holding his jacket open to display a large gold watch-chain on his waistcoat. Apart from their colour, they could have been a respectable working-class couple in Britain.

[2] Some of those who were thus trained are still alive and are men of importance among the Mambwe, holding posts as councillors and officials.

pressures to work are much more complex. Wage-labour is now an accepted part of a man's life; he is expected to go out and earn wages in the same way as most men in our own society. This social expectation is a strong compulsion; a man would be considered odd if he did not wish to earn money. I met only one adult male who had not been away to work, an old traditional chief who had succeeded to his title while young, and thus never had an opportunity of going away.[1]

But more than anything else, men need money, and they can only get it by working. Money is needed for taxes, marriage payments, court fines, bicycles and their licences, bus fares, clothes, sewing-machines, household goods of all kinds, brick houses, even for such 'luxuries' as wireless sets and guns. Their wives and children too need clothes and store goods.[2] It is on young men that the pressure to work is greatest, for a young man needs a considerable sum for a marriage payment before he can marry. The essential item in the Mambwe marriage is an exchange of money and cattle, although a man also works in the garden of his parents-in-law. In the old days, cattle, goats, sheep, calico, hoes, axes, spears, and arrows formed the marriage payment, but since the 1914–18 war cattle and money have taken the place of this wider range of goods. When a marriage payment is written down today, as many of them are, the total sum handed over is equated with the traditional items such as hoes, spears, etc. Formerly seventeen such items were handed over, each with a special name, and each representing a specific strand in the marriage bond. Each was given to the bride's parents at a specific time and place, thus forming a 'score' for the whole wedding transactions and ceremony.[3] All of these are now subsumed in the cash payment.

---

[1] The Mambwe consider that the land would suffer in the absence of the chief. Chiefs are not expected to take paid employment, for manual labour would lower their dignity; this applies even to those traditional chiefs who do not receive a salary from the Administration. As one chief said: 'A chief does not work; he walks about and looks after his people.'

[2] Throughout Africa money debts provide a means for applying pressure on men to undertake labour contracts. In South Africa traders were for many years the chief recruiting agents of the mines. Cf. Stent, 'Migrancy and Urbanization in the Union of South Africa', p. 168 ff.

[3] The Ngoni had a similar list of transactions. See Barnes, *Marriage in a Changing Society*.

TABLE IV

Marriage payments made in 24 primary marriages between 1920 and 1929, and in 27 primary marriages between 1950 and 1953

1920 to 1929				1950 to 1953	
Cattle	Goats	Sheep	Cash	Cattle	Cash
			£ s. d.		£ s. d.
4			2 4 6	4	12 10 0
4			—	4	5 3 6
2			1 5 0	3	8 19 0
2			—	3	1 0 0
1			3 0 0	2	10 0 0
1			2 12 0	2	4 0 0
1			1 0 0	2	2 0 0
				1	12 7 0
				1	8 17 6
				1	7 0 0
				1	5 10 0
	5		2 0 0		
	4	1	—		
	3		—		
	2		2 10 0		
	2		2 10 0		
	2		2 8 0		
	2		2 0 0		
	1		1 5 0		
	1		1 0 0		
	1		—		
	1		—		
			5 0 0		17 2 6
			4 5 0		15 2 6
			3 0 0		13 0 0
			2 15 0		11 1 9
			2 15 0		10 2 6
			2 10 0		10 0 0
					10 0 0
					9 10 0
					8 5 0
					7 5 0
					7 5 0
					7 3 0
					7 0 0
					6 10 0
					3 0 0
					3 0 0

Note: *Primary marriage*, a girl's first marriage

To compare the change in the form of payment, I have shown in Table IV the difference in marriage payments in twenty-four primary marriages in the period 1920 to 1929, and in twenty-seven primary marriages in the period 1950 to 1953. A primary marriage is a girl's first marriage; the payment is always highest for a previously unwedded girl. The Mambwe place a strong emphasis on the virginity of a bride, and prenuptial conception is extremely rare.[1] If a man seduces a virgin, and she bears a child, the courts award damages of fifteen pounds or more against him.

Table IV shows the rise in cash value of the marriage payments in the thirty-three years covered by the marriages.[2] This was generally true of all marriage payments recorded; they have grown greater over the years. I have omitted the goods (calico, hoes, and axes) handed over in the 1920s, for even then they were being omitted from many exchanges. Hoes and axes could be bought cheaply in the stores, and their former scarcity-value had disappeared. The number of cattle has increased, and goats and sheep have entirely disappeared from the recent marriage payments, while the amount of money handed over has greatly increased. Mambwe marriage payments absorb much of the money earned by wage-labour.

The Mambwe say that men marry at a younger age today than they did in the past. In the eight villages of my census, there were thirty-five men between the ages of twenty and twenty-five; 56 per cent of these were known to be married. It

---

[1] The Mambwe have a word for the hymen, *katowa*. Evidence of virginity is sought on the wedding night, and a marriage may be declared void if the girl is found not to be a virgin. She is inspected after intercourse by an old woman, who makes a statement to the families of the couple. If the man is impotent, the girl can call off the marriage. A special relationship exists between a husband and a wife who was a virgin when she married, and they address each other as *kapundu*. The same value is not attached to subsequent marriages, nor are the marriage payments so high.

[2] The increase in real value is perhaps not so great as the gross figures of cash handed over make it appear. Although the number of cattle handed over is the same in the first marriages shown in each period, the cash payment in the second period has increased $5\frac{1}{2}$ times. But in the intervening period inflation has reduced the real value of the pound. If we accept that inflation has reduced the value of the pound in 1950 to one-third of its value in 1920, the real value of the cash handed over has only doubled. The significant change appears to be that higher payments are given nowadays in more marriages than in the past, and that cash is now almost universally substituted for other goods.

seems likely that the ability of young men to earn wages and thereby obtain the price of marriage payments, may have lowered the age at which a man gets married. As all the living men today have been involved in wage-labour, no comparison with the past is possible.

Thus a young man wishing to get married must either raise a considerable sum by himself, or appeal to his agnatic kin for aid. When he does this, he must go out to work to repay his obligations. Even to be considered as a potential husband, a Mambwe youth must be smartly dressed, able to give presents, socially accomplished, adept in the Sava-Sava (a popular African ballroom dance based on the foxtrot), and generally he must have the sophisticated air and fashions of the urban worker. The consequence is that young men are eager to go out to work as soon as they can.

Some men have other financial obligations to their kin besides those incurred for marriage payments. The best-paid jobs go to skilled men, and one of the most useful skills which can be readily acquired is the ability to read and write English well. This demands a standard of education higher than that provided by the Native Authority schools, and many Mambwe go to the school at Lunzuwa, fifteen miles from Abercorn. Education here is free, but the boys must pay £8 4s. a year for uniforms and other items, and this must be paid in full at the beginning of each year. Older brothers give the fees to younger brothers to keep them at this school for three years or more, and in view of the low wages (between 30s. and £5 a month according to the market and age and experience) earned by unskilled adult Mambwe, this amounts to a considerable outlay.

Besides these purely economic compulsions, there are other pressures. A young man wishes to visit the marvellous world of the Europeans and to see the wonders of the Copperbelt towns. European civilization as represented there is at its most attractive to the Mambwe. The 'big city', with all the attractions, dangers, and excitements that it holds for the countryman, exerts a strong pull. A visit there marks out a man as being as sophisticated and experienced as his fellows. Indeed, a man who had never been away to work would be hard put to it to take a lively part in social affairs, for village conversation today includes a great many subjects that their forefathers could rarely have envisaged. The

Mambwe discuss politics and the desirability or unpleasantness of different kinds of work; they endlessly discuss the Europeans they have met and their different attitudes and behaviour towards Africans; they are interested in world affairs.[1] Wage-labour is the most important school for all Mambwe, much more important than the formal schools of the missions and the Native Authorities.

The women exert considerable pressure on the men to go out to work. Single women are prevented by law from going to the Copperbelt to find work by themselves. Apart from the legal restrictions, Mambwe ideas of decorum forbid women to attempt to seek work on their own. A woman showing such a degree of independence would be considered immoral. I came across only one young woman who could be described as a wage-earner. She worked in an Indian store over the border in Tanganyika, and the proprietor had 'married' her with the consent of her parents.

If a married woman wishes to go to the towns, she must have in her possession a Marriage Certificate issued by the Native Authority, or the town police will return her to the reserve.[2] But when a wife does accompany her husband to the town, the Mambwe see no objection to her working for wages, provided she lives with her husband. The pressure that women bring to bear on their men appears in the number of married labourers who take their wives with them to their place of work, or who send for them after they have found a job. I have shown the marital status of all the absent labourers from eight villages in Table V. Of forty men absent on wage-labour from these villages, twenty-nine had their wives with them.[3] A number of these men were working locally, but the majority were on the Copperbelt.[4]

---

[1] The headman of the first village other than the chief's that I visited began our conversation, after greeting me with the usual civilities, by asking: 'Do you think that our policy at the London Conference last year was wise?'

[2] The police check all the buses bringing in people from the country.

[3] According to the Administration Census of 1952, 462 men from Chief Mwamba's area were out of the reserve earning wages. This includes both married and single men. During that year Chief Mwamba's court issued 153 Marriage Certificates, so that a large number, perhaps 40 per cent, of the wives joined their husbands at work that year. Marriage Certificates are rarely sought for any other purpose.

[4] The number of wives who can join their husbands is, of course, limited by such factors as the availability of housing, the amount of wages earned, etc.

TABLE V

Age and marital status of 67 wage-earners absent from eight villages in 1953

Age-groups	Single men			Married men			Total	
				Residence of dependants:				
	Unwedded	Divorced	Widowed	With him	In migrant's village	In wife's father's village	Single	Married
15–24	21	1	–	9	–	1	22	10
25–29	4	1	–	6	4	–	5	10
30–34	–	–	–	5	–	–	–	5
35–39	–	–	–	5	3	–	–	8
40–44	–	–	–	3	–	1	–	4
45–49	–	–	–	1	–	–	–	1
Totals:	25	2	–	29	7	2	27	38
Not known:	–	–	–	–	2	–	–	2

A trip to the Copperbelt is an experience that a young woman never forgets. For at least once in her life she is free from the everlasting duties of fetching water and stamping meal, and acquires the outward appearance of European women, if not their leisure. Mambwe women have a hard life, and the indirect effects of these educational visits to the Copperbelt undoubtedly affect their whole attitude towards tribal life on their return. Girls are no longer willing to have their husbands chosen for them by their parents, but insist on choosing their own lovers, and they do not choose young men who cannot or will not go out to work to provide them with European clothes and household goods.

Some women will go to extraordinary lengths to get to the towns. One woman left her husband and went to live with her sister, who was married to a man contemplating a trip to the Copperbelt. Eventually this man 'took' her, and when her husband divorced her, married her.[1] He took both his wives to the town. The former divorcee paid a holiday visit to the village while I was there. She had acquired a bicycle, was smartly dressed in European clothes, and had some money. Her material

---

[1] The Mambwe have sororal polygyny.

prosperity was the subject of much envious admiration by the other women and a source of conversation long after she left, despite the general condemnation of her morals—or perhaps because of it. It is quite usual to see a smartly-dressed young woman living in a village, on holiday from the Copperbelt. This constant stimulation sets up standards of what can be done through wage-labour, and the women are not backwards in pressing their men-folk to go out and get money. In a divorce case before Chief Mwamba's court, the woman freely admitted her adultery. The court awarded her husband a divorce and eight pounds in damages against the lover, who was present. Immediately the case was over and the divorce pronounced, the woman asked the court to give her a Marriage Certificate, so that she could go off at once to the Copperbelt with her lover. The whole court, officials and spectators, burst out laughing at the naïveté of this demand. The senior assessor told the woman he now fully understood why she had given such shameless evidence—she wanted to go to the Copperbelt for an easy life. He upbraided her for breaking her marriage for such a purpose, and read her a lecture on the virtues of Mambwe marriage and true Mambwe wives. He stressed the importance of the marriage bond, that was not to be lightly broken, and told her she had exchanged a husband for a lover and might find her new position less agreeable than she had imagined. He told her to go off: the court would issue a Marriage Certificate only when her lover married her, and brought her parents before the court to prove that he had made a proper marriage payment.[1] The lover did marry her subsequently and she achieved her trip to the Copperbelt.[2]

Wage-labour can also afford an escape from village life and unpleasant circumstances. A nagging wife may find herself without a husband, who goes off to work and does not return. One such woman, with four children, was deserted by her husband,

---

[1] Before the court will issue a Marriage Certificate, the parents of the wife must testify that they have received a marriage payment, and the amount that they received.

[2] The women have always been avid for European goods. Gouldsbury stated that before 1911 the balance of money earned went to the stores for 'gauds and trinkets to tempt fickle females'. He blamed the increase of adultery on this, but he was writing generally of all the natives on the plateau, and probably meant the Bemba here. Op. cit., p. 346.

and forced to go to live in her brother's village, as she had not heard from her husband for four years. Her husband had successfully concealed his place of work from her. A young man who committed adultery with the wife of a chief, fled the country and went to work on the Copperbelt. A young married man, who had already made several wage-earning trips, was sued for his adultery with the wife of an absent wage-earner, the case being brought by the husband's brother. The adulterer told me that he intended to go off to Tanganyika to work before he was brought before the court, but his brothers prevailed on him to stay and face his responsibilities. But the possibility of escape was present in his mind. Thus, apart from the direct economic and social pressures to go out to earn money, wage-labour offers an escape from unpleasant or intolerable social and economic situations at home.

THE LABOUR MARKETS

The migration of workers to distant centres of European enterprise is only one aspect of Mambwe wage-labour, although the most important in quantity. Migrant labour is really only part of the more general participation of the Mambwe in a system of monetary relations.

As we have seen, the first source of employment available to the Mambwe was the missionaries and explorers who traversed their territory. Shortly afterwards the British Administration arrived and opened up new sources of wages. The Administration was followed by European farmers, and by 1914 there were a number of these in the locality, together with two stores. The work they made available to the Mambwe was either labouring or clerical or domestic service. The discovery and exploitation of minerals in Central Africa, not only in Northern Rhodesia but also in Southern Rhodesia and the Congo, opened up new opportunities. The exploitation of the country as a whole changed from the haphazard operations of individuals to the wholesale organized effort of large companies, particularly the mining companies, both copper and coal. In addition, development proceeded in neighbouring territories, particularly on the sisal plantations and the goldfields at Lupa in Tanganyika. This change in the Europeans' relations to the country's resources inevitably affected the pattern of Mambwe wage-earning.

The present position is that the kind of work available to the Mambwe falls into five broad categories: Administrative, Mining and Industrial, Agricultural, Trading, and Domestic Service.[1] These categories, as far as the Mambwe are concerned, differ in only two ways: one, that some jobs are further away from the reserve than others; and two, that some require skills and others do not. They therefore regard labour in these two ways: it is either local or distant, and skilled or unskilled. The skill that a Mambwe can bring to the market obviously determines the wages he can earn, but most of the Mambwe are unskilled, as there are few places near home where they can acquire skills. On the whole the unskilled men prefer distant markets, for they have more opportunities of acquiring cash on the Copperbelt. Within the reserve or in local European employment the unskilled labourer can rarely earn more than one-and-fourpence a day, the Administration's rate for unskilled work.[2] Other things being equal, a Mambwe prefers to work locally, whether he is skilled or not, for he can see his family often and constantly visit his friends, besides drawing food from the subsistence economy, which helps to raise his real wages. But the local market is limited.

The Administration is the dominant employer in the local market; it provides jobs with the police, schools, agricultural and veterinary departments, Native Authorities, and public works, besides employing clerks and officials in the lower branches of the administrative system. The government of Northern Rhodesia was in the hands of the British South Africa Company until 1924, when the Colonial Office took over. In 1930 the policy of Indirect Rule was introduced, and three salaried chiefs with their Native Authorities were created, and thus a class of paid officials round the chiefs. The Administration also employed African clerks from the very beginning. Further jobs became available to the

---

[1] In 1952, the three largest categories of employment for Africans in Northern Rhodesia were: mining, 40,000; agriculture, 30,000; domestic service, 30,000. *Colonial Annual Report, Northern Rhodesia*, 1952.

[2] The towns have always offered higher wages, to bring in the men. In 1911 the mines in Southern Rhodesia were attracting men from the Abercorn District, because they offered higher wages. The mines did not have to offer very much, for the local wage was only 4s. 2d. a month, including a calico ration. That the Africans were prepared to walk all the way to Bulawayo to gain a few extra shillings well illustrates the strength of the desire for money, even in those days. See Gouldsbury and Sheane, op. cit., p. 346.

Mambwe with the development of the technical services, mainly the agricultural and veterinary departments. On the whole this market demands skills from the Mambwe, although many are employed by the public works department in unskilled labour, with some semi-skilled workers such as woodworkers and brick-layers.

Some local jobs in agriculture, domestic service, and general labouring are also provided by European farmers and traders. There are not enough of these to form an important market for the Mambwe. By far the largest local private employer now is the International Red Locust Control. This organization's task is to control the breeding and swarming of the Red Locust in two areas, the Mweru marshes to the north and west of Abercorn and the Lake Rukwa valley in Tanganyika to the east. It main-tains a large workshop to service its fleet of vehicles and special spraying equipment. This workshop employs some 130 Africans, many of them in semi-skilled work, as well as a body of about sixty African drivers. In addition, the administrative side of the organization employs clerks and messengers, and the European staff also employ Africans as domestic servants and gardeners. This organization therefore forms a considerable addition to the local wage market for Mambwe, both skilled and unskilled. It also serves to demonstrate the pull of a local market against the in-dustrial market of the Copperbelt.

The distant markets fall into two main areas, lying in opposite directions: the Copperbelt and Tanganyika. Work on the Cop-perbelt varies from copper-mining to employment in factories and in domestic service and building. It is largely unskilled work, as far as the Mambwe are concerned, but the pay is relatively good. In 1952 the copper mines paid an African surface worker from 80 to 370 shillings for thirty working days, and an underground worker from 90 to 405 shillings for the same period. In other industries wages for unskilled Africans ranged from 25 shillings to 70 shillings a month, and for semi-skilled Africans from 50 to 120 a month. Skilled men, such as typists, carpenters, bricklayers, and trade-tested transport drivers, could earn up to £20 a month. Most of them got free accommodation and food, or a cash pay-ment in lieu, in addition to their cash wages.[1]

---

[1] African wages have risen steadily since the war. In 1946 the average monthly cash wage was 34s. 2d. for surface workers and 42s. 5d. for under-

In Tanganyika, the principal employer is the federation of sisal planters, which operates a company to collect and distribute labour to the plantations. This work is almost entirely agricultural. There are also jobs in domestic service, trading, and industry to be found in Tanganyika, but not on the same scale as on the Copperbelt. The gold field at Lupa also attracts some Mambwe, though fewer now than in the past. This too is unskilled work.

Although a Mambwe prefers to work locally if he can find a suitable job, so that he can keep his wife with him and raise his real wages by drawing food from the subsistence economy, he is affected by other factors in the general situation besides the purely economic. The curiosity and interest of European town life can be enjoyed only by a trip to the Copperbelt, or some other town. The market to which a Mambwe applies for work largely depends on his age and marital status.

In the past, before the Copperbelt developed, the Mambwe ranged further afield in their search for work—to the Congo, Southern Rhodesia, and South Africa. Very few men go to these places today, although all provide much higher wages than they can earn locally. They say they resent the pass laws and other devices which restrict their movements and freedom in these places, and the indignity of their status as Africans. They prefer to go to the Copperbelt and to Tanganyika, where they consider they are more liberally treated. In 1952, the last year for which full figures are available, there were 2,407 Mambwe males, estimated to be eighteen years of age or over, absent earning wages, out of a total male population of 6,045.[1] Only twenty-one of these (less than one per cent) were thought by the Administration to be working in either the Congo, Southern Rhodesia, or South Africa. In the eight villages in which I took a census, none of the absent workers were reported to be in any of these countries. But in the labour histories of returned workers at present living in these eight villages, I found that men over forty years of age had often made journeys to these territories in the past. There

ground workers. In 1951 the surface worker's wage ranged from 45s. to 320s. a month, and the underground worker's from 55s. to 355s. Real wages did not go up at this rate, for the cost of living went up 23 points during the year, and has gone up 55 points since 1943. The largest increase was in the price of food. *Colonial Reports, Northern Rhodesia,* 1946, p. 16, and 1952, pp. 13, 14.

[1] Administration Census.

were forty-one men over forty who had made 138 trips between them. Forty-five of these trips, or 33 per cent, were made to the foreign territories other than Tanganyika, most of them to the Belgian Congo[1] (Table VIII, p. 61).

The canalization of the labour flow may also have affected their decision not to venture to the Congo or the other territories. In 1921 the European population of Northern Rhodesia was only 3,634,[2] and there was no industrial development that could be compared with these other territories. The lack of roads and the cost of transport forced the men to walk to work in those days, and they moved from job to job ever further afield. European labour recruiters also recruited them for territories outside Northern Rhodesia. There are no recruiters in the Mambwe area at present; they are not needed. No one now walks to the Copperbelt; they all go by bus. A social survey of the Copperbelt recently found that of 140 men who had come there from the Northern Province, 104 arrived by bus and only 27 by foot, the remainder going part of the way by various forms of transport and the rest by foot.[3] Abercorn is the most distant part of the Northern Province from the Copperbelt; my own experience with the Mambwe was that no one walked to the Copperbelt. The journey by bus is a significant change from the past. A man no longer expects to go ragged and on foot to the Copperbelt and return clothed and by bus. Now he both goes and returns by bus, properly dressed. If he cannot find the money for both suitable clothes and the bus fare of £2 10s., his relatives must stake him.

The route into Tanganyika has also been organized. This route is the easiest and cheapest way to regular work, and consequently attracts most of the youths on their first trip. The Labour Bureau of the Tanganyika Sisal Growers' Association (Silabu) maintains an African agent at a village just over the border from

[1] Regulations now hinder the entrance of Africans from Northern Rhodesia to the Congo. They must have a signed medical certificate of fitness in their Identification Certificates, an irksome formality for Africans, who do not like to approach the District Commissioner and the doctor. The Belgian mining company, the Union Miniere, prefers to attract permanent workers, and its policy opposes the use of migrant labourers.

[2] *Census of Population*, May, 1921.

[3] Niddrie, 'The Road to Work: A Survey of the Influence of Transport on Migrant Labour in Central Africa', p. 42.

Northern Rhodesia, and therefore only a few miles from Mambwe country. When a Mambwe youth reports to this agent for work, he is given free transport on a Silabu bus to Mbeya, in Tanganyika, and issued with rations of meat and mealie meal for the journey. At Mbeya a European interviews him and directs him to a particular place. The terms of the contract are not onerous. The labourer can have a Casual Labour Ticket and work by the day. The system is a kind of piecework, with a certain amount of work recognized as justifying a mark on the labourer's ticket. A bonus payment is earned when a labourer completes a *kipande*, a period of thirty completed working days, within a period of forty-two consecutive days. Rates of pay vary according to the kind of work he is set to perform, and earnings range from about fifteen shillings to £2 a month. A man can take a day off when he likes. The men are issued with rations, clothing, and a blanket, and live together in a compound. Normally they go for a contract of twelve months, and if they complete this satisfactorily are brought back free to the border where they started.

For a young man without money or clothes, the whole process is simple and easy; he need make no other effort than to walk the few miles to the border and present himself for work. His initial contact is with an African, an important point, for his lack of a decent suit and his inadequate English do not endanger his chances of employment, besides offering less psychological difficulties. In the towns, a man's general appearance and ability to speak English, in however limited a way, are assets in finding work. The work is not so well paid as on the Copperbelt, but on the other hand it is agricultural and simple, and easy to learn. The youths almost invariably go in small groups from the same village, under the guidance of a leader who has already made the trip. Occasionally a father will conduct his son. According to the Mambwe, the authorities in Tanganyika are not so insistent on passes and regulations as those in neighbouring territories, including Northern Rhodesia, and Africans can move about freely, without fear of molestation or unlucky clashes with regulations they do not understand. It is in fact a kind of apprenticeship to labour conditions, made in the helpful company of kin and friends. The initial contact with Europeans and their customs and language is made under the most favourable circumstances. Capital is accumulated for suitable clothes and the bus fare to the Copperbelt, as well as a fund of useful experience in European habits and demands.

There are therefore two main routes to the labour markets: the bus route from Moze village in Tanganyika which leads to the sisal plantations, and the bus route from Abercorn to the Copperbelt. Labour within the Province is a third choice; this is confined almost entirely to the European centre of Abercorn, and to the capital of the Northern Province, Kasama, some 110 miles from Abercorn. The age, skill, social status, and labour experience of each individual who seeks work all help to determine his choice of market in which to sell his labour.

The Labour Supply

Precise statistics of the Mambwe population are difficult to obtain. The Administration makes an annual census of the population, which is the basis of the tax registers, and these counts are the only available figures for the Mambwe population. This annual census does not differentiate the population into age-groups. The only division is between Adult Males and Adult Females, and Male Children and Female Children. A Male is any adult over the estimated age of eighteen, when the men become liable to pay tax. A Female is any married woman or a girl of marriageable age. The parents of girls are asked whether or not they are betrothed or married. When the answer is 'yes', the girl is classified as a Female Adult and not as a Child. These classifications are therefore somewhat vague and arbitrary, and the accuracy of the figures depends greatly on the experience of the European officer who conducts the count.

To combine a numerical account with my descriptive and analytical material, I chose eight villages which I considered representative, and made my own census within them. The relevant data collected are shown in Table VI. Where there were written records of births, marriages, and deaths, I used these, and estimated the ages of the rest of the population by five-year age-groups. I took a genealogy from every adult person at present living in these villages, and checked the present residence of adults and children who appeared on these genealogies. This method accounts for most of the members of a village who are absent at the time the census is made, but it does not necessarily

TABLE VI

Demographic data from eight representative villages in 1953

Area:		Grassland Mambwe					Tr. chief	Woodland Mambwe		Totals
Status:		Royal headmen			Commoner headmen			Adm. chief	Commoner headmen	
Title:		Kasunga (1)	Kosam (2)	Aron (3)	Simukulwa (4)	Luembe (5)	Kowa (6)	Mpande (7)	Ponde (8)	
Population										
1. 0–14 years	Male	17	18	10	13	20	21	37	26	162
	Female	16	20	14	13	15	15	21	27	141
2. 15 years upwards	Male	25	22	23	18	12	26	39	28	193
	Female	31	29	22	18	25	27	48	45	245
3. Total pop.	Male	42	40	33	31	32	47	76	54	355
	Female	47	49	36	31	40	42	69	72	386
4. No. of wage-earners		11	6	8	8	6	11	14	3	67
5. Resident pop.	Male	14	16	15	10	6	23	25	25	134
	Female	28	25	20	15	22	26	43	44	223
6. Proportion women to men resident		2·0	1·6	1·3	1·5	3·7	1·1	1·8	1·7	1·6
7. No. of huts		31	22	24	27	22	40	42	45	253
8. Aver. per hut	Total pop.	2·9	4·1	2·9	2·3	3·3	2·2	3·5	2·8	2·9
	Present res:	2·4	3·6	2·5	1·9	2·9	2·1	3·0	2·7	2·6
9. Polygynists		4	6	1	4	4	4	5	8	36 (28%)

uncover all of them. Although Mambwe villages are stable, in the sense that they move within a limited area and that the agnatic core to which the headman belongs retains its association with a particular village, people do move between villages. Residence is virilocal, so women are constantly moving between villages, primarily from their fathers' villages to those of their husbands. But other people move as well, for various reasons, e.g. because they are discontented with life in one village and want to try another, or because a kinsman has returned from work with some money and they decide to join him in his village, or because they prefer to live with other persons of the same religion as themselves. There are a large number of reasons why people move from village to village. Thus men who are permanently lost to the tribe are easily overlooked, and sometimes they have been forgotten. However, the number of such men is likely to be small.

I have used the Administration's census figures only for broad generalizations, and depend on my own census of eight villages for most of my conclusions on Mambwe wage-labour.

The eight villages were chosen as representative of the four main categories of Mambwe village. These categories are:

A—Villages of an administrative chief

There are only three of these, but as the seats of government, they have an obvious importance. All of these chiefs are members of the royal clan.

B—Villages of a traditional chief

There are thirteen of these, of which ten are members of the royal clan. I have selected Kowa village from this group. Kowa is a traditional chief of a commoner clan, now reduced to the status of headman.

C—Villages of royal headmen

These form about one-half of the total number of all Mambwe villages.

D—Villages of commoner headmen

These form the remainder of Mambwe villages which are not in the above three categories.

Categories C and D form the bulk of Mambwe villages; there

are 190 villages in all. I further selected the villages from the two main divisions of the people into Aisa Mambwe and Maswepa Mambwe, the grassland and forest people. Six of the villages were grassland and two forest. There did not appear to be any significant difference between the two groups, apart from their methods of cultivating, but the forest sample is too small for me to be dogmatic on this point.[1] The census is therefore based on the grassland Mambwe, among whom I lived longest, and the two forest Mambwe villages were chosen as a control.

Category A is represented by Chief Mpande's village (7). Chief Mpande is the next senior chief to Nsokolo, and rules an entirely forest population.

Category B is represented by Chief Kowa's village (6).

Category C is represented by three villages, Kasunga (1), Kosam (2), and Aron (3). These are all old-established royal villages, whose headmen have titles. Aron village was included, as the majority of the population were members of the Watch Tower Bible and Tract Society. The present headman's father was sympathetic to the movement, and when the original community of Jehovah's Witnesses was broken up,[2] he accepted many of them into his village.

Category D is represented by three commoner villages, Simukulwa (4), Luembe (5), and Ponde (8). Ponde is a forest village, the other two grassland. Each of these commoner villages was founded for a different reason; Simukulwa and Luembe are described in Chapter IV. The present headman of Ponde was the second, and succeeded from his elder brother who founded the village; he was linked cognatically to Chief Mpande.

The villages selected cover all types of Mambwe village. The Administration treats all the headmen equally, except Chief Mpande, but they represent quite different social elements to the Mambwe. The history and social connections of each village have affected its response to the wage-labour markets. They do not represent a random sample, but a selected sample.[3]

---

[1] I visited many more forest villages, but did not collect the precise data given here. But my general impression was that there was little difference in the wage-earning patterns of the two groups.

[2] See p. 200.

[3] I believe that this method, taken together with my wider observations of Mambwe life, is the best use I could make of the time available for research. A

I have also shown in Table VI the number of men engaged in wage-labour. I have omitted from this group those men who are working and earning wages within their own villages. Opportunities for paid employment within the reserve are limited and are mainly confined to the villages of the three administrative chiefs. Most of such men are employed by the Administration, as agricultural and veterinary assistants and messengers, etc., or by the Native Authority, as clerks, court assessors, etc. There are also three large stores, two owned by European companies and one by an African. The two missions employ some men, and the London Missionary Society sends a few paid evangelists to live in villages. Altogether, probably no more than fifty Mambwe earn wages within their own villages. I have not included them among the number of men working locally for wages, for their inclusion in my small sample would unduly distort the proportion of men working in local markets compared with the number of men working in distant markets, who form the bulk of Mambwe wage-earners.

Nine men earned wages within their own villages. Six of them worked in the village of Chief Mpande, the seat of the Native Authority and Court attached to his chieftaincy. The other three men each lived in a different village. Between them they held the following jobs:

Assessors at the Native Court	2
Messenger at the Native Court . . .	1
Mailman for the Native Authority . . .	1
Dispenser	1
Storekeeper	1
Evangelist for mission	1
Hawkers, self-employed	2

All these village wage-earners were over thirty years of age, and had been out of the tribal area to work at one time or another, except the storekeeper, a young man of twenty-one. He planned to make a trip to Tanganyika the following year. Both

scheme was drawn up to use a team of African research workers to make a census of all Mambwe villages to check the findings of this representative sample, but it could not be carried out because of the political situation at the time. At some future date, when the Mambwe are more settled, this scheme may be taken up again.

F

he and his employer were members of the royal clan, and both were related to Chief Mpande, in whose village the store was situated.

The number of men at present engaged on wage-labour that I have shown in Table VI is therefore the number who have gone out of the reserve to work. All these men are absent from their villages while at work, except those from two villages, Kowa and Luembe. These two are close to the local European labour market of Abercorn, Kowa some seven or eight miles away and Luembe four or five. This proximity to a labour market has given the men of these villages an opportunity to earn wages locally while continuing to live at home. None of the men from these two villages worked for a Native Authority. They thus represent a small but significant proportion of all Mambwe wage-earners. Eight of the Kowa wage-earners lived in the village and travelled to work each day, or else visited the village every weekend. This had a considerable effect on their village (see pp. 124 ff). Luembe had one wage-earner who cycled to Abercorn each day to work. The men from these two villages earning wages are included in the analysis of the local market to which I turn later. All other wage-earners in the sample working in the local market were forced to live out of their villages, because of the distance to their places of work.

The population figures for the eight villages are divided into two groups in Table VI, those under the age of fifteen and those over. I have also shown the proportion of women to men actually resident in the village at the time of census. This proportion varied between 1·1 for Kowa, the most successful village in earning money, and 3·7 for Luembe, which, for all its advantageous situation, was tending to disintegrate (see pp. 129 ff). The average was 1·6, and indicates the high rate of labour migration among Mambwe males. There were no female migrants although a large number of married migrants had taken their wives with them. The proportion of men absent earning wages as shown in this way is similar to that recorded by Read among the Ngoni and Cewa of Nyasaland in 1939, where it ranged from 1·5 to 1·8 in a much larger sample.[1] A number of men in each village had more than one wife; the majority of these were over thirty-

---

[1] Op. cit., p. 620.

five and were returned labourers, and unlikely to go off to work again. The total number of polygynists was 36, forming 28 per cent of all married men. There is only one polygynist in Aron village, which had a population of Jehovah's Witnesses. He was also the youngest polygynist, being only twenty-three years of age. His father was a leader of the Witnesses in Aron village, but the young man had rejected the sect. I have included women living in concubinage among the plural marriages. The main difference between a concubine and a wife is a legal one; as no marriage payment is made for a concubine, the man has no rights over her services. If she commits adultery, he cannot claim damages. The children of concubines are illegitimate, and a fee must be paid to legitimize them. Although the Mambwe disapprove of concubinage, it is fairly common; generally the woman is a divorcee. A previously unmarried girl would never live as a concubine. A proportion of the surplus women left in the villages are therefore attached to some man through marriage or concubinage; the others are widows and old women dependent on their agnatic kin, and wives and sisters left behind by the workers.

The universality of the phenomenon of wage-labour became immediately evident when I made the census. There were 155 males over the age of twenty; all had worked abroad at one time or another, except one chief, to whom I have previously referred. Every other Mambwe I met had been away to work. Wage-labour is therefore quite definitely an integral part of the Mambwe mode of life. It is not something additional to their lives, a paid holiday or voluntary widening of experience, but an inherent part of the economic structure of their present society.

In Table VII I have compared the Administration census figures for the year 1951 with my own genealogical census. There is a slight discrepancy in the ages of the adult males, for the Administration definition of a male starts at the age of eighteen, while I have given the population over fifteen. Some of the boys under eighteen go off to work in Tanganyika without an Identification Certificate, and work as water boys, or in domestic service for a few months. But the figures are sufficiently close to show a resemblance.

The percentages of men absent on wage-labour are slightly misleading, for they show the number of labourers against the total number of adult males. But few Mambwe go out to work

TABLE VII

Sex and age composition of Mambwe population from (*a*) 1951 Administration
Census and (*b*) Genealogical Census in 1953, showing numbers and percentages
of men estimated to be absent earning wages

	Male	Female	Absent labourers	Percentage of total	No. of women per man
		(*a*) 1951 Administration Census			
Adult . .	5,783	6,292	2,169	37·5	
Juvenile .	4,837	4,476	—	—	
Totals:	10,620	10,768	2,169	—	1·03
		(*b*) 1953 Genealogical Census of Eight Villages			
Adult . .	193	246	67	34·7	
Juvenile .	162	141	—	—	
Totals:	355	387	67		1·09

Note: Administration defines adult male as 'man over apparent age of eighteen'.
Genealogical Census figures are for persons over the estimated age of fifteen.

after the age of forty-five, and my own investigations showed
that 54 per cent of the men between twenty and twenty-five years
of age were absent. The vast majority of the men actually working
away from home are all between eighteen and fifty years of
age, and they form a higher percentage of the total male population between these ages than appears from the Administration
census.

I have shown in Table VIII the number of men aged between
fifteen and forty-nine years of age by five-year age-groups who
are at present working in the two main labour markets, local
and distant. The local market is the Northern Province, and the
distant markets are the two areas served by the buses. Excluding
the men whose ages are not known, fifty-six of the men between
the ages of twenty and forty-nine were absent at work out of a
total male population of this age of 118.

Only nine of the age-group 15–19 were absent. The remaining
twenty-nine were most of them still too young to go, and were
awaiting assessment for tax, which entitles them to an Identification Certificate (*situpa*). Without this Certificate a boy would find

TABLE VIII

Number of males between fifteen and forty-nine years of age absent from eight villages in 1953 earning wages, showing place of work, compared with total male population of this age-group

Age-groups	Total number of males	Number of men absent on wage-labour			Total
		In Northern Province	In Copperbelt and other N. Rh. towns	In Tanganyika Territory	
15–19	38	1	1	7	9
20–24	35	7	3	13	23
25–29	23	4	10	1	15
30–34	15	1	4	1	6
35–39	17	2	2	2	6
40–44	13	2	2	1	5
45–49	15	1	—	—	1
Not known	3	—	—	2	2
Totals:	159	18	22	27	67
Percentage:		27%	33%	40%	100%
		By larger age-groups with percentage			
15–24	73	8	4	20	32
Percentage:		25%	12%	63%	100%
25–49	86	10	18	5	33
Percentage:		30%	55%	15%	100%

difficulty in finding a job.[1] The Certificate is issued when a boy reaches the age of about eighteen, i.e. when the District Commissioner estimates his age to be eighteen, therefore rendering him liable to pay tax. Some boys manage to find paid work locally before this age, either with a farmer or as a domestic servant in Abercorn. Some go to Tanganyika, even without the Certificate, for the Mambwe say that the authorities there do not often bother Africans from Northern Rhodesia to produce a Certificate. They say that if a boy is big enough to work, no one in Tanganyika asks any questions. But they never attempt to go to the Copperbelt without a Certificate. Many boys apply to be

---

[1] The employment of children and young persons is controlled by Chapter 191 of the Laws of Northern Rhodesia (Employment of Women, Young Persons and Children Ordinance) as amended by No. 49 of 1950.

taxed long before they are big enough to work, and there are usually two or three lads hanging about the District Commissioner's office waiting for him to judge them fit for tax, and therefore for work.[1]

The Identification Certificate has the man's fingerprints, and has pages on which receipts for poll tax and levy are recorded. It also contains a labour history, which is supposed to be completed by each employer when a man is discharged. It is therefore a form of passport, and if an African is accosted by the police he must produce his Certificate.[2] When a man leaves for work in another territory, the District Commissioner must sign his Certificate, and for travel to the Belgian Congo a medical section must be completed. This may affect their decisions whether or not to go out of Northern Rhodesia to work. This Certificate controls the labour flow to a certain extent, for the buses arriving at the Copperbelt are boarded by the police who check the passengers' Certificates. An African without a Certificate is arrested.[3] Employers will not engage a man without a Certificate.

Tanganyika Territory attracted the largest number of labourers, 40 per cent of the total. Most of these were the youngest men, for twenty out of twenty-five were under the age of twenty-five.[4] The majority of these were making their first journey to work. The Copperbelt and other towns attracted 33 per cent of the labourers, most of them over the age of twenty-five, and the majority making their second or third trip. The local market

---

[1] I saw the District Commissioner in Abercorn inspect five such lads one day. He thought three of them were old enough but dismissed the other two. One of these protested that he must be fit for work, as he was married the week before. Now he was married, he said, he must go off to work. The District Commissioner, who had spent eight years among the Mambwe, sent him off, saying he was not big enough to build a hut, let alone work for wages. Of course the boy was not married.

[2] This Certificate is very similar to the documents issued to workers in European countries during the Industrial Revolution, such as the 'Wanderbuch' issued by the Bavarian Government in 1808. The British and French had similar devices. See Redford, op. cit., pp. 77, 78.

[3] A man on a visit to the Copperbelt and not seeking work must carry a Native Pass showing his name, village, district, and province, where he is going and the purpose of his visit. Either the chief or the District Commissioner may sign it.

[4] The five older men had all made at least one previous trip to Tanganyika, had found jobs outside the sisal industry, and had taken their wives with them.

drew an approximately equal percentage of men in both age-groups, but unlike the other markets, employed skilled men only.

Thus, of the distant markets for unskilled labour, Tanganyika attracted the majority (63 per cent) of the unmarried or newly-married young men under the age of twenty-five, and only a minority (15 per cent) of the married men over that age.[1] The Copperbelt and other towns showed the opposite picture: they attracted the majority (55 per cent) of the older men, and only a minority (12 per cent) of those under twenty-five.

I believe that these differences are related to the age and status of the labourers seeking work. The methods of getting to the distant markets, which I discussed previously, and the varying conditions of work and pay in each market, make quite different appeals to the younger and older men. Young men prefer to make their first wage-earning trip to the sisal industry, which costs nothing, and marry when they get back with some money. Most Mambwe men marry between the ages of nineteen and twenty-five; thus, only 31 per cent of the age-group 15–24 were married, and the majority of this age-group went to Tanganyika.[2] Eighty-eight per cent of the age-group 25–49 were married,[3] and the majority of these went to the Copperbelt and other towns. The trip to the Copperbelt is almost invariably a second wage-earning foray, after a first trip to Tanganyika. A man is now established in the village, able to pay the bus fare, better dressed,

---

[1] This cannot be said to be due to the difficulties of accommodation for families in Tanganyika. The sisal industry now offers good accommodation for labourers' families, together with free transport and food en route.

[2] The few men in this age-group who are already married before their first trip are usually in debt for their marriage payments. They leave only when their wives are pregnant or when the first child is very small. Only one married man under twenty-five took his wife with him to Tanganyika. Eight other married men in this age-group worked locally, mainly in Abercorn.

[3] Only five of the thirty-three men in this age-group were reported to be single. All of these had been away from their villages for some years, and may well have married at their place of work without informing their relatives. One had been married and divorced, and was not known to have married again. I suspected that two of the other four were indeed married, but could not check the information. The relatively long absence of these men, and their lack of contact with home, suggests that some may have decided to become town-dwellers, and are now living abroad with women they met and married there.

and more familiar with European ways. He goes to the Copper-belt alone, and sends back money for his wife's bus fare once he is established. It is a longer trip than that to Tanganyika, for few of them spend less than two years on the Copperbelt; a shorter period is not economic. The wife travels alone to join her husband, or takes only a child in arms that cannot be left behind. Older children are usually left at home in the care of kinsfolk.

The men who held jobs locally had skills denied to the majority of Mambwe. The Administration employed eleven out of the eighteen working locally, four of them as agricultural assistants and messengers, two of them as schoolmasters, one as a carpenter, and four in the public works department. Two of these were foremen, one on the roads and the other over bricklayers. The only two unskilled men employed by the Administration were labourers, one on the roads and the other making bricks. Five others were employed by the International Red Locust Control, either in the workshop or as drivers. Only two were privately employed, one as the foreman on a European farm and the other as a clerk in a store. Eleven of them worked in Abercorn or nearby, four in Lunzuwa, two in Isoka, the administrative centre of the Isoka District, and one at Provincial Headquarters in Kasama. Eight of them were under twenty-five years old, and only one of these had an unskilled job, as a road labourer. These locally employed men therefore represented a relatively highly-skilled and highly-paid group. Those employed by the Administration and the International Red Locust Control had a considerable degree of security in their employment, with good conditions and prospects. Most of them had held their jobs for a number of years, and even the two privately-employed men had had long periods of service. The European farmer's foreman had been eight years with his employer, and the store clerk had held his job for five years. This local market is valued by the Mambwe and there is keen competition for jobs within it. Local work, when it is skilled and consequently well-paid, gives the Mambwe the best of both worlds. A local worker can keep a job much longer than one who goes to the Copperbelt, and therefore continues to benefit from a cash income for a much longer period. Further, local work eliminates the nostalgia for home and village life that plagues the worker in a distant market.

It will be seen that the number of men absent drops sharply

after the age of forty-five. If we examine the number of absent labourers by ten-year groups, the proportion of absent to resident males is seen quite clearly to be related to age. Only 24 per cent of the age-group 15–19 is away, and this small number is due to the limitation of movement and employment imposed by the Identification Certificate. Of the age-group 20–29, 65 per cent are absent; 33 per cent of age-group 30–39; and 13 per cent of the age-group 40–49. The highest percentage of men absent to men resident is therefore to be found among the men between twenty and twenty-nine years of age. The percentage drops between the ages of thirty and thirty-nine, and it is very small between forty and forty-nine. Apart from the assessors at the Native Courts and other officials of the Native Authority, who are selected because they are senior and experienced men, the oldest man earning wages whom I encountered was forty-five. He lived in his own village near Abercorn, and cycled each day to work. His wife and family lived in the village.

I have already referred to the canalization of the labour flow to the Copperbelt and Tanganyika Territory, and stated that men over forty years old formerly went as far afield as the Congo and Southern Rhodesia in their search for work. In the eight villages on which the figures under discussion were based, there were sixty men over forty years of age who had been away to work at one time or another in their lives. Their period of wage-earning, with few exceptions, may be said to be over. There were also forty-one men under the age of forty who had been away to work and returned, and were now working in their gardens. These men had not all completed their labour periods, for some of them would undoubtedly go off to work again. From these two groups I selected forty-one of the over-forties who could clearly remember their labour histories, and thirty-one of the under-forties. I have shown in Table IX the different markets to which these two groups applied for work, the number of trips they made, and the time spent on each trip.

The number of trips made by the two groups differs. The over-forties had made 138 trips between them, an average of 3·4 per man, and the thirty-one under-forties had made 70 trips, an average of 2·2 per man.[1] The difference in the average number

---

[1] I ignored those short periods of labour on road-making and brick-making for the Native Authority which most men engage in to pay their tax, for these

TABLE IX

Length of time spent in different labour markets in 138 wage-earning trips made by 41 men over the age of forty, and in 70 trips made by 31 men under the age of forty: from the eight villages covered by the Census

Market	Age	Length of time spent on each trip						Totals
		Less than one year	One to two years	Two to three years	Three to four years	Four to five years	More than five years	
Northern Province	Under 40	3	1	—	—	—	1	5
	Over 40	3	2	4	—	2	4	15
Copperbelt and other N.Rh. towns	Under 40	—	13	4	—	3	—	20
	Over 40	9	12	2	—	—	—	23
Tanganyika Territory	Under 40	17	17	6	1	3	1	45
	Over 40	23	18	5	8	—	1	55
Congo and Southern Rhodesia	Under 40	—	—	—	—	—	—	—
	Over 40	32	10	2	—	—	1	45
Total: Percentages:	Under 40	20 29%	31 44%	10 14%	1	6	2	70 100%
					} 13%			
Total: Percentages:	Over 40	67 49%	42 30%	13 9%	8	2	6	138 100%
					} 12%			

of trips is not entirely due to the fact that the over-forties have completed their working periods and that the under-forties still have trips to do. The length of time spent on each trip by the older group is less than that spent by the younger group. The over-forties worked for less than one year on 49 per cent of their trips, while the under-forties worked for this short period on only 28 per cent of their trips. The older informants say that they used to go away for only six to eight months. They tried to leave on a trip immediately after the main cultivation was finished for the year, in the lean period before the harvest, March and April. They tried to return from their wage-labour in time for the arduous work of cultivation that begins with the heavy rains at the end of December and the beginning of January. Hence they had a period of six to nine months in which to earn money. The labourers still tend to leave in the period before the harvest, and in the past this was apparently a universal habit. Most of the older men spent the short period of work in Tanganyika or in the Belgian Congo, and they had to walk many hundreds of miles there and back. Only a few went to Southern Rhodesia, and usually for a period longer than one year, owing to the great distance involved.

This change reflects the change in the markets to which the Mambwe apply for work. Since the 1939–45 war they no longer go to the Congo, and those who go to Tanganyika usually sign a contract to work on the sisal plantations for a minimum period of twelve months, which guarantees them a free bus ride home. Most of the under-forties who have worked less than twelve months are either men who have broken their contract and come home by themselves, or men who went to the Lupa goldfields to work. This goldfield generally attracts them for periods of three to six months only, even today, as the work is desultory and casual, and the amusements are few.[1]

Two years seems to be the maximum period that most men of either group worked on one trip. Only 13 per cent of the under-forties and 18 per cent of the over-forties spent three years or more on one trip. Why this is so I cannot say. It may be related to the

---

periods are seldom more than two or three weeks or a month, and seldom take them away from their own villages.

[1] The Lupa goldfields are not organized in the same way as the gold-mines of South Africa or the copper mines of Northern Rhodesia.

former taboo on sexual intercourse with a wife who is suckling a child, for intercourse was not resumed until the child was weaned, at about three years of age. Hence, if a married man went off to work after a child was born, he could resume normal married life after an absence of about two years. The Native Courts still consider that a man who has been absent for three years without communicating with his wife has given her sufficient grounds on which she can bring an action for divorce for desertion. However, Gluckman states that the Central Lozi Court has reduced the period of absence without communication which entitled a woman to bring an action for divorce from six years to two.[1] This similarity of period seems to suggest that the estimate of the period after which the husband may be assumed to have deserted his wife may be based on the conditions that prevail among the workers in the towns, and not on any indigenous social factors.

The change in the minimum period spent away is therefore from a period of six to eight months to a period between one year and two. The over-forties spent up to two years away from home on 79 per cent of their trips, and the under-forties on 72 per cent of their trips. The distribution over the different markets of the trips of more than three years again reflects the changed conditions of these markets. None of the over-forties spent more than three years on the Copperbelt whereas some of the under-forties did. Tanganyika attracted most of the men of both groups who spent more than three years on one trip, fourteen out of a total of twenty-five. Five worked locally, and only three on the Copperbelt, all of them from the under-forty group. The increase in copper production during and since the 1939–45 war increased the demand for labour on the Copperbelt. The boom in copper stimulated the development of secondary industry, and there are many attractive and varied jobs for Africans.

The duration of labour trips, particularly on the Copperbelt, has undoubtedly increased over the years since 1945. I have shown in Table X the reported length of absence, from the eight census villages, of sixty-seven men at present working abroad. These men are still working out their labour periods. One-quarter of them have already been absent for more than three years—more

---

[1] *The Judicial Process Among the Barotse of Northern Rhodesia*, p. 288.

TABLE X

Reported length of absence of 67 wage-earners from eight villages in 1953, and the markets in which they are reported to be working

Market	Age-groups	Reported length of absence						Totals
		Less than one year	One to two years	Two to three years	Three to four years	Four to five years	More than five years	
Northern Province	15–24	3	3	1	–	1	–	8
	25–49	1	5	1	–	1	2	10
Copperbelt and other N.Rh. towns	15–24	1	1	2	–	–	–	4
	25–49	3	–	6	1	4	4	18
Tanganyika Territory	15–24	15	2	1	–	1	1	20
	25–49	2	–	1	1	–	1	5
*Not known		–	1	1	–	–	–	2
Totals: Percentage:		25 37%	12 18%	13 19%	2	7	8	67 100%

(Three to four years, Four to five years, More than five years: 25%)

*Included in the 25–49 group, as they are both married

than half of these on the Copperbelt. Only 18 per cent of the men
on the Copperbelt have worked there for less than one year,
against 68 per cent of the workers in Tanganyika. While the
majority (40 per cent) of the absentees are in Tanganyika, they
are drawn mainly from the age-group 15–24, most of whom
have contracted for only twelve months' labour in the sisal
industry.

Some general conclusions emerge from considering these
figures of labour migration. The increasing tempo of industrialization in Africa since 1939 has had a potent effect on Mambwe
wage-earning, and all Mambwe now go out to work for wages
at some time between the ages of eighteen and forty-five. Some
go to the Copperbelt for periods of three or four years at a time,
only returning to their villages for short holidays. The Mambwe
on the whole offer only unskilled labour, and this puts a premium
on youth and strength. Young men between twenty and thirty
years of age form the majority of the wage-earners abroad, whereas
the majority of men over thirty are present in their villages.
If we regard the total male population as a labour force deployed
on two fronts, agricultural and industrial, we find that the young
and more adaptable men are out at unskilled work in industry
while the older men remain at home to maintain the fields with
the aid of the women. This arrangement appears to suit both the
indigenous social system and the labour markets. The social and
economic pressure towards earning money by working abroad
is greater on young than on old men. The young men want to
earn money for marriage payments, or to repay debts already
incurred for these. Also they need money for the European goods
now considered necessary for setting up a home, and to buy
clothes and other necessities. The older men have already achieved
all this. Their eyes are turned in other directions. All the positions
of importance within the tribe are held by older men, for example,
chieftainships, headmanships, councillors' posts. In a society where
years of experience are necessary before a man acquires a compe-
tent knowledge of its law and customs, positions of authority
inevitably go to older men. By the time a man is forty-five, he
has retired permanently from wage-labour to his village. He has
raised a family, which aids him in the fields. Status depends on
the number of dependants a man can gather, and his family are

his first followers. The mode of life in Mambwe villages determines the number, age, and status of the men who go out to earn wages, and the village itself is part of a wider system of relationships that includes the whole Mambwe polity.

CHAPTER IV

THE MAMBWE VILLAGE

Stockaded and Open Villages

MAMBWE villages radically changed in form after the arrival of the Europeans. Until then each village was in effect a village state: chief, officials, and people all lived within the same enclosure. The village was surrounded by a ditch and a palisade of tree-trunks about four to five feet high, with earth banked up about the base.[1] The surrounding countryside was the domain (*icialo*) of the chief, and the boundaries between chieftaincies were well-defined. Sentries were posted on ant hills and at other strategic points round the village to guard both the herds and the people at work. The villagers normally left their enclosure only to work in their fields, but at those times when they least feared attack, they moved into temporary huts closer to the fields. These protective measures were a response to the unsettled conditions of the time; during the nineteenth century the Mambwe were almost constantly at war with the Bemba and other peoples.

The size of these village states varied, but from the accounts of travellers, and the extent of the old ditches that can still be seen, I estimate that the smallest had at least 100 huts within it. These huts were divided among a number of administrative sections (*ivitente*), with the cattle kraal in the centre. Each section had a public building (*nsaka*), a thatched open-sided round enclosure in which business was transacted, visitors were entertained, and cases were heard. Each enclosure was in charge of a junior judge (*nkombe*), whose duty was to carry out the day-to-day administration of his section and deal initially with the legal disputes of the members of the section. Another official, whose duties were military, administrative, judicial, and ritual, was placed in charge of two or more sections and their junior judges. These captains [2] (*amusika*) were chosen primarily for their skill

---

[1] See Decle, op. cit., p. 296.

[2] I was told that 'big' chiefs, like Nsokolo and Kela, had four or five captains, but 'little' chiefs, like Fwambo, had only two or three.

in war, and led the men of their sections into battle. But they also acted as senior judges, to whom the junior judges referred difficult cases, and they played a crucial part in the installation of a new chief. The captains and the chief sitting together formed a court of appeal for all sections of the village.

The chief appointed one man to represent him in the day-to-day running of the village as a whole. This executive officer (*mwene muzi*, 'the owner of the village', or headman) organized the tribute labour in the chief's own garden (*usonga*) and the gardens of his wives, entertained strangers, and issued beer and food to those whom the chief wished to reward. He also performed the daily ritual at the village shrine, which was situated inside the village near the main gate. The executive officer was the senior of the chief's civil councillors (*ivilolo*), a body of senior men selected from the various sections of the village. The executive officer was invariably the chief's sister's son, but the councillors, junior judges, and captains were not necessarily related to the chief. Men of the royal clan could not hold any of these posts, although they sat together with the chief and these officials to form a council of state.

The chief lived in a separate enclosure (*isano*), cut off from the main part of the village by a guarded gate. This palace consisted of a number of buildings. The chief had a separate hut near the gate into the village, and each of his wives had a hut for herself and her children. One wife was appointed to be the great wife (*wacitindi fukamila*).[1] She was in charge of the other wives, and had important ritual duties to perform in connection with the chieftainship. She was distinguished from the other wives by her dress: she wore both a special distinctive cloth and heavy anklets of copper wire. The largest building in the palace was a barrack-room (*chenza*) in which slept a number of unmarried youths (*yakalume vya mwene*). This building had no door to it, in order to keep the lads alert in case the village was attacked, when they were supposed to jump up and rouse everyone with their cries. The chief's royal drum (*kamangu*), which was (and is) only beaten when danger threatened or a chief died, was then beaten. The youngest of these youths acted as pages and servants

---

[1] *Citindi* is the word for coils of yellowish copper. *Ukufukamila* is to worship, derived from *ukufukuma*, to kneel.

to the chief, and the eldest as bodyguard and police (*alukaluka*). These were selected for their physique and bravery. There was also a sacred hut (*ng'anda ya vianzo vya mwene*) which contained the relics (*vianzo*) of the former chiefs, consisting of spears, bows and arrows, stools, and ceremonial axes (*inzewe*).[1] The palace was out of bounds to the ordinary villagers, and only the officials had daily access to the chief. The chief's brothers and grown sons lived in the main part of the village. The palace was a place of sanctuary, and a murderer who managed to flee there could not be killed by the relatives of his victim.

Thus each Mambwe village was a separate state, containing within itself a complete array of political, administrative, judicial, military, and ritual officials. These states were virtually independent, but were linked together through the kinship ties of the chiefs, who, with a few exceptions, were all members of the royal clan. I estimate from the records of the Administration and from the accounts of Mambwe informants, that in 1890 there were sixteen of these large villages. All of them had chiefs of the royal clan, except three.[2] One of these, Chief Chindo, was the head (*cikolwe*) of the Simwinga clan, whose daughter is said to have married the royal founding ancestor Changala. Chief Chindo thus stood in the relationship of father-in-law to the Mambwe senior chief, a relationship which has been repeated through subsequent marriages into this clan by successive Nsokolos. The other two commoner chiefs, Chileshya and Kowa, are on the perimeter of Mambwe country. Chief Chileshya is the head of the Sinfukwe[3] clan, and it is said that he is of Nyika origin. His chieftaincy is on the east of Mambwe country, and the story goes that one day when Changala was hunting he met a Nyika,

---

[1] Chief Mwamba told me that this axe was carried in imitation of the Bemba chiefs, and that in the old days Mambwe chiefs did not have them.

[2] This estimate applies only to the Mambwe living in what is now Northern Rhodesia. I have no information of the situation at that time in Chief Muti's area in what is now Tanganyika Territory. It seems unlikely that there were more than three or four villages there, if that. One of these may possibly have been a commoner village, for two titled heads of commoner clans live there now: Mwene Misansa (Simusokwe clan), and Mwene Upundu (Simpungwe clan).

[3] Usually translated as Eland. But the Mambwe use the word *nsefu* when referring to this animal. The Sinfukwe clan is also found among the Inamwanga people.

PLATE II

A TRADITIONAL CHIEF

Commoner Chief Chindo is the oldest Mambwe chief. He is wearing the traditional cloth headdress and carries a ceremonial axe of office.

Kalembi, and a group of his people, looking for a place to settle. Kalembi agreed to recognize Changala as his chief, and gave him his daughter to marry. Changala gave his new father-in-law the small district of Chileshya. Chief Kowa is the head of the Siuluta[1] clan, which is also found among the neighbouring Lungu people. Chief Kowa's territory is on the northern border between the Mambwe and the Lungu. Chief Kowa married a daughter of Chief Nsokolo, a marriage which has been repeated each time a new Kowa succeeded, and he paid tribute to the nearest Mambwe chief of the royal clan, Chief Fwambo. The internal organization of these non-royal chieftaincies was similar in most respects to that of the royal chieftaincies.

Each stockaded village was in effect a fort: it was compact, densely populated, and easy to defend. Safety was their principal justification, for they had many disadvantages. They were over-crowded and unhealthy; Decle describes them as 'dirty beyond words'.[2] Their size and elaborate defences ruled out any frequent change of site, and the process of shifting cultivation moved the people's fields ever further away from their huts. Decle states that the fields of Chief Fwambo's stockaded village were five miles away.[3] The arrival of the British in the 1890s heralded their decline and the rise of a new form of Mambwe village, for the stockaded village at once lost its primary function of defence. The *pax britannica* freed the Mambwe from the raids of the Bemba, their traditional enemy,[4] and the people were able to move safely into smaller undefended villages nearer to their fields. The stockaded villages disappeared entirely in a few years, and the number of open villages grew rapidly.

ROYAL AND COMMONER VILLAGES

The older villages were all ruled either by chiefs or by royal headmen who stood in a perpetual relationship of son or grandson

---

[1] No English equivalent. [2] Op. cit., p. 296. [3] Op. cit., p. 296.
[4] The British incidentally may have saved the Mambwe from extinction as a people, for the Bemba had already driven out one chief, Mpande, and absorbed his subjects into the Bemba polity under the rule of Chief Makasa. Chief Nsokolo had fled the country, and the Mambwe were being pressed to pay tribute, although they now deny this. Gouldsbury claimed that the British saved the Mambwe from extermination. Op. cit., p. 11.

to the chief. I will deal more fully with these relationships when discussing the political structure of the Mambwe, for they are essentially political relationships expressed in kinship terms. In the old days a new village was created by the chief. Under the Mambwe rules of succession to chieftainships, only a son born after his father had succeeded to his title was eligible to be considered for succession in turn. Thus the chief tended to appoint his elder sons, born before he succeeded, to be headmen over villages. He allocated a specific area and gave the prince some followers. These appointments in theory were made for the lifetime only of the first incumbent of the headmanship. The reigning chief reserved the right to appoint one of his own sons to a royal headmanship when the incumbent died.[1] But these royal headmanships tended to become hereditary in the lineage section of the first incumbent, and his relatives resisted the right of the chief to appoint his own sons. In effect, the names of the first royal headman became titles associated with specific villages and estates. A title can be inherited, and with it the right to rule the village to which it is attached. A commoner cannot inherit a title belonging to the royal clan. In the early days of the *pax britannica*, when the stockaded villages were giving place to smaller open villages, the new villages almost invariably had royal headmen. Thus in 1893 Chief Fwambo had one large stockaded village, but in 1918 he had ten villages in his chieftaincy, and eight of these had royal headmen.[2] Of the two commoner headmen, one was the executive officer of the stockaded village, and the other a councillor from one of its sections.[3] The former executive officer was still alive in 1953,[4] and both he and the councillor's successor addressed the present Chief Fwambo as mother's brother. Thus the emergence of commoner headmen is a phenomenon of the past thirty years. By 1953 the number of villages in Fwambo's chieftaincy had grown to nineteen. The original eight royal villages continued to

---

[1] This right is still the cause of friction between Chief Nsokolo and the chiefs of the other lineages of the royal clan.

[2] District Commissioner's records, Abercorn.

[3] Individual sections of the village states may have moved out as separate units, but I could not definitely establish this.

[4] Headman Selemani must have been at least ninety years old at this time, for he was executive officer of the Fwambo village state in 1893 when Decle passed through Fwambo village. He was much too old and weak to attend to village affairs, and died in 1954.

exist, but the number of commoner villages had grown to eleven. The Silungwe clan had acquired two headmanships: this clan stands in a special burial and joking relationship (*mayombo*) with the Fwambo lineage of the royal clan. The Sinkonde clan had also acquired two headmanships, but no other clan had more than one. Similar developments took place within the other traditional chieftaincies. Thus, after the initial movement out of the stockaded villages which created a number of royal villages, the increase in the number of Mambwe villages has tended to be an increase in the number of commoner villages.

In 1953 members of a chief's clan held between them almost exactly half of the total number of headmanships, while the other commoner clans held the rest between them. Almost every commoner clan had at least one headmanship; the largest number held by any one of these clans is four. This is a significant change from the past, and an increase in the authority of the commoner clans relative to the chiefs' clans. Today new villages are almost invariably founded by commoners.

I have shown in Table XI the clans of chiefs and headmen of six traditional chieftaincies in 1953. Two of the royal chieftaincies are grassland and two woodland. One of the commoner chiefs, Kowa, lives in the grasslands, and the other, Chindo, in the woodlands. The Administration recognizes only two of these chiefs, Mpande and Mwamba, and they both have courts and salaries. The other traditional chiefs are treated as headmen; cases arising within their traditional chieftaincies must be taken to the court of an administrative chief.[1] Thus Chief Fwambo is now a headman under the rule of Chief Mwamba, although he is traditionally senior. Chief Kowa is also under Mwamba. Likewise the administrative Chief Mpande rules over royal Chief Chivuta and commoner Chief Chindo.

Today Chief Mwamba has 27 villages within his traditional chieftaincy, of which 15 have royal headmen; Chief Fwambo has 19 villages, of which eight are royal; Chief Mpande has 24 villages, of which 10 are royal; Chief Chivuta has 16 villages, of which 10 are royal. Similarly, the commoner Chief Chindo's Simwinga clan holds 10 out of 15 headmanships in his area, and Chief

---

[1] I have seen traditional chiefs trying cases, and there is no doubt that they are in the habit of doing so, although the Administration would not enforce their findings.

TABLE XI

Clans of chiefs and headmen in six traditional chieftaincies

Chiefs	Royal				Commoner	
	Grassland Mambwe		Forest Mambwe		Forest	Grassland
Title:	Mwamba	Fwambo	Mpande	Chivuta	Chindo	Kowa
Clan:	Sichula	Sichula	Sichula	Sichula	Simwinga	Siuluta
Headman's clan						
Sichula	15	8	10	10	1	–
Simwinga			1		10	
Siuluta						7
Simunyola	2					
Simuyemba	1					
Sichiliya	1					
Sikazwe	1					
Silupiya	1					
Simwala	1					
Simusokwe	2			1		1
Simpokolwe	1					
Sinyangwe	1	1				
Simbeya	1	1				1
Silungwe		2				
Sinzumwa		1				
Siluamba		1				
Sikalumba		1				
Sinkonde		2				
Simutowe		1	1		1	
Simpungwe		1	1			
Simukwasa			1			
Sinchangwa			2			
Sichinsambwe			1			
Sichilima			1			
Sikapite			3			
Sikalamba			1			
Sichitalwe			1	1		
Simazuo			1	2		
Siulemba				1		
Sichivula				1		
Musukuma					1	
Mwambazi					1	
Sikasula					1	1
Sichiliango						1
Sinjela						2
Sinfukwe						1
Totals:	27	19	24	16	15	14

78

Kowa's Siuluta clan has seven out of 15 headmanships. Chief Chindo is exceptional in that he has one royal headman in his chieftaincy.

Each chieftaincy has a different set of commoner clans holding headmanships within it (this is clearly shown in Table X), although individual members of all clans are to be found dispersed throughout the whole Mambwe area. The core of a village is usually the segment of an agnatic lineage, of which the headman is the senior member. A headmanship tends to attract other members of the headman's clan, thus creating a local concentration of this clan's members. Only three clans, apart from the chiefs' clans, hold headmanships in both royal and commoner chieftaincies. The Simusokwe clan holds four headmanships in three chieftaincies. This clan is large in numbers and influence: one of the full-time councillors of the Native Authority is a Simusokwe, and the senior member of the clan bears the title of Mwene Misansa. The present holder of this title lives in Tanganyika, but often visits his clansmen among the Mambwe in Northern Rhodesia. The Simutowe clan holds one headmanship in three chieftaincies; this clan has a joking relationship with both Chief Mpande's lineage of the royal clan and the Simwinga clan of Chief Chindo.

A man must have permission from both chief and Administration to form a new village. Formerly the Administration insisted that a man should have a following of at least ten taxpayers, but this rule has been rescinded.[1] The chief often refuses permission for an aspiring commoner to build a new village, with its consequent independence. The history of Simukulwa village shows some of the reasons why a commoner seeks headmanship, and the ensuing change in relations with other traditional headmen and the chief. This village is also an example of the simplest form of Mambwe village organization. A skeleton genealogy is given in Figure 1. The people in the genealogy are numbered by generation, and when their names are mentioned, the number is given in brackets for convenient reference.

George Simukulwa (C14) has been both an evangelist and a trader, and for a number of years was an assessor at Chief

---

[1] The District Commissioner still prefers to know that a man has a fairly substantial following before he allows him to build a village on his own.

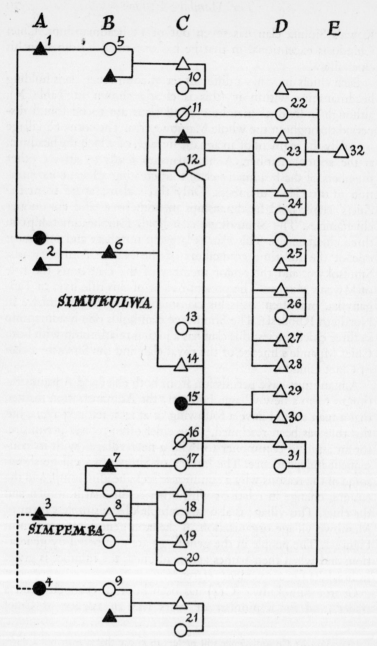

FIG. 1.—GENEALOGY OF SIMUKULWA VILLAGE.

Mwamba's court. Through trading he acquired some wealth, and he is regarded as a man of substance and influence. George conducted his trading from Kosam village, which had a royal headman. George decided to build a <u>brick house</u>, the symbol of success for the Mambwe, and sought permission to do this. Permission was granted on the usual condition that he built in the vicinity of an established village and recognized the rule of its headman. A man is not allowed to build a brick house wherever he pleases. George built his brick house under Ng'ina Hill, about a mile away from Kosam; it had a separate brick kitchen, and a wattle-and-daub storehouse. Some time later he inherited the widows of no less than three brothers who died, and thereby acquired a following of considerable size. He built wattle-and-daub huts for his new wives and their children near his new brick building. The older sons went off to work, and on their return they too built huts for their wives and families near George's brick house. These sons and their wives and children form the bulk of the village population. At this time George and his dependants continued to recognize Kosam as their headman. Then headman Kosam died, and his brother succeeded. This change of headmen caused a split in Kosam, and a number of persons began to leave. George was now in effect headman of a village almost as large as Kosam, and he now applied to be recognized as headman in his own right. The chief refused him permission. George had broken his connection with the mission when he became a polygynist on inheriting his brothers' widows; he now married Linile (C13), who was from the chief's own lineage and called him 'brother'. Shortly after this marriage, the chief gave George authority to become a headman of his own village, and his attachment to Kosam was severed. A number of the Kosam villagers now came to join the new headman. John Simpemba (B8), who was related to George through one of his wives (C17), brought his two wives and their children, together with a widow (B9) and her son (C21) and his wife, who were connected to him. Another man (D22) came because his wife's mother's sister (C12) was married to George. Some time later another widow (B5) brought her son (C10) and his wife into the village; this woman claimed kinship with George through his father's mother's brother (A1), and George addressed this woman as mother.

The core of this village was a group of men, the segment of an agnatic lineage, of whom George was the senior member, and their wives and children. Attached by cognatic and affinal ties to this core was a number of other agnatic groups, and a fringe of individuals whose links to any other group were weak. This is the common pattern of Mambwe villages, whether the central core is a segment of the royal or of a commoner clan. However, I did not find any members of the royal clan resident in a commoner village, with one exception to which I will refer later. The solidarity of the agnatic groups holds the Mambwe village together. Other Mambwe villages differ from this one only in the size and complexity of the relationships between the agnatic core which holds the headmanship and the other groups.

The villages of chiefs are organized on the same principles, except that the chiefs do not themselves administer their villages, but appoint an executive officer to act for them; he combines the duties of headman and lieutenant to the chief. The chief spends most of his time attending to the business of his chieftaincy. In the villages of the three salaried chiefs, who had courts and paid officials, each one of the executive officers was the chief's sister's son, and therefore all were commoners. Chief Mpande's village may be regarded as typical. There were twenty-two men over the age of twenty-one in the village. Seven of these were members of the chief's own lineage; four were sisters' sons; one claimed to be mother's brother to the chief; three were consorts (*lumbwe*) married to women of the royal lineage; one was the father-in-law of the chief's son. The remaining seven had no direct connection with the chief's lineage: most of these were officials of the Native Authority.

George Simukulwa represents a new class of men who obtain wealth and influence through money. His mission education and his ability had helped him to acquire considerable wealth. George was born in the Mambwe chieftaincy in Tanganyika, but had broken away from his kin to live and work in another chieftaincy. This break had assisted him to acquire his wealth, and more important, to keep it. He built a brick house, the outward symbol of his success. When he inherited the wives and children of his brothers, they were only too glad to come to him, as a man of wealth and influence. Finally, he attempted to consolidate his gains in wealth and followers by establishing himself as an independent headman, and astutely exploited the opportunity to attract more followers created by the split in Kosam village when the headman died. But the chief at first refused him permission to become a headman, until George married into his family, and thus established a firm political tie. George's history is typical of many commoner headmen of new villages. The money economy has enabled them to acquire wealth, and thereby followers, outside the traditional channels, which were monopolized by the royal clan. But the political authority of the chief is maintained, and the commoners must find some firm tie with the royal family before they can establish themselves. If they do not establish firm ties with the chiefs, their successors are in danger of losing their gains, for the chiefs claim the right to appoint their sons even to the headmanships of villages founded by commoners. The chiefs often exercise this right.

In Chief Nsokolo's area, a commoner of the Sinzumwa clan founded a village. His wife was royal, but belonged to a different lineage from that of Chief Nsokolo. The headman was a Christian, and did not make another marriage. When he died, Chief Nsokolo refused to allow his son to succeed, and appointed one of his own elder sons to the vacant headmanship. The brothers of the original headman were all dead, and his eldest son, who was also a Christian and a perambulating evangelist for the London Missionary Society, had the strongest claim to succeed his father. However, he accepted Chief Nsokolo's action, and continued to live in the village with his sons and their wives, but continually grumbled. Finally Chief Nsokolo told him, 'My son is always sick while you are living here.' This was of course an accusation of using sorcery against the royal headman. The commoner was compelled to leave with his sons and their families, and moved to Kasunga village, in Mwamba's chieftaincy. The chiefs therefore exercise their rights to intervene in the succession to headmanships, even when the original incumbent was a commoner. It is therefore imperative for a commoner headman to establish a firm connection with his chief, and keep his goodwill, and the best way of doing this is to marry a woman from the chief's lineage. The husbands of a chief's sisters or daughters are consorts (*lumbwe*), and today most commoner headmen, no matter how they first obtained their headmanships, are careful to establish this relationship with the chief.

New villages also arise from the splitting of the lineage section within an established village. One such split occurred in 1952 in Wilson village, and again the brick house was used as a device to make a spatial move away from the home village. Wilson, a royal headman, died and his younger brother James succeeded. James quarrelled with Wilson's son Len over the distribution of the property, and Len then applied for permission to build a brick house. This was granted, and he moved about a mile away from his uncle's village. He persuaded his half-brother Simon to join him when Simon returned from a wage-earning trip. Simon too built a brick house. Both men had two wives each and some young children. Len's mother took her son's part in the quarrel and joined her son. James had refused to inherit her as she was too old to bear children. Later a divorcee with a grown son and his wife joined them. This woman was related to Len's mother. There were now eight huts round Len's brick house, but it was still officially part of the original village. This group may become an independent village, for Len will find less difficulty in getting a headmanship than a commoner. But he is also the potential heir to his father's brother, and has a strong claim to be considered for succession. If he does succeed in time, Len's present site would become the centre of the village, and the villagers at present living with his uncle would come under his rule. Whether or not Len decides to try to become an independent headman will depend on the number of followers he can attract, the conduct of his uncle as headman of the parent village, and finally the personal relations between the two men.

Another innovation is the emergence of villages based on a residential group with a common religious belief and not on kinship or affinal ties, thus introducing a new principle into Mambwe village organization. There are four of these among the grassland Mambwe, all composed of members of the Watch Tower Bible and Tract Society, usually known as Jehovah's Witnesses. These people prefer to live with their co-religionists and not scattered among the pagan population. The Witnesses do not practise polygyny, nor do they drink beer, so that life in their villages is more austere than in others. The largest grassland Mambwe village was a community of this kind. There are none among the forest Mambwe, who fall within the sphere of influence of the White Fathers, who have resolutely refused to allow the Witnesses to proselytize in their area. Three of these villages sprang from one village, called Galilee, founded in 1919 by Anok Simpungwe, who brought back the tenets of the new faith from a spell of wage-labour in the Wankie Colliery in Southern Rhodesia. Anok finally announced himself head of his own sect, and appointed deacons and other church officials, and even founded a colony of followers in Tanganyika. The Administration ordered him to leave his village, and his people to find places for themselves in other villages. Chief Nsokolo supported the Administration. The group split into three parts under this external pressure and through internal dissensions. One part followed Anok, another formed a new village under the headmanship of a royal convert, with the authority of the chief, and the last section was taken into the royal village of Aron, whose headman was sympathetic to the movement. Since then one other village of Witnesses has been formed. Galilee was burned down. Anok subsequently died under suspicious circumstances suggesting that he was poisoned, and his personal followers dispersed into existing villages.[1]

It will be noticed that the royal clan still exerted its authority over all these different villages. George Simukulwa was linked to the chief's family through marriage; the section of Wilson's village broke away under the leadership of a member of the royal clan with an interest in a royal headmanship; and the Jehovah's Witnesses were allowed to live in two other villages, both under members of the royal clan.

Kasunga village is an old-established royal village, and I shall examine it in some detail. The core of the village is a segment of the Luwandi lineage of the royal clan. The head of this lineage is Chief Kela, and the headman's title of Kasunga stands in the perpetual relationship of son to father to the title of Kela. A skeleton genealogy of Kasunga village is given in Figure 2. In 1953 the village had thirty-two huts, in which lived forty-two males and forty-seven females.

Headman Kasunga (D39) had succeeded from his father (C12). His elder half-brother, Moses (D31) was passed over for the title, as he was born before his father succeeded, and was thus debarred. This group, with their cognatic kinsmen and their wives and

---

[1] See pp. 197 ff.

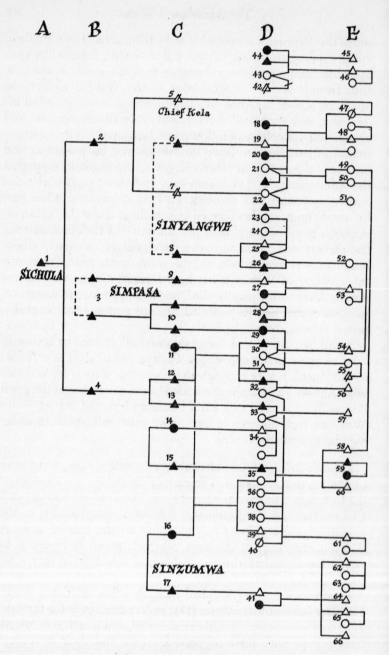

FIG. 2.—GENEALOGY OF KASUNGA VILLAGE.

families, formed the largest group in the village. Kasunga's sister's son, Adam Sikaombwe (E58), was born in the village, in which his father too had lived during his lifetime. The Sinzumwa group had lived in the village for only a few years. Samson Sinzumwa (D41) had been born and lived in a village in Chief Nsokolo's area, of which his father was headman. Samson left this village after a dispute with Chief Nsokolo about the succession to this headmanship.[1] He brought his sons and their families to join Kasunga village. Samson came to this village because he was Kasunga's mother's brother's son.

The relationship of a Mambwe to his mother's brother is important in their kinship system. It forms a strong and permanent link between two agnatic groups, for it is a tie of common descent. Outside the members of his own agnatic group, a Mambwe looks to his mother's brother for aid and assistance. He can even inherit from his mother's brother,[2] failing other heirs, except where a title is involved. Particularly, a Mambwe can demand cattle or money from his mother's brother to assist him with his marriage payment. This claim arises from the manner in which marriage payments are distributed. The mother of a bride gives her share of her daughter's marriage payment directly to her brother. The mother's share is always slightly less than the father's. Thus, if the payment is two cattle and eleven pounds, one animal and £6 goes to the father, and the other animal and £5 to the mother. The father and the mother's brother keep the cattle, but distribute most of the money among the members of their own agnatic group, in sums of one pound or ten shillings, so that quite a large circle of relatives receive something. When a man's sister is married, therefore, almost half the marriage payment goes to his mother's brother. The Mambwe consider that this obliges the mother's brother to contribute towards the marriage payment of his sister's son, when his time comes to be married. In normal day-to-day life, the relations between a Mambwe and his mother's brother are marked by respect and affection.[3] Samson therefore

---

[1] See p. 83 above.

[2] I did not record any instances of such inheritance. Almost invariably there are some agnatic kin with a prior claim, which is always superior to that of another clan.

[3] The significance of the connection appears in the form of address used by a Mambwe to his mother's brother. The common term is *yama* (mother's

had a strong claim on Kasunga's services, and Kasunga accepted him into his village without demur.

The other large group in the village consisted of two related men of the Sinyangwe clan and their wives and families. They were connected to the headman's lineage by marriage. One Nanyangwe girl (E52) was married to a Sichula (D54), and two Nanyangwe sisters (E49, E50) were married to the headman's sister's son Adam (E58). Elliam Sinyangwe (D25) acted as lieutenant and adviser to Kasunga, a position held by his father in the days of the present Kasunga's father.[1] Elliam had a local reputation and practice as a diviner, and was the most important man in the village next to the headman. He was son-in-law to Chief Kowa, the head of the Siuluta clan, through his marriage to Kowa's daughter Oripa (D24). Elliam formerly had a big following in the village. His young brother Isaac had lived there, together with two sons and a daughter whom Elliam inherited when his elder brother Wangwe (D26) died. But Isaac was converted by the Jehovah's Witnesses while serving in the Army during the war, and on his discharge he went off to join his coreligionists in Aron village. The two inherited sons left after a quarrel with Elliam.[2] These losses had been partly restored by the arrival of Kari Sinyangwe (D19) with his wives and family. Kari's connection with Elliam was not clear; they claimed that their fathers called one another brother, but could not give the precise relationship. Kari said he had come to join Elliam, but his son-in-law, Adam (E58), also lived in the village. Kari was also connected to the headman's own lineage through his wife Ismel (D22), who was the daughter of Chief Kela's brother. This link was strengthened when Chief Kela himself married Kari's daughter Silika (E47). Kari was notoriously quarrelsome and aggressive, and had moved from village to village throughout his life. He seemed unable to live peaceably anywhere. He had inherited many wives and cattle, but lost most of the cattle in

---

brother) and this is used when referring to such a relative. But I often heard a Mambwe greet his mother's brother with the words *yamayo* or *yamangu*. *Mayo* is the common word for mother, *mangu* a rarer alternative. The prefix *ya-* is the plural, and is customarily added to kinship terms as an indication of respect.

[1] He was addressed as *nkombe*, the rank of the section leaders and junior judges in the village states (see p. 72 above).

[2] See p. 153 f.

fines and damages, for he was constantly brought to court for quarrelling. None of his affairs prospered: he seemed born to bring trouble on himself and others. His daughter's marriage to Kela brought disaster on the village, for through her Kela hanged himself. This suicide had significant repercussions which I will discuss later. When Kari arrived in Kasunga, he was welcomed because of his large following.

The small group of the Simpasa clan were linked to the royal clan through the deceased wife (D29) of the headman's brother Moses (D31). Chole Simpasa (D27) was also a recent arrival. He had been a widower for a number of years and could not find another wife, as he suffered from leprosy. He brought his family to Kasunga, together with a widow, Eleni (D28), who was of the same clan and claimed kinship with him. Chole had lived for many years in the nearby village of Kosam, but left when the old headman died, after a quarrel with his successor. In spite of this the new headman of Kosam was pressing him to return, for he was a cheerful man and an industrious worker.

Another man, Island Simpemba (D34), who had two wives, was linked to the royal clan through a mother's brother relationship with the deceased husband of the headman's older sister (D35).

The only group not claiming any link whatever with the headman's clan was brought into the village by a widow, Eli (D43), of the Siinga clan. Eli had brought two young men with her, both sons of her deceased husband. One (E46) was her own son, the other (E45) a son of her husband's other wife (D44), now also dead. Eli had married again after her husband's death, but her second husband had divorced her. Subsequently this man went mad, and Eli was given refuge in Kasunga village.

The permanent residential group in this village, therefore, was the segment of the royal clan which held the title Kasunga, and its associated estate Mwansa. The village site had often been moved[1] within the bounds of the estate which formed the cultivating area round the village. The other groups were less stable, residentially. Apart from Elliam Sinyangwe (D25), who was born in the village and whose father too had lived there, the other groups had a history of movement between villages before coming to

---

[1] I traced five former sites.

H

Kasunga. This stability of the Kasunga lineage segment reflects the dominance of the royal clan as a whole, for lineages and segments of lineages within the royal clan are closely identified with particular districts, and their titles are associated with particular estates. Commoner clans are not identified with particular districts (with the exception of the clans of the three commoner chiefs), and hence commoners are free to move between villages. This freedom of movement allows for adjustment within the society, for it checks the authority of individual royal title-holders, since the people can leave them and go to live with another title-holder. The members of the royal clan tend to display a certain arrogance towards commoners. This may have been even more marked in the past when they practically monopolized control of Mambwe villages. Chief Mwamba told me that he favoured the appointment of commoners as headmen of new villages, for the royal headmen 'oppressed the people'.[1] The members of a royal lineage segment are tied to their title-holder by bonds of kinship and common interest in the title, but the commoners must be treated with care and their interests consulted, or the headman will lose them to a more just and generous title-holder. The commoners depend on a title-holder for rights to cultivate land, for justice, and for the performance of rituals upon which depend the fertility of both land and people. The personality of a headman is therefore an important factor in determining the size and prosperity of a village, for if he cannot satisfy his villagers, they will leave him and go elsewhere. He must be circumspect and tactful in all his dealings.

Kasunga's character and personality had a palpable effect on the fortunes of his village. He succeeded to the title and headmanship in 1931. When his father died, Kasunga was working in Tanganyika, and his brother Moses looked after the village until

---

[1] This statement must be considered in the light of Mwamba's own position. The Administration appointed Mwamba to the chieftainship when it deposed his father's brother in 1950. The Mambwe continued to recognize the deposed man, who had succeeded in the traditional way, as the 'true' chief. He still lived in Mwamba's village. Furthermore, the Administration created the present dominance of Mwamba's chieftainship by incorporating within its administrative area the chieftaincies of Kela and Fwambo. Both Kela and Fwambo are senior to Mwamba in the tribal system. Mwamba therefore had an interest in building up loyalties to himself to perpetuate his new authority and to undermine the traditional loyalties to Kela and Fwambo.

he returned to take up the succession. Kasunga ran the village until 1937, when he found a job in Abercorn, where he chose to live as well. He left the active administration of the village to Moses, but was able to supervise, as Abercorn is only about thirty miles away. During these thirteen years the village grew in size, for Moses was popular. In 1950 Kasunga returned permanently to the village, and took over the active conduct of its affairs. Difficulties arose at once. A good deal of tension developed between the brothers, for Kasunga was not so popular as Moses. He forced men out of the village, mainly because he interfered with their women, and the village began to decline in numbers. A former inhabitant told me that no one would join Kasunga, for he treated other men's wives as his own. One man left while I was there, because Kasunga had an affair with his wife. This man took Kasunga to court, and was awarded damages, but his wife remained in the village as Kasunga's concubine. This did not please Kasunga's wives. He had five wives, two of them (D32, D33) inherited from kinsmen. Two of his wives left the village, but were brought back. The whole village was much disturbed, and many said that Kasunga 'knew something', the Mambwe euphemism for practising sorcery.[1] Finally his reputation involved him in serious trouble with the head of his own lineage, Chief Kela.

Chief Kela married a young girl from Kasunga village, the daughter of Kari Sinyangwe. This girl resented the marriage, which was forced on her, and it proved unhappy, full of quarrels and beatings. She used to run off home to Kasunga village to visit her father. Chief Kela was extremely jealous of the girl, and accused Kasunga of having an affair with her. Kasunga denied this, both in public and in private, but Kela was not satisfied. He blamed Kasunga for corrupting the girl. Finally the girl ran off to Tanganyika with a lover from another village. Kela pursued them, but failed to find them, and returned without his wife. He then came to Kasunga's village, asked for the use of a hut for the night, and then hanged himself with a neck-cloth from the rafters. This was not entirely due to jealousy, but had other and more complex causes, which I will deal with later.[2]

The suicide laid a curse on the village. Kela's followers came in

---

[1] This is a common accusation against headmen.
[2] See p. 176 below.

a rage for the body, and Kasunga was fortunate to escape un-hurt.[1] The suicide hut was doctored and shut up.[2] The people talked about moving the village to another site, and the following dry season began to build new huts. Kasunga went off to Aber-corn to work, and Moses resumed the administration of the village.

At this time the proportion of women in the village to men was 2·0,[3] and this seems to be about the limit of tolerance before a village begins to break up. However, the Kasunga title is an important one, and the Sichula brothers, both dead and alive, have many young sons. After a time, the village will probably once more start to grow.

During the sixty years of British rule, the number of Mambwe villages has considerably increased, and the most significant development has been the emergence of a large number of com-moner villages, ruled by headmen of clans other than the royal. The stockaded village has entirely disappeared. The new villages are smaller, and at first arose through the breaking-up of the village states. The chief's brothers and sons were the first to be made headmen of their own villages. Former officials of the chief's court also became headmen of separate villages.

The Mambwe population appears to have increased since the break-up of the village states. In the last twenty years it has grown by 50 per cent. The new small villages may be healthier than the crowded village states, which were extremely dirty, and were constantly scourged by smallpox. Whether or not this is so, the new population has been accommodated in new vil-lages, and the number of villages is related to the increase in population.

The spread of villages over the land multiplied the number of headmanships and thus the number of political offices open to

---

[1] Formerly Chief Kela would have killed Kasunga for adultery. As it was, Kela's followers were so furious that they might easily have killed Kasunga. However, they knew that the Administration had been informed of Kela's death.

[2] When I left this hut was still not safe for habitation. Kasunga had not carried out the final rite of purification, an act of ritual intercourse with his chief wife. If he was really guilty of adultery with Kela's wife, he may have been afraid to do this, for fear of the anger and punishment of the ancestors.

[3] See Table VI.

aspiring commoners. Today the commoner headman has a position of authority he could not achieve in the past. The new villages are also more distant from the chief, which gives them a certain independence from the chief's surveillance. The hold of the royal clan has been weakened to a certain extent, for commoner headmen now compose half the total number. But the royal clan retained the chieftainships, and thereby major control over the people. The increase in the number of villages has also decreased the number of intermediaries between people and chief. Formerly a tribesman had to apply first to a junior judge, then to a captain, then to the council, before he was taken before the chief. Today he can apply through his headman to the chief, or even directly to the chief. The smaller village ensures that the inhabitants are in direct contact with the village headman and in more intimate association with him.

The form of the village state was largely dictated by military considerations, as a defensive enclosure or fort, and each section was also a military unit. It is significant that the men of authority in the village state were the captains. Peace made this form of organization unnecessary and the people were able to spread out over the land. The actual form of Mambwe villages has therefore adjusted to new conditions. The village has ceased to be a state and stronghold, but retains its economic function as a corporate productive group. Although the new villages are far smaller than the village states, they are always of a certain size, seldom less than thirty huts. A family cannot live on its own with the present methods of agriculture, for it would not be able to release men to wage-labour. Numbers are necessary to carry out the co-operative tasks of cultivation that enable men to leave.

Each village forms a discrete social group, distinguished by the name of the village. This name is that of its estate, the area of arable land and pasture on which the villagers cultivate and herd their cattle. When a Mambwe is asked to which village he belongs, he invariably replies with the name of his village estate. He rarely gives the name of the headman unless this is specifically sought.[1] This Mambwe practice differs from that of many other

---

[1] The Administration always use the headman's name. When speaking to Europeans, Mambwe follow this practice for convenience.

Central African peoples, among whom the village is known by the name of the headman.[1]

The modern village is therefore the main residential and productive unit of Mambwe society. The villagers co-operate in productive, ritual, social, and political activities. Mambwe pass their whole lives in one village or another, and a villager is in constant contact with his own agnatic and affinal kin. Every villager has traditional rights and duties towards his headman, and through him to his chief.

VILLAGE LAND AND LABOUR

Village membership gives a Mambwe the fundamental right to the use of land. A Mambwe receives permission to use land from the headman, who in turn receives his rights to allocate his village land from the chief. The Mambwe use the same word, *mwene*, for both chiefs and headmen. There is no distinctive form of address used either for royal chiefs or headmen, or for commoner chiefs and headmen. This word may be loosely translated as 'owner', but ownership in the Mambwe sense does not imply the right of the 'owner' to dispose of the land as he thinks fit. A chief or headman cannot sell the land or give it away. His rights are clearly defined, as are those of the men who cultivate the land. The word *mwene* is also used in connection with people. Chief Nsokolo is styled Mwene Mambwe, the 'owner of the Mambwe people'. This does not mean that he could enslave his people, in the days of slavery. A free man was under the protection of the law. The chief had claims on his labour and loyalty, but in turn the chief had to uphold his rights as a subject. Similarly, the heads of some clans are styled Mwene, and I found six such titles: Mwene Kowa, Chileshya, Chindo, Upundu, Misansa, Chipoko.[2] The headman of a village is styled *Mwene muzi* (owner of the village), and even the heads of families are sometimes addressed as *mwene*. Mitchell translates the similar Yao word *asyene* as 'the person with whom an object is identified' and in regard to people,

---

[1] Cf. Gluckman, Mitchell, and Barnes, 'The Village Headman in British Central Africa', p. 89, and my own paper 'The Kaonde Village', p. 7.

[2] The first three of these clan title-holders lived among the Mambwe in Northern Rhodesia, the next two among the Mambwe in Tanganyika, and the last among the Lungu in Northern Rhodesia.

quotes Wagner's definition of the Logoli word, 'Thus the *omwene* (owner) of a person is the one who has not only the foremost rights over him but also the foremost obligations towards him.'[1] The Mambwe use of the word *mwene* is identical. The chief 'owns' both land and people, but the concept of ownership to the Mambwe embraces clusters of rights and duties towards the land and persons 'owned'.

Chief Nsokolo, as Mwene Mambwe, is the source of all Mambwe land rights. Nsokolo grants what Gluckman has called 'estates of holding'[2] to the lesser chiefs, who recognize his authority. In turn these lesser chiefs grant estates to village headmen within their chieftaincies, and the headmen allocate holdings to the members of their villages. In return, each holder of an estate admits the political authority of the superior from whom he derives his estate, and pays him respect. Thus the series of 'estates of holding' reflects the distribution of political authority within the tribal community. Sheddick has described the similar authority of the chiefs over land in Basutoland as 'rights to administer land', and distinguishes between these rights and 'rights to use land'.[3] He found in Basutoland that 'all chiefs and subordinate authorities are regarded as nothing more than "caretakers" acting for the Paramount Chief'.[4] This distinction between the control exercised by chiefs and headmen over the distribution of the land, and the rights to use the land for productive purposes, is a valid one. The chief himself, like his subjects, has the right to use some land within the chieftaincy for production, but he cannot take away land that a subject is already cultivating. The hierarchy of 'estates of holding' is an aspect of political control. Thus when Chief Nsokolo asserts his right to appoint one of his sons to the Mwamba chieftainship on the death of the incumbent, he is also asserting his rights over the estate that is attached to the title.

Any man, even of another tribe, can claim the right to use land from the chief, and will be given that right. But before he can exercise this right, he must find a headman who is willing to accept him into his village. Once a man finds such acceptance,

1 'The Yao of Southern Nyasaland', pp. 318–19.
2 'Lozi Land Tenure', p. 29.
3 *Land Tenure in Basutoland*, p. 2.
4 Ibid., p. 141.

and has cleared land for his own use, the rights in this land are his own, and no one can take them from him. His heir can inherit this land, but only on condition that he comes to live in the deceased's village. If the heir refuses to do this, the land reverts to the headman, who may reallocate it as he wishes.

The close association between land and the political hierarchy of 'estates of holding' appears in the customary Mambwe description of political units by the place-names of the districts in which they are situated.[1] The Mambwe describe both chieftaincies and villages by places: Mbiriya, Atuntu, Mwansa, etc., and rarely by the names of the personages who are socially and politically dominant there: Chief Mwamba, Chief Kowa, Headman Kasunga, etc. Within his estate the chief had rights over the distribution of land among his headmen, over animals killed by hunters, and over the ores found in the earth. Trespass on these rights by persons from another chieftaincy led to conflict between the chiefs. The guild of elephant hunters (*mwami*) could follow and kill an animal only within the bounds of their own chief's territory. If a wounded elephant escaped into a neighbouring chieftaincy, the hunters had to let it go. However, they had some claim on a wounded animal that escaped. If an elephant died as a result of wounds not inflicted by his own hunters, a chief might consider sharing the meat and ivory with the chief whose hunters had wounded it in the first place. Even then the hunters' chief had to inform the other when and where his men had severely wounded the animal. He could do little to enforce his claims. I cite these examples from hunting to show that the territories of the separate chiefs were clearly distinguished and the rights of each chief within his own territory were paramount.

Boundaries between village estates are not so clearly demarcated. Village boundaries have not been distinctly defined by the chief; there are no boundary marks, such as boulders, mounds, fences, etc. Each headman roughly distinguishes his area by reference to natural features, hills, streams, outcrops of rock. Precise definition only emerges when villagers quarrel over land. I watched one man from Kasunga village breaking virgin soil

---

[1] The place-names Aisa and Maswepa describe the largest social division of the whole tribe, viz. between the grassland cultivators and the forest people. In conversation among the Mambwe the extent and political affiliations of any social group are implicit in the geographical definition.

for a garden. He was quite close to the site of Aron village; some men from this village had gardens only a hundred yards away. The Kasunga villager made a row of mounds to mark out the area he wished to cultivate. The Aron villagers protested that the field lay within the estate of Aron. Headman Aron thereupon consulted Kasunga, who agreed at once that the land was Aron's, and told his villager to cultivate elsewhere. The dispute was not taken before the chief. It was settled amicably because land was available elsewhere. Increasing pressure of population on the land may lead to an exact definition of boundaries in the future. At present land does not appear to be scarce among the grassland Mambwe. The Citemene Control Scheme clearly distinguishes boundaries for the woodland Mambwe. As a result, few disputes arise concerning the boundaries between village estates.

The headman's considerable authority rests on his power to refuse a man admittance to his village, thus denying him access to land. The chief will not give a man the right to cultivate anywhere he pleases: he must live in a village. This sanction of acceptance by a headman is naturally a political control. A man must accept the rule of chief and headman if he is to get land to work, and must continue to behave in a reasonable way if he wishes to remain in the village. If none of the headmen will accept a man, then his only recourse is to move elsewhere. The headmen frequently exercise their power. For instance, many headmen will not accept Jehovah's Witnesses, on the grounds that they make too much trouble. When the original Watch Tower village was destroyed, the chief ordered the Witnesses to disperse to ordinary villages. But many headmen refused to take them, and thus a large number were rendered homeless. Some were accepted by a royal headman who was a convert, and the chief permitted another royal convert to set up a new village. But many of the more militant had to migrate to Tanganyika before they found a headman willing to take them. These Witnesses founded a new sect there.[1]

The headman is solely responsible for allocating the village land among his people. He must approve the specific strips of land that a man wishes to cultivate. When a man leaves the village, or when a man dies and his heir refuses to come and live in the

[1] See p. 199.

village, the land reverts to the headman. He can then allocate it as he thinks best. He settles disputes about the ownership or use of land, and protects the interests of the men who are absent at work. He must be consulted whenever some change in the ownership or cultivation of the land is proposed.

But once a man is accepted as a member of a village his rights to the land allocated to him by the headman are secure. The labour that he expends on breaking virgin soil establishes his rights to it, and it becomes his field. He may dispose of his fields to fellow-villagers as he pleases, but not to outsiders. Young boys help their fathers to cultivate, and to herd cattle. When they are about fourteen they are given some of their fathers' land to cultivate by themselves, but they do not get fields of their own until they are ready to be married and have built huts in the village for their wives.

A man can give the temporary use of his land to another villager, and this person may work it and take off a crop; but an owner can always demand back his land whenever he wishes. When a man goes off to work, and leaves his wife behind, she continues to work his fields.

A man cannot sell his land. He may, however, sell the potential crop. If a man has prepared virgin soil, thrown up mounds and planted seed, he can allow another person to continue to work the land and take off the crop, in return for a cash payment. A man in a royal village offered to hand over the crop from a field he had prepared in order to discharge a debt of £3 he could not pay. The creditor accepted the arrangement, worked the garden for about a month before the harvest, and took away the crop. Most men leave for work abroad in the period before the harvest. At this time the main work of cultivation is over, there is not much for the men to do, and there is little beer to drink, as supplies of millet are short. If a man takes his wife with him when he goes off to work, he can sell the crop he is expecting from his fields. This is sometimes done to help raise the bus fares and expenses for a trip to the Copperbelt. This arrangement can be made either with a fellow-villager or with an outsider. The land still belongs to the owner. Some absent workers give their fields to kinsfolk to cultivate for them while they are away. If they happen to find work locally, they take part of the crop as a kind of rent. The use of the fields reverts to the owner on his return.

A man's rights in village land can be inherited. The heir takes both the hut and the cultivated fields of his predecessor. But he must live in the village if he is to use the fields. If the heir wishes to cultivate the fields, he must take up residence in the village. Thus if an heir does not live in the village, and refuses to come to live there, he forfeits his rights to his predecessor's fields. He may dispose of the hut as he thinks fit, either by taking away the heavier beams, which are in short supply among the grassland Mambwe, or by selling the hut to someone already living in the village. Should a man living in the village inherit more land than he can work, he can distribute it among his relatives, provided that they too are resident in the village.

When a man leaves the village and goes to live elsewhere, he forfeits all rights to the land he works, save that he can continue to cultivate his fields until harvest, when they revert to the headman. One villager brought a case against his headman, alleging adultery with his wife. The villager won his case, was awarded damages, and divorced his wife. He then left the village and went to live elsewhere. This happened in November, and he had already prepared his fields. He returned each day to cultivate his fields until the following May, when his mother and sister came to reap the crop and carried it off.

Women's rights to the use of land differ from those of men. There are no 'estates of holding' for women; they must work land whose rights are held by men. A man must make a garden for each of his wives, and if he does not, his wife may leave him and claim a divorce. This puts a great strain on those men who have more than two wives. Chiefs have many wives, but can depend on tribute labour for the cultivation of gardens for them, even today, when it is supposed to be forbidden. One royal headman had four wives and a concubine, living in his village, and had great difficulty in providing gardens for them all. The concubine was entirely dependent on her lover's bounty for food, for she had lost the use of her husband's fields when he divorced her. The year the headman took the concubine, he inherited the fourth wife, who was a member of Chief Mpande's lineage of the royal clan. As the headman did not at once make a garden for her, this wife left him and returned to Chief Mpande's village. Because she had no garden of her own she had been forced to work for food in other people's gardens, a particularly

humiliating role for a person of her status. The headman followed
her to Chief Mpande's village and threatened to shoot himself
there and then if she did not return with him. Chief Mpande
persuaded her to return with her husband after he had promised
to make her a garden.

Eli (D43), a widow, brought two young men to Kasunga village, a son and a foster-son. Her own son and his wife went
off to work in Tanganyika, and Eli worked his fields while he was
away. Her foster-son, Jackson (E45), also provided fields for her.
Jackson was not married, but was engaged and had built a hut,
and thus obtained land of his own. Eli carried out all the woman's
share of cultivation and also cooked for Jackson. She also worked
for food in the fields of other villagers. Usually a widow can
depend on her male agnatic kin to provide her with fields to work
if she is not inherited by her husband's brother.[1] Kasunga's elder
sister Mika (D35) was also a widow, and she worked in gardens
made for her by her sons. Her position was very secure, for
Kasunga was both her natal and marital village, and she had
both brothers and sons to support her. Daughters help their
mothers to cultivate their fathers' fields until they are married,
when they go to their husbands' villages. A deserted wife loses
her rights to use her husband's fields. When a wage-earner fails
to return after an absence of three to five years, and has not sent
his wife any clothes or goods,[2] or otherwise communicated with
the village, he is assumed to have deserted her. Her rights in his
fields then lapse, and she must seek support in a village where she
has male kin.[3] Such women often claim divorce on the grounds
of desertion, and the courts treat them sympathetically. The
courts communicate with the man, and if he states definitely that

---

[1] Heirs often refuse to accept elderly widows as wives, if they cannot bear
children.

[2] When a returned labourer seeks damages for his wife's adultery in his
absence, the courts consider whether or not he has neglected his wife. Their
judgement on this point affects their assessment of the amount of damages to
be awarded.

[3] I did not come across any women who had been asked to leave their fields
because they were deserted. Most Mambwe wives would not tolerate such a
long period of neglect. The public shame of desertion would drive a wife
either to go off with another man who would provide her with clothes and
care, or to return to her father's or brother's village, long before three years
had elapsed.

he is not coming back, or gives an inadequate reason for failing to support his wife, grant the woman a divorce. When this happens, the husband can no longer claim damages for her adultery.

Rights to pasture cattle are of a different order from rights to cultivate land. A village can graze its herd anywhere that it can find pasturage, except among growing crops.[1] The herd need not be confined to the village estate. In the wet season grass is plentiful, and each village usually herds the cattle nearby on a recognized pasturage (*icemeluwe*) established by custom. If this pasturage fails (which is unlikely), the cattle may be taken further afield, on to the customary pasturage of another village. There is no objection to this, provided that the visiting herd is tended by men, and not by boys.[2] In the dry season when pastures are poor, the cattle may be grazed anywhere, and are often taken far from the village. At this time they are also allowed to graze on the crop stover in people's fields. No one is allowed to reserve his own stover for his own cattle.

Thus each village accords freedom of access to herds from other villages. Mambwe herds are not large,[3] and there appears to be sufficient pasturage for many more cattle than the Mambwe own at present, but there is a further reason for this tolerance. Each village herd is the centre of widespread interest, for it contains animals from many other villages. No village herd is composed entirely of animals owned by the villagers. A cattle-owner seldom keeps his animals in his own village. He prefers to send them to a friend to be herded for a fee (*lusoso*). The herder's fee is the milk of the cattle he cares for, and a heifer calf at the end of three years. If both owner and herder are satisfied, the arrangement is continued, and from then on the owner gives the herder a bull calf every two years. The herder must inform the owner at once if an animal is injured or dies, or is killed by wild animals. The owner comes to take away the carcase and the skin, which must be kept for his inspection to prove that the herder's account

---

[1] If the cattle eat or trample growing crops, the whole village is liable to pay damages to the owner.

[2] To keep the bulls from fighting.

[3] See Table II.

of the animal's death is genuine. The herder has the right to receive the head and right foreleg of the carcase. If the owner cannot come at once to collect the carcase, the herder dries the meat and sends it to him, together with the skin.

A cattle-owner usually employs as herder a man to whom he is not related. If he has a number of beasts he may distribute them among a number of herders. But relatives are rarely given cattle to herd, for they have rights to dispose of the cattle. Cattle are 'owned' only in the sense that one man is responsible for them; he is not entirely free to do what he likes with them. For example, if some cattle came to a man through his sister's marriage payment, her sons will certainly lay a claim to his animals in the future, for their own marriage payments. Brothers inherit the animals when the 'owner' dies, and if they are allowed to herd the cattle in his lifetime, may be tempted to anticipate their rights. One informant said, 'How can you give cattle to your relative to herd? He would use them to pay a fine and then say he was your brother.' The herding arrangement therefore establishes widespread connections between men of different lineages throughout a number of villages. The owner constantly visits his herder to inspect his cattle and check that they have not been sold or killed for meat. Cattle link men of different clans in a common bond of property. The constant visits of owners to their herders extends the interests of the Mambwe outside their own village groups.

Cattle are always the foci of a number of Mambwe social relationships, often of an extremely complicated nature. Different relatives have varied interests in the same beasts. Bonds of the closest friendship, enduring over long periods, connect men in distant villages, through the herding arrangement. But cattle are also a fertile source of disputes. The histories of the following disputes illustrate the complexity and variation of the relationships involved in owning and herding cattle.

A villager, Kauzeni, was friendly with Ndalama, the headman of a village about fifteen miles away. Kauzeni used to visit his friend regularly, and the headman frequently gave him presents of sweet potatoes to take home with him. On one occasion, Kauzeni was short of grain, and offered to buy some from Ndalama, who gave him a full tin. Kauzeni had offered to pay for this, but in fact did not. Ndalama did not press him. Ndalama also performed several other favours. Kauzeni returned various

small presents, including a pipe he brought back from a trip to
Tanganyika, but he did not fully reciprocate Ndalama's gifts and
services. In 1939, Kauzeni went off to Lusaka to work. Before he
left, he gave Ndalama a pound to buy a calf for him, and asked
him to herd it while he was away. Ndalama reared the calf until
it was full-grown. It calved for the first time during the dry
season, but died shortly afterwards. Ndalama skinned the cow and
sent word to Kauzeni's brother, John. John sent his sons to fetch
one foreleg and the entrails, with instructions that Ndalama was
to sell the remainder of the meat, except for the head, his per-
quisite as herder.

Ndalama complied with John's instructions and sold the meat
for eighteen shillings. He sent this money to John at once. John
kept this money for himself and did not forward it to his brother
Kauzeni in Lusaka. Shortly after this, the calf followed the other
cattle into the bush and disappeared. It was a weak animal, and
had been given special care. That day Ndalama happened to be
absent from the village and his people searched for the lost calf
without success. On his return Ndalama sent a message to John
reporting the loss. John did not come to Ndalama's village to
help in the search for the lost calf, for he knew it was weak and
probably worthless. He would have come if the calf had been
bigger and stronger. After the bush fires in the autumn, the calf's
skeleton was found, and this was duly reported to John. At this
juncture Kauzeni died in Lusaka. His other brother, Machi, inherited his wife and property, including some cattle. Machi then
claimed that Ndalama owed him an animal to replace the calf lost
in the bush, and sued him before the Native Court.

The court dismissed Machi's claim to receive an animal from
Ndalama. The chief pointed out that Ndalama was a good friend
to Kauzeni; he had given many gifts and received few in return.
All he had got to show was a pipe. Further, he had not claimed his
herder's fee from his friend. If Ndalama had been a hard man, he
would have claimed his fee, for whether or not the calf died, he
still had had the work of looking after both it and the cow. John,
the brother of the deceased Kauzeni, was the man at fault; he had
kept the eighteen shillings that Ndalama had got for the meat.
Machi was told that if he wanted an animal, he must apply to
his brother John. This judgement suited Machi. His real intention
in bringing a case against Ndalama was probably to expose his

brother's part in the transactions. John's debt to the inherited estate was now publicly established.

I have given this case in some detail, for it illustrates the close bonds of friendship often shared by Mambwe who enter a herding arrangement, the rights and obligations of owner and herder, and the attitude of brothers towards the cattle owned by one of them. The details of the dispute cover a period of fourteen years, and it is not yet ended; John has not given the eighteen shillings to his brother. It is significant that the court did not order him to do so. John and Machi have mutual rights and obligations towards one another, and towards the property that Machi inherited. The court's findings will affect their relations, but they have common interests as well as rivalries, and will settle the matter between themselves.

Another dispute involved the interests in certain animals of five people: a mother, her brother, her son, and two herders. Mary received two cows when her daughter Sara was married. Mary handed these over to her brother Alec. Alec went abroad to work, and gave the cattle to William to herd, together with another cow he acquired in exchange for a bicycle. This cow had a calf while in William's care. After a time, Mary's son Sandy complained that William was neglecting the cattle, took them away, and transferred the herding to a friend of his, Dawson.[1] Sandy did not give William a herding fee. Sandy then went off to Ndola to work, taking his mother with him.

The first herder, William, then applied to the second herder, Dawson, to give him the calf as his herding fee. Dawson refused. He said that he did not know whether or not William had a just claim, and anyway, the demand was irregular, for it should be made to the owner, not to the herder. William then brought his claim for a fee before the Native Court.

The three principals, Alec, his sister Mary, and Mary's son, Sandy, were all absent when the case came before the court. Accordingly, the court wrote to Alec and informed him about the

---

[1] These two animals moved in a short space of time through the kraals of five separate villages, viz. the villages of husband, wife's mother, wife's mother's brother, first herder, second herder. There may have been more, for I do not know where the husband acquired them. The changing constitution of any particular village herd aggravates the difficulties of unravelling the changing clusters of rights that centre on individual animals.

case. Alec replied that Sandy had no right at all to take away the cow with the calf; this was definitely his own property. Regarding the other two animals, Alec suggested that Sandy may have been ordered to change the herder by his mother; she had every right to do this, for the cattle came for her daughter. Further, Alec wrote that he was not satisfied with Sandy's action. As Sandy's mother's brother, he should have been consulted before the cattle were moved. The court upheld Alec's right to dispose of the cattle as he thought fit, on the grounds that he had prior rights to Sandy. But they ordered that William was to have the calf as his fee.

The court assessor told me that Sandy's mistake was to take Alec's cow along with the other two. He had no right at all to interfere with this cow. But the two other cattle were a different matter. Alec had got these two cattle through the marriage of Sandy's sister; Sandy too had rights in them. If Sandy decided that the cattle were not being properly looked after by the first herder, he had every right to look into the matter; but he ought to have consulted his mother's brother before moving them. Sandy's father was dead, and he could expect some cattle from his father's relatives to help with his marriage payments. If they could not supply him with sufficient cattle, then Sandy could certainly turn to his mother's brother to make up the number needed. It is evident that Sandy was attempting to strengthen his claim to the cattle by withdrawing them from Alec's herder and placing them with a friend of his own. But he had exceeded his rights.

In the assessor's view, the difficulties in this case all arose through the absence of the two men at work. Sandy would not have dared to move the cattle if his mother's brother had been at home. The assessor said that matters were always being muddled because men were absent from home.[1]

The village herd is therefore of interest not only to the people within the village but to many people outside. Rights over particular animals are constantly passing from one group of

---

[1] While this is true, the absent workers nevertheless keep in close touch with affairs at home. In another dispute between a wife's father and her husband concerning the marriage cattle, the court adjourned the case until one of the wife's brothers made a special journey from the Copperbelt to give evidence before the court. Absent workers are contacted when necessary, and they maintain a lively interest in their families and social affairs generally.

persons to another, and at the same time the cattle themselves move from village to village. Each village herd binds the people of the village to many other people and villages, even in other chieftaincies. Woodland Mambwe have their cattle herded by grassland villagers. Grassland Mambwe have their cattle herded by the Mambwe in Tanganyika. The Mambwe, like the Plateau Tonga,[1] are interested in ownership rather than in immediate possession of cattle, and the animals represent to them a complex of social ties and obligations.

In addition to land rights, village membership ensures that a man's family becomes part of a corporate working-group. He can depend on assistance for such tasks as preparing new fields, thatching roofs, fishing, and many other essential activities. The villagers work in one another's fields in voluntary co-operative groups, in which women supply the bulk of the labour. The Mambwe system of agriculture makes this co-operation possible, and the absence of a great number of men makes it essential. All the heavy fieldwork in Kasunga village was performed under this system of co-operative labour during a three-week period for which I kept records of every person's activities. This was the time of year (January and February) when the heavy rains set in, and the preparation of the seed-beds is an urgent task. Every day the villagers divided into groups which went by invitation to the fields of the man whose wife had brewed beer for that day. The work-party drank the beer when they returned from the fields, in return for their assistance. The people left the village at about eight o'clock in the morning, and returned between twelve and two o'clock in the afternoon.[2] These work-parties occurred in all the villages I visited, including those of the woodland Mambwe.

Richards has described similar work-parties among the Bemba.[3] She states that they last for about four hours, and that these outings are a 'useful means of breaking the back of a big job such as clearing the bush or putting new grassland under the hoe'. The amount of grain used each year by the Bemba for these work-

---

[1] Cf. Colson, 'The Role of Cattle Among the Plateau Tonga'.

[2] The women had stamped and ground flour, and fed their families, before the work-parties set out for the fields. The men had worked for about an hour on individual tasks.

[3] *Land, Labour, and Diet*, pp. 146 ff.

parties was appreciable, and most householders brewed at least once during the season for this purpose. But Richards states that the system among the Bemba is 'inefficient from the economic point of view perhaps, since the proportion of the day spent in beer-drinking is very large compared with that spent on actual work'. She adds that it was not uncommon to find the party returning at eleven or twelve o'clock in order to have time to enjoy the beer. The impression I form from this account is that the Bemba work-parties are occasional and for short sharp spells of work. It is not so among the Mambwe.

It can be said that for the Mambwe the work-party is the funda-mental method of production. The heavy hoeing necessary to rotate the crops is best performed by groups working together. It is true that the Mambwe too spend only four to five hours a day in the fields, but turning over wet ground with a hoe is very heavy work. Four or five hours of this labour seems to me to be an adequate portion of their available working hours, in view of their diet and mode of life. They have other work to do in the village as well. Work in the fields is only one part of subsistence production, although the most important. There are many other subsidiary tasks which must be done every day. The women have to attend to their village gardens, to fetch firewood and water, to stamp and grind flour for two meals a day. Children must be washed and tended, and water boiled for the men's baths.[1] The men have to keep the hoes and axes in working order, maintain the huts and the paths around the village, seek for strayed cattle and attend to those that are sick or injured, and fulfil the social obligations that keep the whole system going.

Beer is not considered repayment for work done, but rather as an essential refreshment for the workers. The basis of Mambwe co-operative work is reciprocity. A man who attends another's work-party obliges the other to work in his own fields in return. Beer is not pay: it is the work which is reciprocated. The Mambwe therefore do not hurry home from their fields to spend the rest of the day carousing. Most work-parties take place in the months between January and April, when grain is running short, and often enough the beer pot is a small one. A man cannot get his

---

[1] When a girl is married, she is instructed that she must boil water every day for her husband's bath.

gardens dug simply by providing beer for others to come and
work for him; if he does not work in return, no one will again
accept his invitations. The constitution of the work-parties reflects the reciprocal obligations between villagers. In Kasunga
village, Chole (D27) was a widower. He was a popular man, and
willingly joined work-parties. But when Chole's daughter-in-law
(E53) brewed beer for the villagers to come to work in Chole's
garden, not one of the women turned up. Chole had no wife to
return the reciprocal obligation and so men only came to work
his garden. The reciprocal nature of the obligation was implicitly
stated here. When Eruda (E62), whose husband was absent at
the Copperbelt, wished to have her garden dug, only seventeen
members of the village came to help. Eruda had spent much of
her time away from the village at her father's village, where she
was helping with the preparations for her sister's wedding. She
was absent from her husband's village during the time of intensive
hoeing and seeding, and had not been able to play her part in
all the work-parties of the period. Only those who owed her an
obligation to work turned up at her own work-party.

The villagers arrange these work-parties among themselves,
but the headman supervises the arrangements in the general
interest. Mambwe millet beer takes three or four days to prepare
and quickly loses its quality. Thus if two people brew beer for the
same day and one lot must be left over, it is likely to go off. No
one wishes to waste grain, and any clash of dates leads to quarrels.
The headman must settle such conflicts with some delicacy, if he
wishes to retain the confidence of both parties. In Kasunga village,
Chole (D27) announced that he would provide beer for a work-
party on a certain day. A few days later, Kari (D19) nominated
the same day. The two men were not on good terms at this time,
and Kari undoubtedly hoped to upset Chole. Neither man would
budge from the day he had announced. The men in the village
had obligations to both, and the night before the work-parties
were due the headman called them to a meeting. Chole was a
widower and therefore none of the women except his daughter-
in-law intended to join his work-party. Kari could command the
work of his wives and children, but only a few other women
owed him work. Kasunga said he wanted to keep the peace and
ensure that everyone's gardens were properly prepared. He suggested that all the men except himself should go to Chole's

garden. He would go to Kari's garden and bring his five wives.
This arrangement worked successfully.

The largest work-party I observed in Kasunga village worked
in the gardens of Itelesi, who was the wife of Stanley (E61),
the headman's son. Stanley was at that time working abroad.
The whole village turned out for Itelesi; she had brewed plenty
of beer, and her garden was finished in two days. Itelesi was the
headman's daughter-in-law and could therefore appeal to kinship
ties, but the large turn-out was not wholly due to this. Itelesi was
a good worker and an unfailing attender at every work-party in
the village. Industrious women can always command help. Eli,
whose kinship relationships with the rest of the villagers were
tenuous and obscure, also had a large turn-out, and again this was
due to her assiduity in attending other people's work-parties.

Cultivation is not carried out entirely by means of work-parties.
Weeding is largely women's work. A woman generally weeds
her own field, although her husband helps her to hoe and seed.
Each wife is provided with her own garden by her husband, and
from this she is expected to provide food and beer for her husband
and family. But when a man has more than one wife, they often
work as a group, dealing with one field at a time. Such an extended
family work-party may be sporadically assisted by others, particularly widows, under the arrangement of working for food
(*ukupula*).[1] A person in need may be rewarded immediately for
such assistance with a basket of flour, but generally, if she does not
need the food at once, she will be given a share of the crop.
Women and indigent persons are expected to earn food in this
way, but ordinary people with fields of their own regard such
work as shameful. The Mambwe consider that persons with fields
of their own who have to find food by working for others must
be either lazy or incompetent, and little better than beggars.
This is why the newly-inherited wife left her new husband.[2] He
had not provided her with a field of her own, and she was forced
to work for others in order to feed herself and her child, a humiliating situation for a young and able woman who was both a
chief's daughter and a headman's wife. She said that the other
women's commiserations (particularly those of her co-wives)
were motivated by spite. I noticed that she confined her work to

---

[1] This word is often used as a synonym for begging.
[2] See p. 99 above.

the fields of her husband's male relatives, so that she worked only for her clansmen.

The only set of gardens in which work-parties never take place are the kitchen gardens (*ivizule*). Women sell the surplus crops (mainly maize) from these gardens and use the money to buy clothes and personal goods. As a result, these gardens are personally tended and jealously guarded. Women often quarrel over these gardens. Disputes regularly occur concerning the ownership of the kitchen refuse, garbage, old leaves, etc., that the women sweep up and use as top-dressing.

Co-operative labour affects village life in many ways. Communal work is more efficient and sociable than solitary labour, and increases production. The constant brewing and drinking of beer helps to distribute the consumption of crops. The work-party ensures that no woman left at home need fear that she will be bereft of labour to cultivate her fields. When a young man goes off to work, he knows that his wife and family will be fed, and will not have to beg. There is also a moral constraint inherent in the communal work principle. A person who co-operates with others and works hard and willingly in work-parties is highly regarded, and considered an asset to the village: a lazy, selfish person is despised. The absence of large numbers of active men does not halt the agricultural process, as men and women both use the hoe and few tasks are specialized. This applies mainly to the grassland Mambwe; woodland men have the special task of lopping the trees. This is strictly men's work, and women never attempt it. However, tree-cutting too is carried out by means of work-parties. The available men in the village work systematically on one another's trees until all have enough wood to make gardens.

But in spite of this system of mutual aid through communal work-parties, the absence of 50 per cent of the active men might be expected to produce a serious effect on the subsistence economy.[1]

---

[1] In 1935 the authorities in the Belgian Congo estimated that serious difficulties would arise if more than 5 to 10 per cent of the adult males went away (*The Recruitment of Labour in the Colonies*, pp. 113 ff.). The value of such estimates is not very great; the percentage of absent men that can be tolerated must depend on a whole constellation of factors: the ages of the absentees, length of time away, social organization of the people concerned, type of tribal economy, and finally, the agricultural system and the division of labour between the sexes.

We have seen how production is maintained, but a man cannot work in two places at once, and if he is mining copper, he cannot be growing millet. It is true that the absent men do not have to be fed, but, often enough, the local wage-earners continue to draw on village production of grain to help raise their real wages. How can this great force of able-bodied men be withdrawn from the economy and yet it still keeps producing?

This difficulty may be resolved, I suggest, by examining the changes brought about in the general pattern of Mambwe activities by the arrival of the Europeans. At that time they lived in the stockaded villages, often five or more miles distant from their fields. The daily journey to and from the fields must have taken up time at the expense of agricultural work. Further, a considerable number of sentries were regularly posted in the neighbourhood to protect both cattle and people from marauding Bemba and others. Each village had to maintain a constant force of men ready to give battle. When the raiders came, cultivation had to be abandoned for flight or battle. The grassland Mambwe in troubled times used to drive their cattle into a series of natural caves near the present Tanganyika border and keep them there for safety. Men had to be sent to herd and guard these cattle; boys could not be detailed for herding as they are today.[1] It is more than likely, therefore, that the men spent a good deal of their total time at war or on guard, and that the bulk of agricultural work fell to the women. The *pax britannica* liberated the Mambwe from the confinement of the stockaded village, brought them closer to their fields, and freed them from military duties. They have always been assiduous cultivators, according to Bemba accounts; indeed it was their wealth in crops and flocks which tempted raiders.[2] Now their production was no longer interrupted by raiders, and the Mambwe could keep the crops to themselves. The Europeans did not radically alter their system of agriculture, so that the task of winning their subsistence from the soil now left them with some leisure. A new productive method would have absorbed this leisure, but there has been little change.

---

[1] The Mambwe say that in the past young men herded the cattle; only in recent years have boys been entrusted with herding.

[2] When the first Europeans arrived, they asked the Bemba where their gardens were. It is said that the Bemba pointed towards the north, towards the Mambwe.

Men have no specialized role in the productive process, except among the woodland Mambwe, where they must lop the trees. But this tree-lopping, although vital to their system of cultivation, occurs only once a year and can be successfully performed by a few men working together. Both men and women hoe. Provided, then, that the land is of good quality, and a village is strongly knit round its agnatic core, half the active men can go off without seriously hampering subsistence production.

I propose now to examine some villages in relation to the absence of men, and the effects of their wage-labour on the social life of these villages.

VILLAGE ADJUSTMENT TO WAGE-LABOUR

Mambwe males are often attached to the same village and the same land for the whole of their lives. A man's neighbours are usually his agnatic and cognatic kin, who have obligations towards him and an interest in helping him. The solidarity of the agnatic group holds the Mambwe village together, even when the actual site of the village is moved because the trees are cut out. The stability of Mambwe village organization appears at once when it is compared with Bemba village organization.

The Bemba are a people with a matrilineal succession system who practise uxorilocal marriage. Both the Bemba and the woodland Mambwe cultivate on the ash-planting system in adjacent areas with very similar soils, although the Mambwe system is superior.[1] Bemba villages are extremely poor, and the Bemba suffer from a hunger period of about two months immediately before the millet is ripe. The poverty of Bemba agriculture is ascribed both to their primitive methods of cultivating and to the difficulty of finding enough men to cut sufficient wood for the gardens.[2] The practice of uxorilocal marriage, and the lack of permanent economic interests between the men in Bemba

---

[1] See p. 24 above.

[2] I visited a Bemba village which had only one elderly man to carry out tree-cutting for a whole village of some twenty huts, and the women were forced to hire the labour of men from other villages to get the gardens made. Miss E. Richardson informs me that this is common. I never heard of this happening among the woodland Mambwe, nor do they suffer a hunger period.

villages, seem to account for their unstable residence.[1] Richards states that 'the Bemba man . . . is born in one village, moves to another to marry, goes to a third to inherit a title, or to join some of his own relatives, or sets up a new village of his own. The local community not only changes its geographical position owing to the custom of shifting cultivation but absorbs new households and loses old ones at each change.'[2] Mambwe villages show much greater geographical stability, for each village is attached to its own estate, and even when it moves its site, moves within the boundaries of its estate. The headmanship is held by an agnatic group whose interest in the title and the estate holds it together, so that often a Mambwe is born in his father's natal village, among his own agnatic kin, brings his wife to live there when he marries, and looks to inherit there. Many Mambwe are born, live, and die in their father's village, particularly members of the royal clan and of those commoner clans whose head holds a chieftainship. But for various reasons members of commoner clans sometimes move between villages, for example, when a man is dissatisfied with the rule of his chief or headman and wishes to change, or when he wishes to join a kinsman who has founded a new village. When such commoners move they generally take their wives and children with them, and almost invariably they join a village where they can claim kinship with some agnatic group already resident. Thus in a Mambwe village the men are usually related to one another, whereas in a Bemba village the husbands of the women are usually unrelated to one another. The kinship links of Bemba men tie them to other villages.

The essential element in the Bemba marriage contract is service performed by the bridegroom for his father-in-law and not the transfer of goods. Mambwe men likewise work in the gardens of their parents-in-law, but, as we have seen, the essential item in their marriage contract is an exchange of cattle and money, and the wife comes to live in her husband's village. When a Mambwe marries, he pays out a considerable sum, and this sum

---

[1] Cf. the similar situation among the Machinga Yao, of whom Mitchell says: 'Marriage is unstable so that a man has no interest in long range agricultural plans in his wife's village. If he invests capital it is in movable goods, if he builds a substantial house it is in his matrilineage village.' 'Preliminary Notes on Land Tenure and Agriculture Among the Machinga Yao', pp. 6–7.

[2] *Bemba Marriage and Present Economic Conditions*, p. 35.

is provided either by himself or more usually by his agnatic kin. Thus the wives of absent wage-earners represent an investment by the husbands' kin-groups in their marriages, and their interest is to keep the marriage strong. When a husband dies, his widow is inherited by his brother, who usually lives in the husband's village. The Mambwe system of inheritance provides for brother to succeed brother until all have succeeded, when the inheritance drops to the next generation and passes along the line of brothers' sons before dropping to the grandson generation. This form of levirate gives the group of agnatic kinsmen an interest in the marriage quite different from the matrilineal Bemba. The marriage payment in effect transfers the woman's procreative capacity to her husband's lineage, and her children belong to that lineage. When a widow refuses to be inherited by her husband's brother, he still has rights over her. If she marries another man, he can sue successfully for damages for adultery. Thus, when a husband dies, the widow can continue to work the fields that her husband had given her, for she will be inherited, with the fields, by one of her husband's agnatic group. Legal marriage and the domestic group are thus relatively stable among the Mambwe.

TABLE XII

Divorce rates based on the marital histories of the partners
in 127 extant marriages, and other widowed and divorced
persons, in six pagan Mambwe villages

Category	Rate
	%
(1) The number of marriages ended in divorce expressed as a percentage of all marriages	19·8 (48/245)
(2) The number of marriages ended in divorce expressed as a percentage of all completed marriages . . .	40·8 (48/118)
(3) The number of marriages ended in divorce expressed as a percentage of all marriages except those ended by death	27·9 (48/172)

The Mambwe claim that formerly they had 'very little' divorce, but that today it has become more frequent. Most of the elopement charges that I recorded in the courts were with the wives of men absent on wage-labour. A few men go away for three or four years and neglect to send money or goods to their wives.

The Mambwe regard such neglect as virtual desertion and sympathize with a neglected wife who goes off with another man, although this sympathy does not prevent the husband's kin from claiming damages. But usually the behaviour of grass widows is closely supervised by the husband's kin, and most men do take their wives with them to the Copperbelt.[1] A man who refuses to take his wife on a labour trip is considered to be a poor husband, particularly by the women. The Mambwe say that divorce has become common only since men started to go out to work. I have shown some divorce rates based on the marital histories of the partners in 127 extant marriages, and other widowed and divorced persons, in six pagan villages in 1953 in Table XII.[2]

The divorce rate among the Bemba is higher.[3] This high divorce rate must affect the circulation of men round different villages in which they can claim the right to reside.

Mambwe men are therefore tied to one village in a way that Bemba men are not. Even when a woman is divorced her children belong to the agnatic kin of her husband, and when they are grown live in his village. They have some rights in their mother's family, for marriage links two groups of agnatic kin together, and a woman's son has some rights and duties towards his mother's brother. But their main rights of inheritance lie in their father's village. Only unredeemed illegitimate children rank as members of a mother's agnatic lineage, and such children are almost invariably redeemed, for the Mambwe value children. Economic and kinship interests thus tend to draw children almost entirely to the village of their father and his agnatic lineage.

The links between Mambwe wage-earners and their home villages are much stronger than among the Bemba, and the

---

[1] See Table V.

[2] I collected my data on divorce by the methods developed by the Rhodes-Livingstone Institute, particularly by the former Director, Professor J. C. Mitchell, and Professor J. A. Barnes, and published by them in *The Lamba Village: Report of a Social Survey*. Table XII is formed on a similar table in Barnes, *Marriage In a Changing Society*, p. 53. This book deals with marriage among the Ngoni of Fort Jameson.

[3] The figures given by Richards in *Bemba Marriage and Present Economic Conditions*, p. 120, are not strictly comparable with the Mambwe figures, for they were collected twenty years ago under different circumstances. The Bemba divorce rate has risen since then, according to a communication from Dr. A. L. Epstein, but his records have not yet been published.

specialized men's work that must be done in the ash-planting system is carried out by the agnatic kin of the wage-earner. The attachment of Mambwe villages to specific areas, the agnatic lineages that form the basis of village organization, the possession and exchange of property, and the stability of Mambwe marriage, all give village organization a permanence that survives even the constant change of site enforced by ash-planting cultivation, and the absence of 50 per cent of the active men.

In 1953 Kasunga village had a male population of forty-two, of whom twenty-five were over fifteen years of age, and therefore old enough to work for wages. Eleven of them were actually out at work.

Only one of the absent workers, Island Simpemba (D34), was over forty years old, and he worked locally as a foreman of a road-building gang for the Public Works Department in Abercorn. Island had a house provided for him there, and he visited the village about once a month. He spent his 'leave' there. He intended to retire permanently to the village when he had saved enough money to build a brick house and furnish it in what he considered to be a suitable style. He had already collected a certain amount of chairs, tables, etc., in Abercorn. The achievement of this ambition was delayed, however, when he made another marriage; he now had to consider whether or not to build two brick houses, one for each wife. This problem delayed his decision to retire, and he continued to work.

Island's case is of particular interest for it shows how secure local employment tends to prolong the period of wage-earning. Generally an older man has difficulty in finding a job when there are so many younger men in the market, and most Mambwe give up wage-labour when they reach the age of forty. The exceptions are those men with a special skill or those who, like Island, have managed to be promoted to a supervisory position. Headman Kasunga, who was fifty-three, was one of these exceptions. He was trained as a carpenter in the London Missionary Society workshops at Kawimbe, and first went abroad to work in 1919, when he went to Bulawayo for a year. In 1925 he went to the Belgian Congo for a year. In 1929 he visited Tanganyika for two years, and returned to take up the headmanship when his father died in 1931. In 1937 he found a job with the Administration in Abercorn, and kept it for thirteen years. In all these places he worked as a carpenter. Kasunga was exceptional in a further respect: that though a headman, he went off to work. His labour history also illustrates the principle that wage-labour can be an escape from domestic difficulties as well as the cause of them. He had acquired so many wives that he was hard put to it to prepare gardens for them all, or to buy the clothing and household necessities that his wives demanded. He had acquired a good deal of money through his labour, but much had drained away through marriage payments and damages for adultery. He had been involved in three adultery cases since 1950, and now had a concubine to support in addition to his wives. With these heavy domestic commitments, and a desire to build a brick house, Kasunga was somewhat pressed for money. After the trouble over Chief Kela's death he again went to Abercorn to work and found a job at his trade. Each wife paid him a weekly visit in turn, taking a supply of food with her, so that Kasunga could save as much money as possible. In his case the old ambition of the Mambwe, to acquire many wives and followers, came into conflict with the modern ambition to have a high standard of living. Kasunga was unable to reconcile the material demands of his wives with his meagre assets, and was forced out to work. His absence from the village also helped him to escape some of the embarrassment which was created by Chief Kela's death.

I have given the ages and marital status of the other wage-earners from the village in Table XIII. Kasunga himself is not included. The three unmarried youths between fifteen and nineteen were two sons of the headman (by different wives) and the headman's sister's son, who was born in the village. His father had been resident there, and made an intra-village marriage with his mother, the headman's sister. These three had gone off to Tanganyika together, under the leadership of Driver Simpasa (E53, Figure 2), the son of Chole. Driver had married after his first visit to Tanganyika, and was prevailed upon to make another visit to conduct the younger lads. Driver was twenty-one years old. They all left in May 1952, just before the harvest, and all took a twelve month contract. They kept together the whole time they were away, working side by side on a sisal plantation. They returned together in June 1953, each with a box containing goods for himself and his relatives. Driver and one other youth had earned 31s. a month, and the other two had earned 25s. and

TABLE XIII

Age and marital status of absent wage-earners from
Kasunga village in 1953

	Single men			Married men				
					Residence of dependants			
Age-groups	Un-wedded	Divorced	Widowed	With him	In migrant's village	In wife's father's village	Total	
							Single	Married
15–19	3						3	–
20–24	1	1		3			2	3
25–29		1			1		1	1
30–34							–	–
35–39							–	–
40–44				1			–	1
45–49							–	–
Totals:	4	2		4	1		6	5

Note: Total male population over the age of fifteen was 25

20s. a month. They had all brought back cash as well as goods: Driver had £5, the others £5 10s., £4 19s., and £4 10s. When they first arrived in Tanganyika, each bought a wooden box costing 15s. with his first pay. They had a hut to themselves, and built a shelf near the roof on which they put their boxes, which could be reached only with a ladder. Every month they bought some goods with their pay, and locked these away in their boxes. There was great excitement in the village on the night of their return. Although it was after dark, the women began preparing grain for beer. When the beer was ready a few days later, the boxes were opened. During this time there was much speculation about who would get what. Driver distributed the following among his relatives:

To his father
  A pair of trousers, a shirt, and one cloth
To his fourteen-year-old brother
  A pair of shorts and a shirt

To his mother's sister (his mother was dead)
  One cloth and one blouse
To his sister
  One cloth and one blouse
To his wife
  One dress and seven pieces of cloth
To himself (and household)
  One pair of shoes; a hat; two pairs of trousers; two shirts;
  two blankets.

Driver's total cash earnings during the twelve months was
£15 10s. He was provided with food by the company, but spent
31s. on European food, such as sugar, tea, white bread, etc. They
all clubbed together to buy these and bought in small quantities,
a few pence at a time. Driver expended £8 19s. in buying the
above clothes, and brought home £5. The need for European
clothing is illustrated by the contents of Driver's box, and he
was set up with a wardrobe that would enable him to go off to
the Copperbelt the following year. The others distributed their
goods to their relatives in much the same way.

At the time this group went off to work, Peter Sinyangwe
(E48), the son of Kari, also went off, but to the Copperbelt.
Peter was twenty-three and had already made one trip to Tanganyika, to work on the sisal plantations, and he had married on
his return. His father Kari, the trouble-maker, had not been able
to help him with his marriage payment, and his other senior
relative in the village, Elliam Sinyangwe, provided two head of
cattle towards it. Peter called Elliam 'father' (*tata*). Peter was un-
fortunate in his Copperbelt experiences. After his marriage, he
had enough money to get down to the Copperbelt, where he
quickly found a job and sent for his wife. He was discharged from
this job soon after she arrived, and he found difficulty in finding
another job, so his wife returned to the village. Peter then fell ill,
and for a time was kept by some relatives already working in
Mufulira. These people got tired of keeping him, but he could
not come home for two reasons. In the first place he was ashamed
to confess his failure, and to return defeated. In the second place,
he had no money for his fare and owed obligations for his marriage cattle to Elliam. He wrote to his father asking for the fare
to be sent to him, but Kari could not send him any. He next wrote

to Elliam, asking for money and promising to repay, but at first
Elliam would not provide it, feeling that he had expended enough
on Kari's family. At this time Kari and Elliam were at loggerheads
over another matter. Peter wrote again to Elliam, begging him to
help him. Elliam relented when he heard of Peter's debts and
miserable condition, and sent the bus fare. Peter returned, but
within a fortnight of his arrival in the village he went off to
Abercorn, and managed to find work on a road gang.

Peter's experience illustrates the solidarity of the kin group.
His initial trip to Tanganyika had set him up with some money
and good clothes for the more important trip to the Copperbelt.
He had brought back gifts from there for his father and brothers,
and for Elliam. Elliam had contributed two cattle towards
Peter's marriage payment. All had benefited from Peter's trip to
Tanganyika, and expected further and more substantial benefits
from his Copperbelt trip. His failure upset their expectations, and
Peter was now in considerable debt, not only to Elliam for the
cattle, but also to his relatives who kept him on the Copperbelt
while he was sick. The kinship group had acted as a source of
mutual credit; and the importance of fulfilling obligations within
it is seen in the haste with which Peter went off to find himself a
job on his return from this abortive trip.

The two divorced men, Andrew (E64) and Ronald (E66), are
both sons of Samson Sinzumwa (D41). One other brother,
Stanley (E65), is married, and works on the Copperbelt. His wife
lives in the village, but joined him after the harvest. The two
divorced men do not have huts in the village, as they were already
away at work when their father came to live in Kasunga. The
two divorced men will return to Kasunga, which is now their
home. One has already been there on holiday. Another brother,
Elam (E62), also lives in the village, and has two wives. Elam,
who is thirty-one, has spent over ten years on wage-labour,
mainly in Tanganyika, where on his third trip he found a good
job as a hotel waiter. He got this job in 1941 and returned for
one year, when he got married. He took his wife back with him,
and worked as a waiter from 1943 to 1948, when he returned to
help his father move to Kasunga village. He went back in 1949
to his old job, leaving his wife in Kasunga village, and returned
in 1952. He then became involved with a girl from Aron village,
whose husband had been absent wage-earning for two years. She

had no children. This girl left Aron village (where her parents were also living; they were all Jehovah's Witnesses) and came to Kasunga, where Elam provided a hut for her. This case caused a considerable scandal, as the Witnesses do not approve of divorce. Her husband's brothers brought Elam to court to claim damages for his adultery with her. The case was brief, as the girl and Elam both admitted the adultery. Elam was charged eight pounds damages and five and sixpence court fee. This case came up when Elam was involved in another matter concerning attempted rape; he was fined five pounds in this other case. He had only three pounds by him in cash, as he had helped his two younger brothers with their marriage payments. Elam wrote to two of his brothers on the Copperbelt, Andrew and Stanley, asking for money. They both sent money, but to their father Samson, to give to Elam. Stanley wrote that he was sending the money to settle the case 'so that shame would not overtake Elam'. Samson handed over the money to Elam, but kept one pound for himself. He said he wanted to buy a new pair of trousers, as he was looking for another wife, and wished to be decently dressed. This deduction left Elam short, and he complained bitterly to his father and to others. The headman, Kasunga, discussed the matter with the other men. Kasunga asked Samson what he meant by taking one pound from the five pounds sent by Stanley. Sampson replied that the money was sent to him. The others (who knew all about the matter, and had read the letters) pointed out that although this was true, Stanley had sent the money for Elam's case; he specifically said so. Samson said that he had done enough for Elam; he had paid the marriage payment for his first wife; Elam had no right to take another man's wife and must suffer the consequences. But in spite of this stand, he was persuaded to give Elam the pound, and the fines were paid.

Here again we see the interaction of the members of the agnatic group in the wage-labour and home situations. Elam had been helped by his father; he had helped his own younger brothers; they now assisted him in his need. Elam has not yet married the girl, who was living in adulterous union with him, and is now his concubine. She is pregnant and Elam wants to marry her, but her parents demand at least three or four pounds. Elam cannot depend on his brothers helping him once again in this matter, and says he will go to Tanganyika to earn the money.

K

Samson's purpose in withholding part of the money needed by Elam was not merely or even mainly to embarrass Elam and express his own moral condemnation of Elam's behaviour over the adultery. When Elam's younger brother Andrew divorced his wife for her adultery, the case was brought by Elam and his father, for Andrew was absent earning wages. Damages were awarded against the adulterer, but he had not paid them. Elam had been too busy with his own affairs to support his father in getting the money (eight pounds) from the adulterer. Samson had approached this man several times without success, and was continually put off with promises. Samson brought Elam's backsliding in his brother's interests to public notice when he withheld part of the money that Elam needed. Andrew's case was brought up at the meeting, and Elam agreed that some action must be taken. He said that either the adulterer must pay at once or he must be brought before the court again. When Elam proposed to go and see this man and do what he could to get Andrew's eight pounds, Samson handed over the pound that Elam needed. If these damages are secured, Elam will be able to marry his concubine and Samson will be in a better financial position to find another wife for himself.

The members of the agnatic group do not help one another only with money. They assist one another in many ways. Adam Sikaombwe (E58), the headman's sister's son, was the eldest of three brothers. Adam was forty-one and had made four successful wage trips. He too, like his mother's brother Kasunga, had been trained by the mission as a carpenter. He had worked at his trade on three trips to Tanganyika, and one to Nkana, where he was employed in the mine. Adam had prospered and his house was the only brick building in Kasunga village. He had a trader's licence, but now traded in a desultory way. His first wife had died, and his present wives were sisters, the daughters of Kari Sinyangwe. His next brother, Petero (E59), was also trained as a carpenter, and after one trip to Tanganyika and marriage on his return, went to Lusaka in 1949, where he found work at his trade with a building firm. He was joined there by the youngest brother, Alfred (E60), who was educated at the Lunzuwa school. Adam paid for his education. Alfred was a smart and intelligent lad, who found work as a clerk. He lived with Petero and his wife, and while there, Petero's wife became involved with another man. Petero fell sick, and while he was in bed his wife's lover came to visit him. Shortly after this visit Petero died. The Mambwe believe that a sick husband will die if his wife's lover visits him. Alfred brought home his brother's widow, together with all his property, and reported to Adam all that had happened. The family took from the widow all the stuff she had brought back: her husband's tools, clothes, sewing machine, cups, plates, etc. The widow was sent back to her own village in Tanganyika. She was not inherited in the usual way.

Here we see an elder brother assisting his younger brothers. Adam paid for Alfred's education. Petero kept Alfred in his house in Lusaka. The younger brother, although he could not prevent his older brother's death in the strange and dangerous environment of the town, brought the errant wife back to the village where the supernatural punishment of the wife would be certain. Like all successful men, Adam is supposed to 'know something' (i.e. to possess magical knowledge). He is said to know how to tame crows through magic, so that they take maize from other people's gardens and grain-bins and bring it to his own. Further, the Mambwe believe that a man's ancestors will work for him to harm or kill his enemies only when the man has suffered some real injury. They will not do this, or rather, are unwilling to harm anyone, if there is no real injury. In these circumstances only a very powerful sorceror (*mulozi*) could get them to 'work' for him. By bringing his dead brother's widow home, Alfred ensured that the ancestors would be given an opportunity to avenge Petero's death.

Kasunga is a royal village of medium size, and is typical. Other villages, because they are closer to centres of European settlement, such as missions or the European township of Abercorn, have responded differently to the wage-labour situation. Some have benefited, others have not. Two sets of influences are at work: first, the operation of the kinship and political system, and second, the intensity of European contact. The interaction of these two influences produces a variety of effects on Mambwe village life. As examples of these differential effects, I propose to examine two villages near Abercorn, that of a traditional chief, Kowa, and that of a commoner headman, Luembe.

Kowa's village is seven miles from Abercorn, and about five miles from the London Missionary Society establishment at

Kawimbe, which has been operating since 1890. Kowa is the head (*cikolwe*) of the Siuluta clan, which has many members among the Lungu people, as well as the Mambwe. Kowa's chieftaincy is on the border between Mambwe and Lungu territory, and Kowa is linked to the ruling clan of each of these peoples. Before the Europeans came, Kowa ruled over a village state, but recognized the political sovereignty of the royal Mambwe Sichula clan. He sent the skins of all lions killed within his chieftaincy to Chief Fwambo, the nearest royal chief. The first Chief Kowa is said to have married a daughter of Chief Nsokolo, and thereby became a consort to a royal princess. This marriage has been repeated by each generation of succeeding Kowas. The present Chief Kowa, an old man, inherited his elder brother's wife, who was a daughter of the present Chief Nsokolo's father. Politically Chief Kowa continues to recognize Chief Nsokolo as his superior.

In the early days the British recognized Kowa as a petty chief, and allowed him to have a court and to try cases. When the present system of administration was introduced in 1930, Kowa was relegated to the status of a headman, and given a small pension for his previous good behaviour and loyalty. Like other village states, Kowa's stockaded village broke up into a number of smaller villages, and by 1918 he had seven villages under his control, according to the Administration's records. Six of these had headmen of the Siuluta clan, and the other a headman of the Sichiliango clan. Today there are fourteen villages within the bounds of his traditional chieftaincy, which is now incorporated into the administrative chieftaincy of Chief Mwamba. Three of these villages are of Lungu origin, and were moved into Kowa's area in 1935 after their land had been alienated to a European farmer. Luembe village is one of these. Kowa is therefore a man of some importance among the Mambwe, although no longer recognized as a chief by the Administration.

The kinship structure of Kowa's village is shown in the skeleton genealogy in Figure 3. There are two main groups: the agnatic members of Kowa's own Siuluta lineage, and a group of cognates of the Simpungwe clan. The senior living member of the Simpungwe, Nsyazye (C7), blind and deaf with age, is Kowa's father's sister's son, but addresses Kowa as mother's brother. He stands in a perpetual relationship of sister's son—mother's brother to the reigning chief. This relationship has been renewed in generation

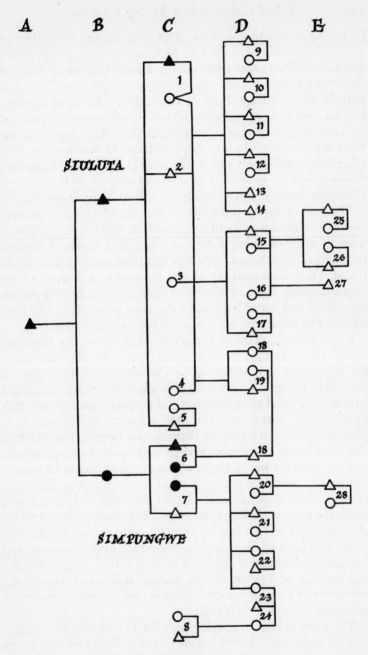

FIG. 3.—GENEALOGY OF KOWA VILLAGE.

D, for Nsyazye's brother's son (D18) has married a daughter of Kowa, thus reaffirming the link between the two groups in this generation. Two other adult men (C8 and D24) are of different clans, and both are of Lungu origin, although one (D24) was born in Kowa village. Both of these address Kowa as mother's brother, but their genealogies did not show any such actual link up to their grandfather's generation. They were linked to the Simpungwe lineage by marriage, and also to one another. One other man and his wife and family lived in the village. I have not shown him in the genealogy as he was a foreigner, an Inamwanga, whom the mission sent to live in the village as an evangelist.

The Siuluta lineage had fourteen men out of a total of twenty-two over eighteen years of age, and four others were cognates. Two of the remaining four men claimed a mother's brother relationship with Kowa, although this relationship could not be traced. One other man (D22) was married to a woman of the cognatic group and had been born in the village, but his parents were dead and his siblings had long since gone off to live elsewhere. The remaining male was the Inamwanga evangelist.

Kowa village had the best material conditions of any Mambwe village I saw. In 1953 the men were completing the removal of the village to a new site about two hundred yards from the old site. All of the new houses were of brick, with brick kitchens and latrines. They had glass windows and properly made doors, with metal hinges, locks, etc. The new village was laid out on a generous scale, with gardens between the houses. The old huts that were being abandoned were of traditional wattle-and-daub, and only half the size of the new houses. The villagers had furniture and household equipment of all kinds to put in their new houses. They were all well clothed and well fed, and had a relatively high standard of education. This happy state of affairs was the result of two factors: first, the influence of the mission, which had been in their neighbourhood for over sixty years and had provided means of acquiring education both in the speaking and reading of English and in manual skills; and second, the proximity of a labour market in the town of Abercorn where they were able to exploit their skills.

The main source of employment for the men of this village was the International Red Locust Control. Four of Kowa's sons were employed in the workshop of this organization. The first to be employed was Amos (D9), aged thirty-nine. After his first trip to work on the Lupa gold-fields in Tanganyika, Amos had been taken on by the bus garage in Abercorn, where he learned to drive and picked up a knowledge of machinery. He worked for twelve years in this garage. When the new organization was first established, Amos transferred there and became a charge hand. In turn he managed to get three of his brothers employed. One of them, Wangwe (D11), aged thirty, had picked up some knowledge of motor mechanics on his previous work trips to Tanganyika, and also found work in the workshop. Nedi (D12), aged twenty-eight, who had worked both in Tanganyika and Fort Rosebery, was first employed as a labourer in the workshop, but graduated to better-paid work. The youngest brother, Yasula (D14), aged twenty, learned to drive at the Locust Control, and eventually came to drive one of the vehicles that carry the spraying equipment. He worked for six months at a time in the Rukwa valley in Tanganyika, where the locusts breed. All of them had a good knowledge of English, and this had been of great assistance to them in getting skilled work. Their half-brother, Lamek (D19), aged thirty-five, worked as a labourer on a settler's farm about six miles from the village, off the Abercorn road. He had held this job for eight years. Their nephew Gentile (E25), aged twenty-four, worked as a carpenter with the public works department in Abercorn. All of these men had bicycles and cycled to and from work each day. Two other Siuluta, Jason (D17), aged forty-three, and Lanwell (E27), aged twenty, also worked locally but too far away to return to the village each day. They too had bicycles and returned to the village at weekends. Jason was a thatcher at the Agricultural Station at Lunzuwa, about twenty miles away, and Lanwell worked as a teacher in the Native Authority school in Chief Mwamba's village, some twelve miles away. Lanwell's mother (D15) was a member of Chief Mwamba's lineage.

For these men their village had become in effect a suburb of Abercorn.

Two of Kowa's sons were working on the Copperbelt, in Ndola. These were Sitbet (D10), aged thirty-four, who had served for six years in the Army during the war, and his brother Kwenlengula (D13), aged twenty-five. Sitbet had been at Ndola since 1946, when he was discharged from the Army. He had his wife with him at Ndola, and returned to the village for a holiday in 1951. Kwenlengula, who was single, returned to the Copperbelt with Sitbet, who found him a job. They were both expected to return to the village in 1954.

The only other man then away at work was Stonelef (D22), who was married to Nsyazye's daughter. He had gone to Tanganyika, on his second trip.

Eleven out of the twenty-two adult males in the village were therefore earning wages, and only three were so far distant that they could not regularly visit the village at least once a week. The eight who worked locally took food from their own grain-bins, and five of them were able to have most of their meals at home. The subsistence economy was playing a full part in helping them to save the maximum amount of cash possible, and to invest it in material goods. I estimate that the eight men working locally were earning a minimum of £300 a year between them. In addition, one of Kowa's younger sons cycled each day to Abercorn with twenty-five bottles of milk, which were sold for sixpence each. Cattle do not give much milk in the dry season, but it is safe to say that another £40 a year was earned from this source.

The local wage-earners worked in their fields at weekends, and also assisted in building the brick houses, although they employed brickmakers and two bricklayers. The men who were not out earning wages, together with the women, were more than enough to keep the fields in good cultivation, in which they were assisted with supervision and advice by a European agricultural expert from the nearby mission. These men also helped to build the houses. The lucky chance of having well-paid work so near at hand, plus their superior education, gave the Siulutas an opportunity to remain longer than usual in paid employment, and they did not have the expense of living far from home. All of the men at home had worked for wages at one time or another, and the village was wealthy. The kinship group acted as a unit, both in the wage-labour and village situations, and their solidarity was paying material dividends.

There were three elements in their success. First, they were united as a group, and had the prestige of a title. Second, they had been exposed to sixty years of mission influence, and this had provided the basis for the skills they exploited. Third, they had the good fortune to be conveniently placed near the expanding labour market of Abercorn. Their skills earned them higher wages and more regular employment than those of most Mambwe. They were making the best of two worlds: on the one hand of the tribal system which gave them land, and on the other of the European economy which gave them wages.

The solidarity of the kin group founded the material success of Kowa village. Luembe village did not have this solidarity, and the impact of the European economy had a quite different effect on it.

Luembe was originally a Lungu village in the chieftaincy of Chief Tafuna, the Lungu paramount chief. In 1935 some of Tafuna's land was alienated to a European farmer, and some villages ordered to move off. Three of these villages were given land in Chief Kowa's area, and Luembe was one of these. Headman Luembe at this time was a Sikazwe clansman related directly to Chief Tafuna.

The village moved en bloc, and settled about five miles from Abercorn, but cut off from Kowa's village by a range of hills, so that a detour of some miles was necessary to get from the new site to Kowa village. The Luembe headman was a messenger in the Administration office in Abercorn, and while he attended to these duties, he left the day-to-day administration of the village in the hands of Henry Sikasula, another Lungu. From the time Luembe village moved, it began to lose people, for many of the Lungu villagers filtered back into Lungu country to join other Lungu villages. When the Sikazwe headman retired from work, he decided to live in Chief Tafuna's village, and surrendered the headmanship. Thereupon Chief Mwamba, within whose administrative jurisdiction the village lay, appointed Henry Sikasula to be headman. I have presented a skeleton genealogy of this village in Figure 4.

The village is much smaller than when it first transferred. There are Lungu, Inamwanga, and Mambwe living in it, but the number of Lungu has fallen away. The people complain that the land is poor, but this is doubtful. The poverty of their agriculture is probably due to the fragmentary nature of the groups which now compose the village, their lack of a common focus of solidarity, and the high proportion of women to men, 3·7 : 1, the highest of any Mambwe village I encountered.

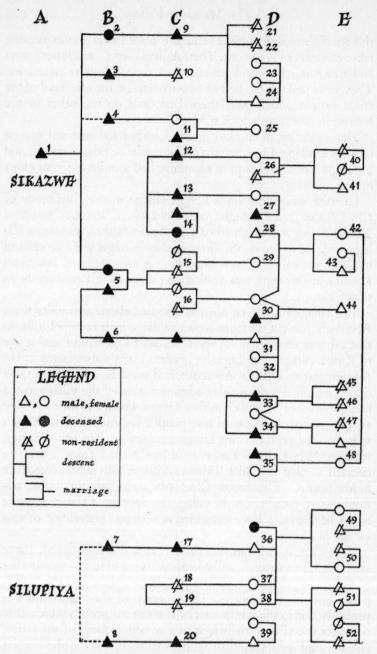

FIG. 4.—GENEALOGY OF LUEMBE VILLAGE.

Today the village population falls into two distinct groups, one attached to headman Henry Sikasula (D28), and the other to Andrew Silupiya (D36). Andrew claims a connection 'long ago' with the headman's lineage, but this was so obscure that neither could trace it, and it was in all probability fictional. Henry had a remote connection with the original headman (C10). He addressed this man as grandfather (*kuku*), and traced a connection through his wife (D29), who had a Sikazwe grandmother. His second wife (D30) is a cross-cousin of the first, and both are connected to the Mambwe royal lineage of Chief Mwamba through their grandfather (B5), who had a Sikazwe wife. This tie with the royal Sichula clan probably supported Henry's claim to be appointed when the original headman retired. Henry had prudently linked himself to the ruling clans of both Mambwe and Lungu through his marriages.

The widow (D35) who is living in her daughter's husband's village, had left Kowa village when her husband died after a serious sorcery case involving the deaths of a number of persons. Another widow (D27) came to the village after a series of deaths. She had lived in her son's village when he died, and shortly after this, her daughter too died in childbirth. This widow then came to join Henry, who was her father's sister's son. Another woman (D26), who had the same relationship to Henry, had been deserted by her husband, who had left her behind when he went off to work. When he failed to communicate with her or to return, she came to Luembe village, bringing with her two of her sons. These two then went off to work in Ndola, the elder (E40) taking his wife with him.[1] Apart from these women linked to Henry through his mother's clan, a smaller group of foreigners was attached to him through marriage. The widow (D33) was a Mambwe from Chief Fwambo's area who married an Inamwanga, and went off to live with him in his own country, where she had two sons (E45, E46). Her husband died, and she was inherited by his brother (D34), who brought her back to Mambwe country and settled in Luembe village. After a time he too died, leaving some children (E47, E48). Three of the grown sons are now working, and have stated their intention never to return to

---

[1] The younger son (E41) is reported to have died in Ndola shortly before I left the Mambwe, but in the genealogy I have shown him as living.

Mambwe country, but to settle with their Inamwanga kin.[1] The youngest son of working age, Dimond (E48), married Henry's daughter (E42) and also the daughter of the widow from Kowa village. He has built huts for his two wives and intends to remain in Luembe and make it his permanent home.

The general impression that these relationships leave is that the people of Luembe were the misfits and unwanted from other villages, with a sprinkling of foreigners. This impression was strengthened when I found in Luembe the only member of the Mambwe royal clan living under a commoner headman that I encountered. This man (D31) claimed a connection with the headman through the Sichula kinship of Henry's wives. He was stupid to the point of idiocy, perhaps through disease, and could scarcely manage to labour in the fields. The main core of Sikazwe had withdrawn, leaving only the cognatic group of three men (D21, D22, D24) who trace a link with the original headman's lineage through their grandmother (B2); a widow (C11) and her daughter (D25), who had been divorced and was now living with her mother; but no other Lungu. Two of the three men (D21, D22) went off long ago to work and have not returned; their younger brother Filemon (D24) was of the opinion that they would never return. The eldest of these brothers (D21) went to Lusaka in 1940, where he married and is now domiciled. The second brother (D22) went to Fort Jameson in 1942, and he too married a woman there and does not intend to return, at least for the time being. Filemon himself has a long wage-labour history. He was a charge-hand (*capitao*) with a government agricultural officer for ten years, and is now a bricklayer with the public works department in Abercorn, and cycles to and from work each day. All of these brothers were born in the 'old' Luembe in the Lungu area, and stand in a sister's son–mother's brother relationship with the original Sikazwe headman. Their connection with the present headman is remote, and traced through their common Sikazwe clanship with his wives.

The headman has no strong agnatic group in the village. He has one son (E43), and also his second wife's son (E44) by her first husband. This man lives in the village at present, but belongs to another clan than the headman's, and is not bound very strongly to

---

[1] Like the Mambwe, the Inamwanga have patrilineal succession.

him. The only other group of persons with kinship ties to the headman are the two widows (D26, D27) who trace their ties through his mother's clan.

The other large group in the village is that surrounding Andrew Silupiya (D36). This man is another of the type who by earning money and saving some capital have successfully set themselves up as small traders and farmers. Andrew is now fifty-seven years old, and was educated by the London Missionary Society. He first worked as a cook in Abercorn, and then the African Lakes Corporation took him on as a tailor. He did well at this, and advanced to serving in the store. Finally the Corporation put him in sole charge of a store at Mporokoso, where he remained for eleven years, till he retired in 1929. He then took out a hawker's licence and engaged in trade on his own behalf. Andrew is a Lungu, and in 1918 married a Lungu woman. He has two surviving daughters of this marriage: one (E49) is divorced and lives in the village, and the other (E50) is married to a Mambwe at present working as a clerk in Tanganyika. She usually lives in Tanganyika with her husband, but at the time I was there was on holiday in Luembe. His first wife died, and in 1928 Andrew married a woman (D38) of the Mambwe royal clan, daughter of Chief Mpenza's brother, and for a time Andrew lived in one of Mpenza's villages. Andrew is apt to be quarrelsome and violent when roused, and after a quarrel he came to live in Luembe, which had already moved to its present site. In 1932 he married another royal Mambwe woman (D37), this time a daughter of Chief Mpenza himself (C18). This marriage thoroughly established Andrew's ties with Chief Mwamba, for Mpenza belongs to the same lineage of the royal clan as Mwamba. Andrew sent his two eldest sons by this wife to the Lunzuwa school, and both are now employed as clerks. One (E51) is a clerk with the International Red Locust Control, and lives in Abercorn with his wife in a house provided by his employers. The other (E52) works as a Government clerk in Mbeya, Tanganyika, but left his wife in her father's village after his marriage in 1953. Andrew has three brick houses in Luembe, and in addition has a plough, oxen, carts, many agricultural tools, and a fine herd of cattle. He ploughs up so much land that a good deal of jealousy arises. His cattle devoured the crops of a man in a nearby village, who brought a case against him. During the course of the evidence in this case, a witness alleged that Andrew ploughed up land within six feet of the aggrieved man's fields, right on the edge of the other village's cultivating area. Andrew won the case, but the Luembe headman and the other villagers showed quite clearly that they found Andrew's material success and wealth anything but agreeable. Andrew is ambitious to become a headman. So far he had attracted only one follower (D39), who came to Luembe in 1950. This man is a Lungu, of the same clan as Andrew, and claims kinship with him.

Headman Henry's followers are old and not tied very strongly to him; and as so many other men have left Luembe for good, Andrew stands a good chance of building up a new village round his own family and his brick houses. The rest of the village shows signs of neglect and dissolution: dilapidated huts, poor thatching, and too many old women. But Andrew's part is impressive, and the new house he is building is a most solid and elaborate affair, better than some of the houses in which the Europeans live in Abercorn.

In this chapter I have described a number of villages that represent three of the four categories of Mambwe villages. Kasunga is an ordinary royal village, typical of its kind. Kowa is the seat of a traditional chief. Simukulwa and Luembe are both commoner villages, Simukulwa being typical of the rising commoner. Luembe has a unique history in that it originated in another tribe. All of them except Luembe have a number of points in common. Each village is a discrete group of people who live and work together. The members are in constant contact with one another, and co-operate in a number of economic and social activities. The core of each village is a group of agnatic kin of whom the headman is the senior member, and associated with this central core are a number of other agnatic groups, linked to the core by affinal and matrilateral ties. Conflicts occur within each agnatic group and also between the different groups. But in spite of internal divisions, the villagers are united as a group against other villagers.

Each village has many active male members who are away earning wages. The traditional obligations of brothers and half-brothers towards one another operate within the labour markets, and give them an opportunity to exploit these markets to the utmost of their present capacities. Apart from its proximity to a local wages market, this is the foundation of the remarkable success of Kowa village. The royal village, Kasunga, has no local market near enough to exploit in the same way, and its gain in wealth is less spectacular. The absent workers have a fixed allegiance to their home village. They hope to return there with the money and goods they have acquired abroad, and to settle there for the rest of their lives. When a labourer goes off to work he knows to which village he will return, and that he will be welcome. The members of the agnatic groups share their economic interests, whether at home or abroad, and support one another. Links between village and labour market are strong.

The one exception is Luembe, the least successful village. Luembe has no firm agnatic core, and consists of a number of small groups loosely connected, and shows every sign of growing even smaller. There are too many old women and too few active men to carry on successful cultivation. But the principles of Mambwe village organization are already asserting themselves within it, and a new leadership is emerging. The new leader, the successful shopkeeper Andrew, is typical of the rising commoners, like Simukulwa, who know how to profit from the new economy; and Andrew's sons, on their return from wage-labour, will form a strong central group that may be able to wrest the headmanship from the present headman.

Much of the increased cash income of the Mambwe has been invested in marriage payments, cattle, and durable European goods. The material conditions of village life have improved since they began to earn money. The brick houses found in many villages, and the number of these now in course of erection, are a symbol of this material progress.

The present system of wage-labour is profitable to the Mambwe only as long as they have sufficient land to cultivate, for subsistence production helps to raise their overall incomes. Mambwe village life is based on the cultivation of the land, and rights to the use of land spring from the chief. The unity of the village as a corporate group is expressed in the position of the headman, and his personality affects the general condition of the village. The headman superintends communal labour and acts as village priest. His ancestors govern the fertility of the village estate, and the headman must act in such a way that his ancestors will be pleased with him. He is involved in disputes between villagers, but must try to settle these disputes in a just way. But the headman's authority too finally depends on the chief. Each village is a political as well as a productive and residential unit. The headman acts as an agent of the Administration. He must see that the people follow the regulations for agriculture and animal husbandry laid down by the Native Authority. He must ensure that paths are kept clear and fit for use, and compel people to dig latrines and use them. The headman is held responsible for the condition of his village when, from time to time, the chief comes to inspect all the villages in his area. The headman is the point of contact between the internal kinship organization of the village and the political system as a whole. The villagers are not only the headman's kin: they are also his subjects. The headman's position is one of inherent strain, for, as Gluckman points out: 'the sanctions on him are dual: the diffuse moral sanctions of kinship, and the organized and legal sanctions supported by political authority.'[1] But in spite of these difficulties, the Mambwe headman's position is one of great prestige, and an ambitious man tries to attract a following so that he can express his importance by achieving a headmanship.[2]

The increased participation of the Mambwe in a cash-economy has been accompanied by an increase in population and in the number of villages. Many commoners have succeeded in winning cash and followers, and have founded their own villages. The appointment of a new headman is a political appointment, and recognizes the importance of the headman's followers within the political system. Headmen have agnatic, cognatic, or affinal ties with their chief. The external relations of all types of village are political relations, and the kinship connections between the chief and headmen of different kinds are the main political bonds between the Mambwe.

---

[1] Gluckman, Barnes, and Mitchell, 'The Village Headman in British Central Africa', p. 91.

[2] Cf. the different types of reaction to a similar situation among the Soga in Uganda, as described by Fallers, *Bantu Bureaucracy*, Chapter VII.

CHAPTER FIVE

MAMBWE INTERNAL POLITICS

CLANS AND LINEAGES

THE political system of the Mambwe can be understood only in relation to the residential arrangement of Mambwe groups, and the social and kinship ties that exist between them. Villages are local groups to which a political value is attached, and villages are grouped within chieftaincies. In this chapter I discuss the Mambwe clan and lineage system, while looking backward to my description of Mambwe villages and forward to an account of the political structure.

All Mambwe belong to widely-dispersed patrilineal clans: the lineages of the royal clan form the framework of the political system and the cohesion of Mambwe society appears to depend on the dominance of the royal clan.

The people say that there were clans in the country before there were chiefs. The members of the royal Sichula clan claim that it brought chieftainship to the country; before, chiefs were not known. In a conversation with the royal Chief Mpande and the commoner Chief Chindo, Mpande corrected Chindo when he said that 'long ago' Chindo was a chief. Changala, the founding ancestor of the royal clan, is said to have married a daughter of the Chindo he found living in the country when he arrived, and from this union sprang the present ruling line of Mambwe chiefs.[1]

Each clan has a distinctive name (*mwiko*). I counted fifty-five of these,[2] of which the Mambwe say that thirty-nine are their own and the others they share with their neighbours, the Lungu, Bemba, and Inamwanga. The clan names sometimes represent natural objects in the environment,[3] or manufactured objects,[4]

---

[1] See p. 13 above.

[2] There may be a few more that I did not record.

[3] Simpemba clan, from *mpemba*, white clay; Sinkala clan, from *inkala*, a crab; Sichalwe clan, from *chalwe*, a zebra, etc.

[4] Singyela clan, from *luela* (pl. *ngyela*), any iron object fashioned by a blacksmith; Siluamba clan, from *luamba*, a fence, etc.

but most often are abstract names, with few equivalents in English.[1] In rare cases a clan claims a special relationship with the object whose name it bears, such as the Caterpillar Clan (Simutowe, from the root *vito*, an edible caterpillar), whose members are said not to eat caterpillars. In fact they do, and members of this clan laughed when I brought the alleged taboo to their notice while they were eating caterpillars.

A number of clans also have a praise name (*inumbwa*), or name of respect, used on formal occasions or as a mark of politeness. The origin of these names is obscure. The Simusokwe clan are addressed as *Kazia* (a little pond or well), the Sichilima as *Asunga* (from *ukusunga*, to take care of, look after), and the Simwinga clan as *Ntenda* (no translation). Some clans have legends of the origin of their clan names, but fellow-clansmen often gave contradictory stories, and many clans could not give any. All those persons bearing a common clan name claim to be related; they are dispersed throughout the whole Mambwe area and clansmen from widely separated districts can seldom state their relationships exactly. Clansmen also claim kinship with persons of the same clan name belonging to neighbouring tribes. The clans never meet together as a whole, nor do they have any corporate activities. The Mambwe patrilineal clan may be defined as the largest number of agnates who claim to be descended from a common ancestor and between whom marriage is forbidden and sexual relations considered incestuous.[2]

A few clans are linked together in joking and burial relationships, whereby the members are permitted without offence to joke with, tease, curse, and vilify each other when they meet. They are also obliged to bury each other, and marriage is encouraged between members of clans bearing this relationship to one another. The burying clan attend the funeral of a joking clansman, dig the grave, and wash and inter the body. Each lineage of the royal clan has several joking partnerships with other clans, and these partners also slaughter the cow in whose skin the dead body of a royal headman or chief must be wrapped. They also assist at the installation of an heir. The Simwinga, Sichilima,

---

[1] Simutame clan, from *ukutama*, to throw a stone; Simunyola clan, from *ukunyola*, to sharpen; Simuchile clan, from *ukumuchila*, to step over; Simyunza, Simwala, Silavwe, and others, I cannot translate.

[2] Cf. Evans-Pritchard, *The Nuer*, p. 192.

and Simpemba clans are always included in the number of joking partners by each lineage of the royal clan.[1]

Every clan comprises a number of lineages. The Mambwe do not have a distinctive, isolated word for a lineage, but use the common word for a hut or house (*inanda*). The royal clan has five major lineages, which have names, and which correspond with the major territorial and political divisions of the tribe. All of these five great lineages recognize the lineage of Chief Nsokolo as the senior, and he is both head of their clan and of the political system. These five royal lineages may marry into one another, but marriage between members of the same royal lineage is forbidden. None of the other clans have named lineages, nor is marriage permitted between their constituent lineages. The royal lineages therefore have some of the characteristics of clans: they have distinguishing names and are allowed to marry into one another. The lineage is not a corporate or localized community, except that the lineages of the royal clan are associated with definite titles and their attached estates.

A commoner usually cannot trace his genealogy further than his grandparents' generation save when he is connected with the royal clan: then the relationship to a royal lineage is precisely stated. These shallow commoner lineages are linked together through the senior members of each lineage, and the senior member of the senior lineage is recognized and addressed as the *Mwene*[2] ('owner' or 'chief') of the clan. The group represented by the *Mwene* of the clan is not a corporate or localized community, although clansmen will point to a certain district as the 'home' of their clan. When this happened, I invariably found that the *Mwene* of the clan resided there.

The *Mwene* of a clan is the senior living *cikolwe*, a word the Mambwe use to describe the living head not only of a clan, but also of a lineage, and of a family. They use the same word to describe the deceased incumbents of these positions, as well as the founding ancestors. Thus the founding ancestor of a clan is the *cikolwe* of all its members; the founding ancestor of a particular lineage is the *cikolwe* of the lineage members only. The word is therefore used in a relative way, and the point of reference depends on the particular person who is selected as the point of

---

[1] See p. 13 above.   [2] See p. 94 above.

departure in tracing the descent of a group. The same word and concept is found among some neighbouring peoples, and Cunnison gives the following description of its use among the Lunda:[1]

Cikolwe describes the man at the head of a matrilineal descent group of any size. He may be alive or dead. He may be the founding ancestor of the clan, or the present head of a house. The position of *cikolwe* is hereditary and the man who takes the place of a recognized *cikolwe* becomes one himself. Every section of a clan of whatever size has a *cikolwe* whose name is associated with the founding and the continuance of the group as such.

With the difference that the Mambwe *cikolwe* is head of a patrilineal group, the position is the same among the Mambwe as among the Lunda.[2] The word *cikolwe* is usually translated as 'ancestor' or 'forefather', but I propose henceforth to distinguish the living incumbent as the 'doyen' of his group.

The doyen 'looks after' his people.[3] He gives advice and attempts to settle such matters as quarrels between fellow-clansmen, marriage negotiations and divorces, disputes about inheritance, etc. An actual instance will make this clear.

Kari Sinyangwe (D19) of Kasunga village (Figure 2, p. 86) had a dispute concerning marriage payments with his son-in-law Adam Sikaombwe (E58), and called in his doyen, Robert Sinyangwe, who was the headman of a village about sixteen miles away. Both Kari and Elliam Sinyangwe (D25) recognized Robert as their doyen. Robert had presided over the inheritance discussion when the father of Daisi (E49) and her sister Elo (E50) died; he supported Kari's claim, and as a result Kari had inherited the widow and her daughters and some cattle. Adam Sikaombwe, at that time a widower, subsequently married Daisi, and for marriage payment gave Kari one cow and twenty shillings in cash. This payment was small because Daisi had been married once before; her husband had divorced her because she was barren. The cow died soon after the marriage and Kari returned the meat and the skin, so that Adam still owed him one cow.[4] All this

---

[1] *Kinship and Local Organization on the Luapula*, p. 13.

[2] The Bemba also use the word. See the *Bemba-English Dictionary*.

[3] *Cikolwe akalolola wakwe vyonsi*—lit. 'the *cikolwe* directs everything'.

[4] Beasts handed over for marriage payments must survive for at least one year after exchange. If they die earlier they must be replaced.

happened before Kari came to live in Kasunga village. Daisi did
not produce any children for Adam. Her sister Elo quarrelled
with her husband and brought her two children to live beside her
mother in Kasunga. She settled down in a hut near Adam's brick
house, and was well treated by Adam, who was well-to-do. He
had a gun and often went hunting, and saw that Elo had a share
of the meat. Finally Adam 'took' Elo, whereupon her husband
divorced her; this cost Adam seven pounds in damages. Elo now
lived as Adam's concubine, for Adam did not regularize their
union by making a payment to Kari. After the birth of a child,
Elo became dissatisfied, complained that Adam did not give her
any clothes, and favoured her sister Daisi, although she was
barren. She did not 'live well'. She wanted to be married to Adam,
and did not relish a status inferior to her sister's.[1] She threatened
to leave Adam, who at once offered Kari thirty shillings as a
marriage payment. If Kari had accepted this, Adam could have
claimed damages from any man who might take Elo. Kari refused
to accept the money, saying that it was not enough. He told his
doyen that if Elo had been happy he might have taken it as part
payment and allowed Adam time to give him some more. But
now he feared that Adam would not give any more, even if he
promised, for he still owed a cow for Daisi.

As soon as Robert Sinyangwe arrived in the village a meeting
took place between representatives of the interested parties. Headman Kasunga represented Adam, who was his sister's son, and
Elliam Sinyangwe represented Adam's wives. Chole Simpasa
(D27) attended the discussions as a witness, for if the case was not
settled at this meeting, and came before the chief, a neutral person
was essential to give an unprejudiced account of the proceedings.
This meeting succeeded in settling the matter amicably: Kasunga
guaranteed that Adam would pay over the cow he owed, and the
doyen said that if he did, he would persuade Kari to accept the
thirty shillings at once, and Adam could pay another thirty
shillings later. The case was not taken before the chief, and Adam
married Elo.

This instance illustrates how the doyen of the lineage is consulted and how he works. In the event of a death, the doyen must

---

[1] Daisi continued to live in the brick house and Elo in a wattle-and-daub
hut.

attend the inheritance discussions and help to decide who is to be the heir. He is the first to be consulted in all disputes, especially when property is involved, and he has a profound knowledge of the affairs of his group.

The doyen represents the ancestors of the lineage at such meetings, for the doyen approaches the ancestors on behalf of the group, and represents the ancestors to the people. When a lineage doyen dies, the senior doyen of the clan attends the funeral and performs certain ritual actions. This sometimes obliges him to travel long distances. Mwene Misansa, the head of the Simusokwe clan, lives in Tanganyika and had to travel over a hundred miles to the south to preside over the death of a clansman who lived in Chief Mpande's country. The funeral was delayed until he arrived. In the old days, if one clansman killed another, he was tried by the chief, but his doyen was consulted about his punishment. The doyen can excommunicate a clan member who has offended, and drive him away. Such a man must leave his kin, go to live elsewhere, and forfeit all rights in inheritance. The doyen also has the power to bring death and disaster on a clansman by cursing him.[1]

Every doyen has a following, by virtue of his position at the head of a patrilineal descent group, but he exercises only a moral authority over his followers: his position is primarily one of family duty and responsibility. Political authority rests only with those men who hold titles and their associated estates. Each village has a core comprising an agnatic group whose doyen is the headman; the doyen of any other agnatic group within the village is administratively and politically subject to the headman. In turn, the headman is subject to the chief whose title is identified with the greater estate within which the headman holds his village estate. The sanctions for the chief's authority lie in his relation to the spirits of his ancestors, who protect the people, guard the land, and control the fertility of both people and soil. Each lineage of the royal clan is identified with a particular territory and its doyen is also the political chief. A commoner doyen who wishes to use his following as the basis of a claim to headmanship must seek permission from the royal lineage title-holder within whose estate he wishes to build his village. As we have seen,

---

[1] I did not observe either of these sanctions being used.

many commoner clans now hold headmanships, but all of them are attached by affinal or matrilateral ties to a royal title-holder. Only three chiefly titles are held by commoners (each of whom is the senior doyen of his clan) and these all recognize the ritual supremacy and political sovereignty of the senior royal chief, Nsokolo. Unlike the commoner clans, succession to the position of doyen in the royal clan invariably carries with it political and administrative, as well as moral, authority. The royal clan dominates the Mambwe political system; commoner clans may be tied to the royal clan by affinal and matrilateral ties, but they are all subject to a royal title-holder, either a headman or a chief. Members of the royal clan never live in villages under a commoner headman, except in one of the few villages consisting entirely of Jehovah's Witnesses.

Specific royal titles and their estates are therefore associated with specific lineages of the royal clan, and the kinship relationships between these lineage heads also express their political relationships. The heads of each royal lineage are ranged in a hierarchy of authority and subordination which corresponds with their genealogical relationships. Thus, Chief Nsokolo is the head of the royal clan and the senior chief; he addresses Chief Mpande as 'son', and Mpande in turn addresses his junior, Chief Chivuta, as 'son'; while Nsokolo addresses Chivuta as 'grandson'. These three titles stand in a *perpetual relationship*[1] of father, son, and grandson, and these kinship terms express their political relationships. The system of fixed titles and their perpetual relationships represents also the spatial arrangement of Mambwe estates attached to titles. The Luwandi lineage of the royal clan shows this (Figure 5). The estates of Chiefs KELA,[2] FWAMBO, MWAMBA, and the headman KASUNGA, are all adjacent to each other: their boundaries touch. I have given these four titles as an example; the other chieftaincies and their dependent headmen show a

---

[1] Cunnison uses this term to describe a similar system among the Lunda of Northern Rhodesia. See his *Kinship and Local Organization on the Luapula*; *History on the Luapula*; 'Perpetual Kinship: A Political Institution of the Luapula Peoples'; and 'History and Genealogies in a Conquest State'. Cunnison's analysis of the Lunda social system greatly assisted my own formulations; I am further indebted to him for many helpful discussions.

[2] For ease of reference in this section I have put royal titles in capitals, except when I refer to the present incumbents, when I give the title in ordinary type.

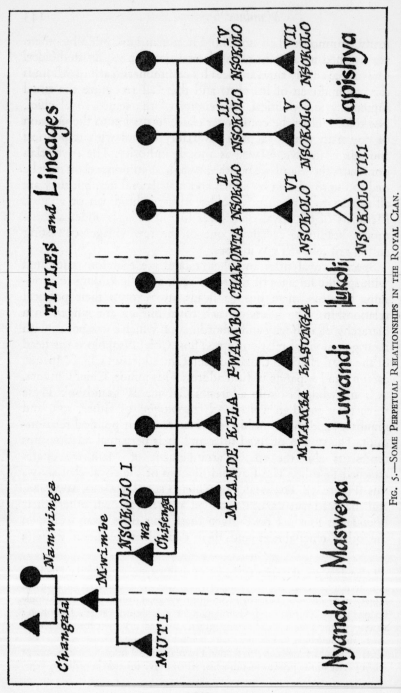

FIG. 5.—SOME PERPETUAL RELATIONSHIPS IN THE ROYAL CLAN.

144

similar connection, in which their territorial contiguity is expressed in kinship terms. The genealogy of the royal clan is therefore a diagram of the territorial and political relationships between existing discrete communities. When a Mambwe is asked who are his people, he generally answers with the name of his village estate, and seldom with the headman's title. He says *Mwansa* and not KASUNGA. If the context demands a broader indication of his position, he says *Aziya* and not FWAMBO. The lineage affiliations of the royal clan are expressed in terms of territorial attachments, and conversely the lineage titles indicate territorial possessions.

POSITIONAL SUCCESSION

All Mambwe titles stand in perpetual relationship to that of NSOKOLO, the senior title, and to each other, irrespective of the actual genealogical relationships between the living incumbents. The actual genealogical relationships between individuals are irrelevant in the context of titles and political authority. The positions of titles relative to one another are held steady through the system of *positional succession.*[1]

When the incumbent of a title dies, his successor assumes his title and authority, and at the same time, his exact place in the kinship system.[2] He takes on the complete social identity of his predecessor and inherits his wives, children, and property, in addition to the title. He becomes the father of his predecessor's children, and takes on all this predecessor's responsibilities, including debts. In a case before Chief Nsokolo, concerning a betrothal that had been broken by a girl after thirty shillings had been handed over to her parents, her stepfather protested that all these arrangements had been made by the girl's father, the dead brother whom he had succeeded. He knew nothing of the

---

[1] Richards first used the term for the Bemba system. See 'Some Types of Family Structure Among the Central Bantu', p. 224, and also 'Mother-right among the Central Bantu', pp. 257 ff.

[2] Mitchell describes the system of positional succession among a matrilineal people of Nyasaland in *The Yao Village*, pp. 121, 181 et seq. Gray states that among the Wambugwe of Tanganyika the single institution of positional succession organizes succession to social positions, inheritance of property, preferential marriage of widows, guardianship for orphans, and adoption. See his 'Positional Succession Among the Wambugwe', pp. 233 ff.

matter. The court pointed out that when he inherited the girl and her mother, he inherited all that his brother had left, including his debts. The case went against him, and he was compelled to pay damages. The identification between heir and predecessor is complete.

Ideally, the Mambwe consider that an elder brother should be succeeded by a younger, until all the brothers and seminal half-brothers of the deceased's generation have succeeded in turn. Succession then drops to the next generation, first to the eldest son of the eldest brother, and then along this line of brothers and half-brothers in order of seniority. In practice, a large number of factors can disturb this ideal pattern. A brother may be passed over because he is too young, or, if he is fully grown, because he is considered too stupid or incompetent to succeed. 'Brothers' may include parallel paternal cousins, in the event that a man has no closer relatives to succeed. An elder brother is not absolutely forbidden to succeed a younger, but this would be considered most undesirable. The Mambwe say: 'It is the red ants that make a man climb a tree',[1] meaning that only the most unusual circumstances would change the proper order of succession from senior to junior. There is always a large number of men who are potential heirs, and the heir is never appointed during a man's lifetime. When a man is passed over for any reason, such as youth or stupidity, he thereupon loses all his rights in succession, nor can his sons succeed in turn.

Normally, a brother does succeed, and takes the wives of the deceased. The Mambwe do not have diverse terms of address to distinguish between a father and his brothers, whether full- or half-brothers, or stepbrothers. A man's son calls all these persons *tata* (father), and where necessary, adds a descriptive term, thus: *tata mukalamba* (father's elder brother) and *tata munono* (father's younger brother). The successor to a dead man automatically becomes *tata* whatever relationship he previously bore to the deceased. A Mambwe younger brother addresses his elder brother formally as *tata lenze*, and in day-to-day usage as *tata*, so that in the event that a man of the sons' generation does succeed, the new relationship has already been anticipated. All men addressed as *tata* address one another's children as *mwana* (child).

---

[1] *Icikakwezya umuntu kumuti inkalandu.*

Where rights to succession and inheritance are involved, children belong to a social position, as it were, and not to individuals. Especially where titles are concerned, it is important that children should be thought of as descended from a title, for this determines their own rights to succeed in turn. All sons of royal title-holders are addressed as princes (*anang'wa*), but unlike commoners' sons, they do not all share an equal right to be considered for succession. Royal titles can be inherited only by sons born after their father succeeded to his title, for they are born 'in the purple' (*pausano*).[1] The elder princes, born before their father succeeded, are excluded from the succession.

The present Chief Nsokolo claims descent from a younger son of NSOKOLO wa Chisenga, the first incumbent of the title of NSOKOLO.[2] The titles held by the Maswepa, Luwandi, and Lukoli lineages are shown as being awarded to elder sons of NSOKOLO wa Chisenga, that is, to princes excluded from succession to the NSOKOLO title. Only the younger sons of a NSOKOLO have ever succeeded to that title. I have shown the order of succession to the NSOKOLO title, as stated by the Mambwe, in Figure 5: the principles of succession to a royal title are clearly enunciated in this charter of titles. Royal headmen claim descent from an elder son of a subsidiary title, and therefore from a grandson of NSOKOLO wa Chisenga. Thus the origins and relationships of all titles are fixed in three generations: those of NSOKOLO wa Chisenga, his sons and grandsons. Commoner chiefs and headmen link in to the royal lineages and titles through marriage, and take their positions in the system of titles through their affinal relationships with the title-holder to whom they are attached.

All the present holders of royal titles gave the original holder at three or four generations remove. Where there had been a large number of title-holders between the original and the present holder, the genealogy showed the title passing from brother to brother in the superior generations. But the number of generations remained invariably three or four, according to whether

---

[1] *Usano* may be translated as the abstract quality of royalty. Thus, *usano unmwene* is the government or rule of the chief, *isano* is the chief's palace, and *asano* are the chief's wives and concubines.

[2] The word *nsokolo* is also used for a small four-pronged thorn, very painful to tread on, that barefooted Mambwe are careful to avoid. They say that the first Nsokolo was a very 'fierce' chief.

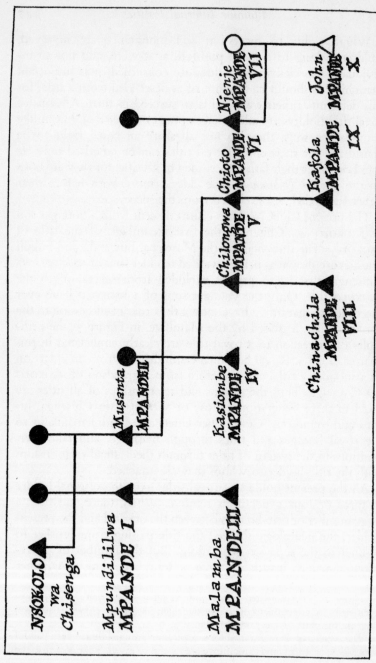

FIG. 6.—MPANDE SUCCESSION.

the royal title-holder was a chief or headman. The genealogy of Chief Mpande, shown in Figure 6, illustrates this process.

The present Chief Mpande, John, claims to be the tenth MPANDE since the title was first given to Mpundililwa, an elder excluded son of NSOKOLO wa Chisenga. Mpundililwa was succeeded by his half-brother Musanta, MPANDE II, and then the succession dropped a generation. In this generation no less than five brothers and half-brothers succeeded in turn, before it dropped to the present MPANDE's generation, in which two other men held the title before John succeeded. The dates when some of these men reigned can be established. The present incumbent, John, MPANDE X, succeeded in 1936 from Kafola, MPANDE IX, who succeeded in 1917; Chinachila, MPANDE VIII, succeeded in 1908; these dates were recorded by the Administration. These are the first local European records, but a comparison of Mambwe events with the chronology of Bemba chiefs prepared by Brelsford[1] can establish dates before this with some certainty. Citimukulu Chitapankwa of the Bemba died in 1887 after a reign of twenty-one years during which he led a raid against the Mambwe in which Chitongwa, MPANDE V, was killed. Before this, the Mambwe say that Musanta, MPANDE II, was also killed by the Bemba, this time under Citimukulu Kanyanta, at some time before the Ngoni came through Mambwe country in 1856.[2] This Citimukulu is not given by Brelsford, who begins his list of Bemba chiefs with Citimukulu Chileshya, who died in 1851. Thus MPANDE II was killed at some time before this date. This genealogy therefore covers a span of more than a century, and would appear to place NSOKOLO wa Chisenga as living about 1830, thereby making him appear half-way through their known history, which goes back to the eighteenth century.[3]

If the actual genealogical relationships between members of different generations over a period of two centuries were precisely remembered, we would expect to find that living members of any

---

[1] *The Succession of Bemba Chiefs,* p. 6 et passim.

[2] Barnes, 'The Fort Jameson Ngoni', p. 194.

[3] Apart from the Bemba account of finding the Mambwe established when they arrived in the middle of the eighteenth century, the Lunda of the Luapula also state that they raided the Mambwe for cattle during that century. (Personal communication from Dr. I. G. Cunnison.) The history of the neighbouring Lungu confirms these Lunda raids.

lineage are removed by many generations from their founding ancestor, and are widely separated from each other in the total kinship structure. Some families may be expected to die out, and others to proliferate, for women are not equally fertile nor do all children survive. Moreover, the ages of many members of the same genealogical generation would show wide disparities. But in fact Mambwe lineages, as the people relate them, do not display the uneven developments that must arise from the same biological and social factors that cause demographic variation. The lineages of both commoner and royal clans are remarkably congruent both in depth of generation and in their relation to one another. They are all shallower than that of Chief Nsokolo, which shows a depth of only eight generations. The reigning Nsokolo is shown as six generations removed from the founding ancestor Changala, and as Nsokolo has sons and grandsons, the whole genealogy embraces eight generations. It is extremely unlikely that Mambwe clans came into existence only six generations ago, in the light of what we know about Mambwe history.[1] The consistency of the genealogies arises, I believe, because they are statements of the political relationships between living people who occupy enduring positions, and not the remembered precise relationships between actual dead or living people. Mambwe genealogies record not only the descent of persons, but also the descent of titles and estates.

The three or four generations stated by chiefs and headmen to separate them from their original title-holders comprises the span of relationships for which the Mambwe have specific terms. The Mambwe have words for father (*tata*), grandfather (*kuku*), and great-grandfather (*sikulu*), that is, for each of a man's forebears who could possibly be alive at any one time, and thus comprehending actual living persons whom he might possibly have known. Everyone before that is a *cikolwe*, an ancestor; except for the founding ancestor of the royal clan, their names are forgotten. Four generations is the limit of reckoning used by an individual, for it fixes the point at which his title originated. Chief Kela of the Luwandi lineage gave me a line of descent of four generations, similar to that of Chief Mpande; headman Kasunga, whose title stands in the relation of son to the title of

---

[1] Cunnison describes a similar genealogical telescoping among the Lunda, where the matrilineages have depths of seven generations. See his 'History and Genealogies in a Conquest State', p. 22.

Kela, took me to the grave of his grandfather, whom he claimed to be the 'first KASUNGA'.[1] It is irrelevant which particular KELA gave an elder son the title of KASUNGA. After the lapse of some generations the existing holder of the KASUNGA title will always state that it originated from the first KELA, since it originated from KELA as a title. The whole relationship of KASUNGA to KELA is fixed in the generations of sons and grandsons of NSOKOLO wa Chisenga.

When the Europeans arrived there were sixteen Mambwe chiefs, thirteen of them royal. Eleven of these claimed that the first holder of their title was a son of NSOKOLO wa Chisenga, and two that the first holder was a grandson. None of the successive incumbents of the NSOKOLO title shown on the genealogy is said to have created a title for a son. New titles do not appear at the generation level of the NSOKOLO who created them; they are added to the number of the original title-holders in the generation below that of NSOKOLO wa Chisenga. All those titles which stand in the perpetual relationship of son to NSOKOLO therefore claim an equal antiquity. The actual genealogical relationships of past title-holders is probably adjusted by each succeeding generation. As at least the father and grandfather of a title-holder are likely to be known, and their actual genealogical relationship appreciated, the adjustment takes place at the higher level of the genealogy, where we find a number of brothers succeeding one another. I believe that this adjustment may, in some cases, happen at the level of the grandfather's generation; I doubt whether the present Chief Mpande's father, for example, was really a son of Musanta, MPANDE II. If the system works in the way I have postulated, we would expect to find that the mothers of men bearing titles are detached from their real husbands and thrust upwards in the genealogy of the royal clan, to become wives of the first NSOKOLO. This theory appears to be borne out by the actual genealogies given. NSOKOLO wa Chisenga, the first incumbent of the title, is shown to have a large number of wives,[2] each of whom gave birth to the original holder of a title.[3]

---

[1] This grave was a former village site within the estate of the present Kasunga village, and could be recognized by the mango trees which surrounded it. There are a number of these former sites; I traced five for this village.

[2] See Figure 5 above.

[3] Cunnison states that in the Lunda matrilineages of seven generations depth, the relationship between any two males is one of the same or adjacent

It is significant that the major modern political cleavage among the Mambwe, that between those living in Tanganyika and those living in Northern Rhodesia, is now shown to have occurred in the lifetime of NSOKOLO wa Chisenga. Now that the Tanganyika Mambwe are under an external authority separate from that of the main body, they have virtually become an independent people. Chief MUTI addresses Chief NSOKOLO as brother, a term that cannot be used to NSOKOLO by any other Mambwe chief. Chief MUTI claims descent from Funda, a brother of NSOKOLO wa Chisenga, who were both sons of a vague figure called Mwimbe, who was the son of the founding ancestor Changala. It is said that NSOKOLO wa Chisenga fell ill, and accused Funda of using sorcery against him; he quarrelled with Funda and drove him and his son out of the country. They went to live in MUTI's present territory. From Funda sprang the whole Nyanda lineage, of which MUTI is the head. NSOKOLO still claims them as part of his own people and subject to his authority, and attempts to interfere in matters of succession within MUTI's area. He has been consistently repulsed, and the Mambwe say that MUTI's people now refuse to attend the funeral of a NSOKOLO. I believe that MUTI is attempting to establish his political independence by claiming descent from a brother of NSOKOLO wa Chisenga, while the present NSOKOLO claims that Funda was not a brother, but a son of NSOKOLO wa Chisenga.

The perpetual relationship between royal titles, and the constant number of generations of descent, provide a fixed system through which actual persons pass; they are adjusted to the system of fixed titles through positional succession. Titles and estates define one another. The land supports the people, and the titles regulate their relations. The whole system of titles and estates forms the enduring tribal structure through which the transient generations pass.

The Mambwe system of succession effectively separates the sons of a title-holder into two categories: the excluded elder sons, and the entitled younger sons. The elder son is the potential ancestor of a new lineage; the younger son hopes to succeed to the title of his father's lineage. When a powerful title-holder creates a new title for his elder son, he gives him not only a semi-

---

generations. Accordingly, he shows that there is a proliferation of siblings in the top generations. See 'Perpetual Kinship: A Political Institution of the Luapula Peoples', pp. 40 ff.

independent status, but concrete gifts: a title, land, cattle, and in the old days, followers. The younger son is left with a right only, the right to be considered for inheritance in his turn. If his father has younger brothers, he may die without ever having had the opportunity to be considered for succession. The creation of a new title not only splits the solidarity of the agnatic group, but it also diminishes the patrimony of the creating title-holder. The younger son sees his elder brother becoming important and independent at his expense. All the stories concerning the creation of titles in the past are tales of quarrels and anger, accompanied by accusations of sorcery. This is the story told of the primary split between the Tanganyika and Northern Rhodesia Mambwe; it is repeated in the quarrel between Chiefs Kela and Mwamba, a quarrel further embittered by the Administration's appointment of Chief MWAMBA to a salaried chieftaincy, which includes his former superior KELA. The chiefs of the main lineages have fought with one another throughout Mambwe history, and within the lineage, the chiefs have quarrelled. Musanta, MPANDE II, is said to have killed his two younger brothers, NSOKOLOS II and III. They did not hesitate to seek outside help in their struggles with one another: MPANDE joined the Ngoni when they invaded Mambwe territory, and helped them to harry NSOKOLO's district. NSOKOLO in turn leagued himself with the Bemba, and defeated both the Ngoni and MPANDE, with the aid, the Mambwe say, of an outbreak of smallpox among the Ngoni. Thereafter, NSOKOLO and the Bemba turned on KELA and defeated him. These rivalries are still current: today Nsokolo, Mpande, and Kela remain at loggerheads.

Strife between brothers and father's brothers is a constant theme in Mambwe life, and is not limited to the families of title-holders. In Kasunga village (cf. Figure 1), Elliam Sinyangwe (D25) inherited two boys, Chisante and Chipingo, their sister Enesi (E52), and their mother, when his brother Wangwe (D26) died. The mother died, and Elliam brought up the children. When the boys were old enough to marry, Elliam gave them cattle for their marriage payments. Elliam and Chisante, the elder brother, quarrelled when Elliam demanded some of the money Chisante brought back from work abroad. Chisante said that Elliam had got plenty of money and cattle from his genitor, Wangwe. Chisante left Kasunga village after this quarrel and joined another

M

Sinyangwe group in a nearby village. Chipingo, the younger brother, then went off to Tanganyika to work, and on his return gave Elliam one blanket. Elliam refused to accept it, saying that it was more of an insult than a present due from a dutiful son. He accused Chipingo of being as unfilial and ungrateful as his elder brother. Chipingo then said that he too would leave the village and join his brother, but first he would sell his hut; he would leave absolutely nothing for Elliam. Elliam claimed that he had built the hut; Chipingo had no right to it. Chipingo had made the door of the hut himself, so they compromised: Chipingo took away the door when he left, and Elliam kept the hut. The rupture between foster-father and sons was complete. Elliam threatened to sever the ties between them publicly (*ukupalokana*, to separate). Only great bitterness will drive Mambwe to this extreme, and as a rule only when charges of sorcery are involved. If Elliam thus repudiated the kinship bond between them, the sons lost their rights to inherit his property. The brothers countered this threat by demanding a cow from Isaac, Elliam's younger brother and likeliest heir, who lived with his co-religionists in the Jehovah's Witness village of Aron. The brothers claimed that their genitor Wangwe (Isaac's eldest brother) had given Isaac a cow for his marriage many years before. Isaac refused to return the cow, and the brothers brought him before Chief Mwamba. Elliam was absent at this time on a visit to his cattle-herding village across the border in Tanganyika, so could not be present to give evidence when the chief heard the case. The chief ordered Isaac to give back a cow. When Elliam returned and heard of this he complained to the chief that this was unjust. He said that Isaac had given Wangwe the sum of fifty shillings when he returned from wage-labour before the war; Elliam had been present at this transaction. If Isaac had to give up the cow, then Chisante should return the fifty shillings. The chief issued a summons for Chisante and his brother to appear before the court to clear up the whole matter. Public sympathy lay with Elliam: he had brought up the boys and acted well towards them and they had returned ingratitude and disobedience. The case was not finished when I left. The conflict of interest between proximate generations, and the solidarity of members of the same generation, appeared clearly from this case. The real dispute concerned the disposal of the property left by the deceased Wangwe.

The general increase in the quantity of material goods brought about by wage-labour is also an increase in the amount of inheritable property over which agnatic kin may quarrel. In addition to the title, a younger brother inherits the wives and property of his elder brother. But the deceased title-holder's elder sons may question his successor's right to some of the property, in particular any which has been acquired through wage-labour, their father's or their own. There are instances of a father making a written will, leaving some of his property to his elder son. The Administration recognizes the validity of such documents. These written wills do not represent a novel change in the system of Mambwe inheritance. In the past, the manner in which a title-holder created a new title for his elder son was a method of handing over some of his own property during both their lifetimes. The father's title, wives, and most of his cattle, would pass inevitably to his successor, who was selected from among his younger brothers and his younger sons. Any disputes concerning what part of the property belonged to the title-holder as incumbent of the title, and what belonged to him as an individual, could be thrashed out by all the interested parties before the property actually left the village. The potential heirs to the title could protest directly to the title-holder against any gift they considered would infringe their own rights. But the creation of a new title inevitably diminished the original estate, even though the heirs would have political authority over the new title. A will prevents the successor to the title from influencing the quantity and character of the property left to the eldest son. The successor cannot argue with a dead man, and the son can bring the power of the Administration to his support when there is a dispute.[1] This action was taken in one dispute between a successor, a younger brother of the title-holder, and the title-holder's elder son, which involved property left to the son by a will.

Samuel, the title-holder who died, was an elder son of Chief Mpepo Mwamba, who died in 1935. During his lifetime, Mpepo favoured Samuel, created the headmanship of MPEMU for him, and gave him cattle. He also set up Samuel in a trading venture

---

[1] The effect of introducing wills on a matrilineal people is quite different, and apparently more disruptive to traditional inheritance. See E. Colson, 'Possible Repercussions of the Right to Make Wills upon the Plateau Tonga of Northern Rhodesia', p. 24.

with part of the money he saved from his salary as an administrative chief. Samuel's younger brother, Moses, resented this favoured treatment, and quarrelled with both his father and his brother.

Samuel had worked abroad and prospered; he left a considerable amount of property. He had a brick house, furniture, a herd of cattle, some of which he had bought with his own money, a plough, and cash. His will gave the purchased cattle, the plough, and the cash to Pinto, his eldest son, an unmarried youth of nineteen.

The succession ceremony (*ukupyana*) took place fourteen days after Samuel's funeral. Chief Yasapa Mwamba, the doyen of the lineage, presided over the family council to determine the heir.[1] At this meeting Moses asserted his right to succeed, and was appointed, in spite of the personal enmity that had always existed between him and Samuel. But Moses was unable to have the will set aside, although he tried; Chief Yasapa Mwamba insisted that it must be recognized, despite all the arguments that Moses brought forward. Moses grew angry, and threatened to beat Pinto and his mother, and other members of Samuel's family. At this the two surviving wives of Samuel refused to be inherited by Moses. One was Pinto's mother and the other her half-sister. The threats of Moses were of no avail, and Moses had to complete the succession ceremony with his own wife playing the role that properly belonged to Pinto's mother. Moses claimed the brick house, and Pinto's mother had to move out. The will did not mention the house.[2] At that part of the succession ceremony where homilies are addressed to the new incumbent of a title, Moses was told again and again that he must put out of his heart any grievance about the cattle and money he did not receive. He was told that there must be peace inside the family: 'If your sisters and daughters are divorced, where will they go if you treat them badly?' Mulefu, another headman of the same lineage,

---

[1] Chief Yasapa Mwamba's active role in the funeral and inheritance ceremonies was instructive, for the Administration deposed him in 1950, and no longer recognized him as chief. But the Mambwe still treat him with the respect and deference due to a chief.

[2] A royal headman should be buried in his own hut. The village is abandoned at the end of the cultivating season in the year of his death, and rebuilt on another site. Brick houses are too expensive and too rare as yet to be used for this purpose. Samuel was buried in an old hut in the gardens at the edge of the village.

told Moses that although the wives had refused to be inherited, he still had rights over them; if they married anyone else, Moses could claim damages. As for cattle, they did not matter; there were other cattle. Moses listened to all this with a sullen air.

A fortnight after this ceremony, Moses attacked Pinto with a stick, when they happened to meet in another village. Pinto ran to his mother, and while she was attending to his bruises, Moses came into the hut. He had been drinking, and set about mother and son with an axe he had picked up and inflicted two wounds on the woman's head. Eventually he was restrained by the villagers. Pinto and his mother complained to Chief Tailosi Mwamba[1] about this. Mwamba told them that Moses was his 'father' and therefore he did not wish to interfere. He advised them to go to the court in Abercorn, which they did. Moses was arrested, tried, and found guilty of assault; he was fined five pounds and given the alternative of three months' imprisonment. His own son, who had joined with him in beating Pinto and his mother, was also sentenced to one pound fine or one month's imprisonment. Moses returned to his inherited village, where his relations with the people were not happy. He spoke bitterly about Chief Tailosi Mwamba, accusing him of reporting the matter to the police, and of influencing the court to fine him.

While the conflict of interest between excluded elder sons and potential successors is inherent in the Mambwe system, it has been exacerbated by the increase in wealth consequent upon wage-labour. Pressure of population on the land has limited the possibilities of creating new titles and estates for excluded elder sons. The acquisition of wealth privately, and not by inheritance, divides a man's property into two parts. The earned property is likely to become more significant in the future. But the distinction between them is not absolutely clear, and the traditional heir naturally presses for all he can get. Moses resented his father giving Samuel money from his chief's salary, which he considered part of the perquisites of the title, and not a private income of the individual holding the title to use as he liked. His father evidently took another view. Similarly, when Chief Yasapa Mwamba was

---

[1] Chief Tailosi Mwamba is the administrative chief, brother's son to Chief Yasapa Mwamba, the deposed traditional chief. Because of his subordinate kinship position to Moses, and his own insecure position at that time, he would not have the case tried in his own court.

deposed, and Tailosi, his brother's son, took his place, Tailosi naturally drew the salary. Yasapa quarrelled with him over this, and demanded that Tailosi should give him some of the money. Tailosi replied that he worked for the Administration and was paid for this work; the money was his. Eventually these two had a serious quarrel, in which a reckoning of mutual obligations was made, and some other property handed over. The occasion of this quarrel too was the disposal of the salary.

It is clear that when the Mambwe work for wages they are involved in a system of economic relations in which the values of a money economy are paramount. These values conflict with some of the values of Mambwe tribal life. While the tribal system persists, tribal values will persist. Reciprocal obligations are still determined by the bonds of kinship, and are not dependent on cash rewards. Nevertheless, relations between men within the tribe are being affected by the money relations which they have experienced in the labour markets. The concept of private property, to be disposed of as the owner wishes, is already present. Private property at the moment consists largely of money, and the cattle and manufactured goods that it can buy. The increase in wealth is still on a superficial level; land, the basis of individual and tribal existence, cannot yet be bought and sold. Land is the final security, and as long as rights to the use of land still depend on kinship affiliations, the kinship relations will retain their importance. No Mambwe at present living in the tribal area has accumulated sufficient money to free himself from the necessity of cultivating his fields. If and when a sufficient number of Mambwe reach this position, the conflict between a man's sons and his brothers is likely to be resolved in favour of the sons, at the expense of kinship ties and obligations.

The preceding analysis shows that the village groups, which form the residential units of Mambwe society, are linked to one another through their headmen and chiefs, and to the other segments of Mambwe society through the kinship of their chiefs. These political ties are not the only ties between villagers. Individual Mambwe in many villages are bound together through the system of cattle-herding. Clan is linked to clan through marriage and joking relationships. Clan ties even extend outside the Mambwe polity, and bind people to fellow-clansmen among the neighbouring Lungu and Inamwanga peoples. Some of the heads of commoner clans, like Mwene Chipoko, belong to other tribes, and are politically part of these tribes. The whole social system is much wider than the area of political relations, and cross-cuts them.

The royal clan forms the framework on which is built the political system. Each lineage of the royal clan is identified with a particular territory, and the head of the lineage is also the political chief. Within each territory, the village headmen are either members of the chief's lineage or commoners linked to his lineage by cognatic or affinal ties. Three commoner clans have separate territories; but each of their chiefs recognizes the political sovereignty of the senior royal chief, and is linked to him both cognatically and affinally. The lineage of the chief dominates the other agnatic groups that live in his territory. The kinship relationships between territorial chiefs express their political relationships.

CHIEFS AND SUBJECTS

Each Mambwe chief was virtually independent before the British arrived. Each lived in his own village state, with his own administrative officers—executive officer, captains, junior judges, etc. The chief exercised juridical, administrative, and legislative authority over his people; in return they gave him respect, obedience, and recognition. They fought for him in his struggles with other chiefs and against invaders from without. The chief had rights over the labour of his people, who had to cultivate his fields and those of his wives, each man working for two days a year. The people also had to bring the chief grain and beer, a share of the catch after a fishing party, and part of any animal slain in the hunt. When a man killed a lion, he brought the skin to the chief, who rewarded him with a bull: if he failed to bring the skin, he was treated as a thief and had his hands and ears cut off. Only the chief and his great wife could sit on a lion skin.[1] The

---

[1] The lion is intimately connected with the chiefs of the royal clan in Mambwe eyes. When a chief dies, the Mambwe believe that his spirit leaves his body by way of a reed placed in his ear for that purpose before interment. This reed projects above the surface of the grave, which was one of the huts belonging to the dead chief. The spirit comes out first in the form of a worm, which gradually grows through stages into a lion. Millet gruel made with cold water

chief was able to accumulate a surplus through this tribute in labour and food, but this wealth did not greatly increase his standard of living, for he constantly returned food to his people, mainly in the form of gifts to dependants. A subject could demand food and assistance from his chief in time of need. Tribute labour did not work only for the chief's benefit; a man became automatically entitled to receive food from the chief's garden by his expenditure of labour on it. Gouldsbury, writing in 1911 after thirteen years among the Mambwe, stated: '. . . it is certainly held that the crops of the chief are the food of the people, since it is his duty to see that his "children" do not starve.'[1] Work in the chief's garden was a form of insurance against want. If the chief did not make gifts to his people, they regarded him as a bad chief, and exercised their final sanction of withdrawal to another chieftaincy.[2] The chief undoubtedly had more security and more material goods than his people; he had more wives, more food, and more beer. From his monopoly of ivory and slaves he could import through the Arabs such goods as copper wire, beads, and calico. But there was little else he could do with these goods except to distribute them among his people. Although the chief gave away so much, his controlling position as the central receiving and distributing agency for labour and goods gave him in return a great deal of power and authority over the people.[3]

(*munya*) is placed in the grave hut for the animal's sustenance while it is growing. When the lion is thought to be grown, the captains (*amusika*) gather outside the grave hut, tell the lion to go into the bush and exhort it to spare the people and bring them meat. No one actually sees the animal, for no one dare enter the grave hut. Today, when a lion kills near a village the people say: 'The chief has killed something for us; he is calling.' They usually seek out the kill to see whether any meat is left, and if there is, call out: 'Thank you, Chief, for the relish,' and take it home. Chief Nsokolo has a great pile of lion skins in his house. Lion meat is never eaten, but is buried. In the old days, leopard meat was mixed with beef and given to the chief's bodyguard, to make the men brave.

[1] Op. cit., p. 58.

[2] Today a man must have written permission from his chief before he can move away. Chief Kowa fined a Jehovah's Witness 5s. for moving from a village within his area to a Jehovah's Witness village in another chieftaincy without first informing him.

[3] This characteristic feature of primitive economies has been noted by Malinowski, Firth, Goldenweiser, Kaberry, Hogbin, and many others. For a full discussion of African types see Gluckman's 'Lozi Land Tenure', p. 34 et seq.

The people treated the chief with great respect; his subjects greeted him by rolling on their backs in the dust and clapping their hands.[1] They could approach him only through the medium of his captains and councillors. The chief's palace was cut off from the main part of the stockaded village and only a subject seeking sanctuary could enter. This social distance did not erect an insurmountable barrier between chief and subjects, for the chief took his wives from among the people, and as a result he was tied to many groups through these women. Thus chief and subject were bound together by a multiplicity of ties, not solely political.

The chief's authority rested finally on two sanctions: one physical, the other supernatural. The chief could employ force to compel his subjects to obey him. He selected from among the young men a group who lived within his palace and acted as his police and bodyguard. These young men were fed and rewarded by the chief. After their spell of duty they were given goods for marriage payments, and left the chief's service to live in the village. Not all young men were selected for this task. They were chosen primarily for their physique and bravery, and the duty was coveted. With this force of men the chief could kill or enslave his subjects for offences. The chief also controlled the poison ordeal (*mwavi*), applied when a man was suspected of practising sorcery. The accused was taken into the bush by the chief's police and made to drink the poison. If he vomited, he was considered to be innocent, and released. If he did not vomit and his stomach swelled up, the police speared him to death. The chief was thus in a position to have his orders enforced. The cruelty of chiefs is a byword among the Mambwe; they emphasize the power and authority that the chief held over their lives and property in the past. One old Mambwe, explaining the difference between the authority of the head of his commoner clan and that of the chief, said that 'the chief could kill anyone': his power to take a man's life was his most significant characteristic.

The supernatural sanctions for the chief's authority lay in his control of the spirits (*imipasi*) of his ancestors. These spirits are considered to be associated both with village life and the estate of the chieftainship. They protect the people, guard the land, and affect the fertility of both people and land. The shrines at which

---

[1] This form of greeting is now rare. I saw it used only twice.

the spirits are worshipped are of two kinds: village shrines (*kavua*) and what I will call land shrines (*myao*). The ancestors of the chief were thought to be present at both shrines in the days of the village states, but there were differences between them. The village shrine was dedicated to the immediate ancestors of the chief, persons known to some of the inhabitants and with whom these were familiar, and they were consulted at this shrine when necessary. This shrine was associated with the village site itself, and with the affairs of the inhabitants. The executive officer made a daily offering of beer at this shrine, which Decle[1] states was sited inside the main gate of Chief Fwambo's village: this was the customary site.

The land shrines are natural objects in the environment: hills, caves, large rocks, or permanent pools of water.[2] Each land shrine has a priest (*simapepo*) and an acolyte (*mulondezi*). The Mambwe do not worship the earth; the land shrines represent the land as the home and nurturer of human beings, the source of food and life. But the land gives crops only when the rain falls[3] and the seasons follow their normal course, and people must plant seed and cultivate. Land, natural forces, and people are all bound together. The Mambwe believe in a being called Leza, who created the earth and all that is on it, but he is so remote from his creation that he is not concerned in the affairs of men.[4] The affairs of living men are of interest only to their ancestors. Thus the spirits to whom an appeal is made are those of the ancestors of the chief, right back to the founding ancestor of the royal clan, and including those immediate ancestors worshipped at the village shrine. There is a mystical connection between the land, the forces of nature, and the spirits of the dead. The people consider that the ancestors can affect the coming of the wind and

---

[1] Op. cit., p. 296.

[2] Old trees are also said to be shrines; I did not see any.

[3] The fact that Mambwe usually resorted to their land shrines during a drought (the commonest cause of crop failure in this area) had led to these shrines being described as 'rain shrines' in official documents and on maps.

[4] The connection between the earth and Leza is obscure, but there is one, for the shrines are sometimes called *Maleza*. On the other hand, the Mambwe have had Christian missionaries living among them for over sixty years, and it is difficult to tell how much of what they say about Leza is now formulated in terms they have acquired from Europeans. They certainly did not worship Leza directly.

the rain, or interrupt the natural succession of the seasons if they are angry with the people for any reason. Conversely, when they are pleased with the people, the ancestors can create conditions in which the land gives forth good crops. Thus the relations of living people with each other are considered to have a prime importance for the harvests, since the maintenance of good relations among the living is a concern of the dead.

The land shrine is resorted to only once a year, in normal times, when the crops have been harvested. Part of each crop is left at the shrine, and the spirits of the ancestors are thanked. In this harvest ceremony, the chief and his great wife, the priest and his acolyte, and the chief's captain, all have roles to play. The priest called on the chief's ancestors by name, from the founding ancestor to the present chief's predecessor. Offerings of hoes, spears, axes, arrows, calico, etc., were placed on the shrine by the priest, together with libations of beer.[1] No one could use the new crop until after this ceremony. Each person attending brought a little of the crop to the priest, who cooked it all together, offered some to the spirits, and then shared it among the people. After this ceremony there was a feast, with beer and dancing.

This ritual emphasized the authority of the chief, and re-stated his position as ruler of the country. Prosperity and well-being were thought to come through the chief and his ancestors, and the land shrine was the material centre of this belief. The mystical values attached to the chief's office and descent were reaffirmed.

Apart from the annual harvest ceremony, the chief and his people appealed to the shrine in times of disaster: drought, failure of crops, locust invasion, outbreaks of disease, invasion of their country, etc. The land shrine therefore referred to both the condition of the country and the condition of the people. Appeal to the shrine was not limited to disasters affecting the whole people: if any section of the people suffered, for example, from a local crop failure or from smallpox, the chief and his priest and the affected group could make an appeal to the ancestors. Even today, the smallest village within a chieftaincy can appeal to the land shrine for aid and assistance. Thus the influence of the shrine

---

[1] Today only cloth and beer are offered. Christianity has affected these ceremonies. Many of the priests will not admit to taking part in the ritual, and large gatherings at the shrines now occur only when there has been a disaster, or when a new chief is installed.

was thought to influence the whole area and all the people over whom the chief ruled.

Each lineage head of the royal clan has a land shrine associated with his title and estate. Chief Nsokolo, the senior chief, has a shrine at Tembo Hill, the prominent landmark near where the founding ancestor Changala is alleged to have settled first when he arrived in the country. However, any royal title-holder can appeal to this shrine, and in times of national disaster, as when the Ngoni overran Mambwe territory, all the chiefs gathered at this shrine for an appeal to the ancestors.

The shrine of the Luwandi lineage is a cave in the tumbled mass of rocks near the Tanganyika border where grassland Mambwe used to hide their cattle during raids. This shrine is associated with the title of KELA, who is the head of the Luwandi lineage. All the title-holders within this lineage can attend at this shrine. The FWAMBO title of this lineage also has a shrine, on the top of the Liamba hills. This shrine, however, is junior to that of KELA, and FWAMBO resorts to the KELA shrine on important occasions, such as a drought affecting both their chieftaincies. The MWAMBA title has no shrine, and MWAMBA resorts to KELA's shrine.

The land shrines are therefore ranged in a hierarchy of importance corresponding with the relationships of the royal title-holders to whom they refer. As all the title-holders claim descent from a common ancestor, the founding ancestors are present at each shrine, together with the particular ancestors of the title-holder to whom it is attached. Thus the influence of each shrine is not thought to be confined to the particular estate within which it is sited; its influence also spreads over into a wider area.

In January 1952 the Mambwe were much disturbed. Chief Kela had committed suicide at the beginning of October, and his successor had not yet been appointed. By the middle of January, when the rains were already overdue, the weather was still bright and sunny, and the country appeared to be threatened with drought. The people were also troubled by the Federation discussions. Some people considered the drought to be a sign of the ancestors' displeasure, because of Kela's untimely death; others ascribed it to the Europeans.[1] The leaders of the royal clan dis-

---

[1] It was said that when the African delegates opposed Federation at the London conference they attended, the Europeans had decided to kill Africans by withholding the rain.

cussed the matter among themselves, and decided to warn the people that they might have to brew beer for an appeal to the ancestors, to be made at the shrine of KELA. While they were still discussing the matter,[1] the rains came, and they abandoned the special intercession at KELA's shrine. In this instance, the land shrine of KELA was thought to be affecting the whole country, and not only KELA's chieftaincy.

The land shrine therefore has an ambiguous nature; its power not only affects the fortunes of the land, chief, and people of the estate within which it is sited, but extends over the whole country and its people. Every estate and its shrine corresponds with a community that is a unit of the social structure; each progressively larger social unit is associated with a larger estate; each is distinguished by a different name and by its association with a different shrine. But each estate is part of the whole Mambwe country and ultimately of the earth that supports all human beings; the title-holders are all members of the royal clan and their commoner subjects are dispersed throughout the whole country. The land shrines symbolize the unity that lies behind all the different divisions of the land, and of the social divisions of the people who live on the land. The mystical power of the land shrine extends over the whole country, and links the living with the dead in the continuing social process for, as Fortes writes of similar concepts used by the Tale to associate people and land: 'Nowhere is the Earth inert; and its mystical powers are a reflex of its relations with human groups.'[2]

The control over the forces of nature exercised by the chief, through his ancestors and the land shrines, gives a strong mystical sanction to his office. This sanction eliminates commoners from the struggle for a royal title. The chief seeks among his kinsmen for a potential usurper, and not among the commoners. The title cannot leave the royal clan. In the constant armed strife between

---

[1] The preparation of large quantities of beer in January was a serious matter, for beer would use up grain needed for food, particularly if the drought continued and caused a crop failure.

[2] *The Dynamics of Clanship Among the Tallensi*, p. 172. A similar association between sacred spots and the social organization is found in the cult of the royal graves among the Lozi. Cf. Gluckman, 'The Lozi of Barotseland in North-Eastern Rhodesia', p. 31: 'Though the grave's power is at its strongest for the neighbourhood, it is not limited by distance.'

rival chiefs throughout the nineteenth century the commoners did not attempt to replace the royal clan, but only attempted to transfer a title from one royal prince to another. As Gluckman writes, '. . . in African political life men were rebels and never revolutionaries.'[1] Royal and commoner clans were united to maintain the system as a whole, but the distinction between the two groups remained absolute. They are even buried in separate graveyards. This separation even in death is so important that it may expose an adultery otherwise concealed. A royal headman committed adultery with the wife of one of his villagers. She gave birth to a son who died a few months later. The headman insisted that the child be buried in the royal graveyard of the village. He gave as a reason that the woman was of the same clan as his sister's husband, and therefore almost one of the royal clan. This stretching of the concept of kinship was accepted by no one; people laughed at the headman for suggesting it. The husband sued for divorce on the grounds of adultery and won his case. The headman had to pay nine pounds in damages, the former husband left the village, and the headman was saddled with the care of a concubine. The chief's court accepted the headman's action in burying the child in the royal graveyard as a full admission of guilt: the headman did not attempt to deny it before the court.

The supernatural power of the chief over the prosperity of the country gives the ritual that surrounds his succession a political significance. The captains of the village states, who were the chief administrative officers, had an essential role in the installation of a new chief, and this gave them considerable control over the chief. The captain and the great wife of the chief were the main functionaries in the ritual of installation, and they were all from commoner clans. The selection of the successor was the prerogative of the royal clan, who discussed it among themselves. The importance of the doyen in such discussions has been mentioned. When a territorial chief died, Nsokolo could try to influence the choice of successor by exerting his authority as doyen of the royal clan. Once the successor has been appointed, the commoner clans played their parts in the ritual of installation, and here they were able to bring pressure on the royal clan.

---

[1] *Rituals of Rebellion in South-East Africa*, p. 20. Gluckman here gives a brilliant analysis of the function of rebellion in repetitive social systems.

The central part of the inheritance ceremony is an act of ritual intercourse (*isumo likukatuka*, 'to make the spear rise') between the successor and the great wife of his predecessor. The great wife was in effect publicly appointed. She was not married especially as a great wife, but was appointed from among the chief's wives, and if she failed in her duties, could be dismissed from her position. Her main duties were ritual: she had to tend the new fire which was kindled at the chief's succession, and which ought never to be allowed to go out; she had to play a part in the land shrine ceremonies; she could sit on the royal lion skins that were forbidden to all other commoners. Her garden was larger than that of any of the other wives, and she gave food to people who were in need. She alone partnered the chief in those acts of ritual intercourse that were necessary on certain occasions. She was deposed when she grew too old or if she committed adultery. When she was deposed, the chief called in the captains and councillors to discuss the choice of her successor; after they had agreed on their choice, the people were called together, beer was brewed, and her appointment announced. She was then given the copper anklets, beads, and special cloth and ear-rings which were the badges of her office. The great wife's sexual and pro-creative powers were (and are) thought to be associated with the well-being of the country. In this sense, therefore, she symbolized the land and the people in their relations to the chief.

After the successor had ritual intercourse with this woman, the captains made new fire with friction sticks (*lusika*) and handed it to the great wife, who lit her own fire with it.[1] From this fire the great wife gave fire to the other women in the village, and the people made new fires in their huts. On the death of a chief, all fires in the huts were extinguished, and not until a new chief had succeeded could new fire be kindled on the hearths, and these only from a great wife's fire.[2]

---

[1] The words *amusika* (captains) and *lusika* (friction sticks) appear to be derived from the verb *ukusika*, to make fire with friction sticks. The verb *ukuzika* means to bury or inter. The Bemba use the same word, *ukushika*, and also have the office of *mushika*, 'steward, manager, officer to a king or chief. See *Bemba-English Dictionary*, and Richards, 'Tribal Government in Transition', p. 8.

[2] There are strong taboos on a woman's use of fire. A menstruating woman cannot touch a hearth fire, and thus cannot cook. For six days her daughter or a neighbour must cook for her. When her period is over she cleans the hearth

Although there are few captains nowadays, compared with the warring days of the past, and the ritual surrounding the chief's succession has been curtailed, the central significance of the great wife remains. When Chief Mpepo Mwamba died in 1935, a dispute arose among the lineage members concerning the choice of his successor, for there were a number of claimants. One of them, Yasapa, a son of Mpepo's predecessor in the title, went secretly to the dead chief's village after dark, broke into the great wife's hut, and forced her to have intercourse with him. The period of mourning was not yet over, and the other members of the lineage were not present. In the morning Yasapa fired a gun, called the people of the village together, and told them that 'the chief has returned to his place'. The other potential successors hurried to the village in a rage, but Yasapa had gone. They took away the great wife, but they had acted too late, and she had to be returned to the new chief, Yasapa.

The ritual duties of the chief were intimately associated with the land and its products: the subsistence of his people. He initiated the agricultural cycle and presented the first fruits to the ancestors. The chief was the source of all land rights. Only the chief could give a man a right to the use of land. The chief and the land are indivisible, and one is dependent on the other. His prerogatives reflect this concept of his powers. Tribute of grain, fish, and meat, had to be given to the chief, a material recognition of his power over the land and its products. The iron ore worked by the blacksmiths belonged to the chief, and the blacksmiths gave him part of the articles manufactured by them after each smelting of ore. The chief nourished the people, not only by giving them land and ensuring the harvests, but also by giving them justice and protection against evil spirits and sorcery. Justice and generosity are considered to be the great chiefly attributes. The subjection of the commoner clans to the royal clan did not lead to tyranny: the chief could neither rule nor perform his ritual functions without the co-operation of his people. Chief and people are indissolubly linked together in a

---

and gets new fire from the fire of an old woman who is past the menopause and is no longer having sexual intercourse. A man cannot take fire from the hut of an old woman. He must ask her to give him fire. When a woman is suckling a child, only children below the age of puberty may touch her fire.

multiplicity of mutual obligations and reciprocal duties. Land, water, and crops represent the capital upon which Mambwe life is based; and the chief and people have a collective responsibility for their use.

The chief was a symbol of the unity of the people: they identified themselves with his title and estate. The chief's justice regulated the relations between man and man, and kept the peace in the interests of all. On his death, the whole nexus of social relations was thrown into temporary disorder, and remained thus until a successor was installed. The rule of justice and order was temporarily in abeyance. The chief's followers pillaged where they could, and committed offences normally abhorred.[1] During this interregnum the captains acted as regents, but they did not have the authority to punish excesses. Only the new chief could focus the multifarious relationships of his people, and allow society to proceed on an ordered course. Thus the speedy selection and installation of a successor was of vital interest to everyone; the temporary confusion served to underline the power and significance of the chief in the social system.

THE CHIEFS AND THE ADMINISTRATION

When the British arrived at Abercorn in 1893, they found the Mambwe largely disrupted by internal conflict. Chiefs Mpande and Chivuta had fled to the Senga for sanctuary, leaving many of their subjects under the rule of the Bemba chief Makasa. The reigning Nsokolo, Kamialile, was living with the Mambwe in what is now Tanganyika, having sought refuge there after a defeat inflicted by the Bemba. Kamialile was blind; his younger brother Kosi had put out his eyes in 1892. The background to this deed is obscure, but was related to Kamialile's alleged defection in battle, and to a division of opinion concerning further resistance to the Bemba.

The Administration at once began to use Kamialile Nsokolo as their principal administrative agent, and for the first time he

---

[1] When Chief Kela's followers came to fetch his body from Kasunga village after his suicide in 1952, the villagers fled in panic at their approach. They took their chickens and small stock with them, and anything valuable they had time to pick up. In the old days, they said, the chief's people would have looted them, and even killed some persons to bury with the chief.

N

found himself backed by a force sufficient to compel the other chiefs to recognize him as the main political authority. The Administration wished to treat Nsokolo as a paramount chief, and to make him responsible for Mambwe affairs in general, and for the conduct of the other chiefs. The British recognized Nsokolo as the sole chief, and the other chiefs either as petty chiefs or district headmen, under Nsokolo's general supervision. Thus, the imposition of colonial rule on the Mambwe began a process of centralization of political authority similar to that experienced by other African peoples.[1] Disputes between chiefs ceased to be settled by armed conflict, and internal order was enforced. In 1898 the British pacified the Bemba and established an administrative centre at Kasama.[2] This relieved the Mambwe of Bemba pressure, which had been considerable during the previous thirty years.

The Mambwe were not slow to see that the new power could be used to help settle their own internal quarrels. Chief Mpande returned to his own area[3] and set to work to recover his authority among his people, and applied to the Administration to restore the boundaries of his chieftaincy. The Administration consulted the villagers in the disputed area, who were asked whether or not they wished to return to Mpande's rule or remain under Chief Makasa. Most of them elected to return to Mpande. Kamialile Nsokolo complained of the injury his brother had done him in 1892, and the new British administrator sent out his police to arrest Kosi. The party succeeded in finding and arresting Kosi, but when they were escorting him back to Abercorn to stand trial, Kosi fell into the Saisi river and was drowned. This 'accident' could scarcely have been fortuitous, for the corporal in charge of the police was a claimant to the title of Nsokolo, and in fact did succeed to that title when the blind Kamialile died in 1907. The death of Kosi therefore appears to be the last certain instance of the removal of a chief or potential heir by violence; thereafter the struggle between chiefs or rival claimants to titles moved on to a new plane, wherein the power and authority of the Administration was the final arbiter.

The British support of Nsokolo's superiority undoubtedly

---

[1] See Fortes and Evans-Pritchard, *African Political Systems*, p. 16.
[2] Kasama is still the seat of the Provincial Commissioner.
[3] See p. 75.

strengthened his position vis-à-vis the other chiefs, and altered traditional relationships between the chiefs. But the junior chiefs did not accept Nsokolo's new dominance with a good grace, and continued to intrigue against him. The Mambwe were familiar with the principle of employing external forces in their internal struggles, as we have seen, and they now employed this principle in attempting to manipulate the decisions of the Administration. When Kamialile Nsokolo died in 1907, the Administration held a meeting at Abercorn to decide on his successor, and all the Mambwe chiefs attended. This meeting agreed to recognize Pembamoto as the new Nsokolo, and it is recorded that the approval of his appointment was 'unanimous'. This unanimity, expressed in the presence of the British administrator, in fact concealed the division of opinion among the chiefs, for Chief Mpande sent a message to the British beforehand stating that the chiefs and headmen had 'failed to agree' on a successor at a private conference. The chiefs who attended this conference were Mpande, Chivuta, Chakonta, and Chileshya, all of them, except Chileshya, members of the Maswepa lineage. The chiefs who had not attended this private conference were Kela, Fwambo, Mwamba, and Mpenza, all of the Luwandi lineage, the core of the Aisa Mambwe. Thus the differences between the lineages was still very much alive. Pembamoto's service as corporal with the police is mentioned with approval in the records; it is not too much to assume that he had the British behind him.

Thus the imposition of British rule introduced a new factor into Mambwe internal politics. The *pax britannica* brought an end to the settlement of disputes by armed conflict, and the decision of the Administration became the final sanction. The Mambwe system at the time of the British arrival cannot be described as either a primitive state or a stateless society. Each chieftaincy was a miniature independent state, with its own administrative machinery, and these were held together only through the perpetual kinship relationships of the chiefs. Nsokolo's territory and following were no larger than those of other territorial chiefs, and he had no centralized administrative machinery, such as that operated by the Bemba paramount chief. Each successive Nsokolo had attempted to widen his authority by establishing in junior titles men with a personal loyalty to himself, and each Nsokolo was in turn confronted with the same problem of resistance from the families of the current title-holders. Even when a Nsokolo succeeded in his attempts, his authority over the imposed chief endured only in his own lifetime; on his death, the family of the imposed chief themselves resisted the encroachments of the succeeding Nsokolo's family. The Mambwe system of succession operates to divide the princes between excluded elder sons and entitled younger sons, militates against the permanent centralization of power in the title of Nsokolo, and strengthens the tendency to independence of the other titles. Nsokolo's seniority was traditionally based on his ritual supremacy, and was expressed in kinship terms, but his relations with the other title-holders varied in the past between armed conflict and peace, as did the relations of the junior title-holders. These changing relations, brought about by the interplay of internal and external pressures, formed and still form the substance of Mambwe politics.

The struggle for appointments and for precedence among the chiefs began to take place at the conferences with British officers held in Abercorn, and continued to do so up to the present. The potential successor to a title must satisfy the Administration that he is the right man. The claimant must seek the support of other chiefs to help swing opinion in his favour. Nsokolo's central position leads him to attempt to impose his will on the others. In 1911 a successor was sought for Chief Kela: Nsokolo attempted to present the Administration with a *fait accompli* by appointing Chipika, a son of the deceased title-holder. This appointment was violently resented by the Kela family, and Nsokolo withdrew his nominee at the Abercorn conference and the family choice was appointed. Chipika then complained that he was being accused of sorcery,[1] but an official investigation found no evidence for this complaint. These struggles appear in all the records of appointment; sometimes Nsokolo succeeds, more often he fails. The British have the final word. In 1912 a successor was sought for Chief Chivuta, whose title springs from Chief Mpande, whom Chivuta addresses as 'father'. Nsokolo suggested a man called Pasasa, a son of the deceased. Mpande objected to this man, giving as his reason that Pasasa had committed adultery with his father's wives. Mpande proposed a younger brother of the deceased, Kapungila. On this occasion the Administration made a decision

---

[1] It is illegal to bring such charges.

worthy of Solomon. They appointed Pasasa to the title, but awarded the wives to Kapungila.

The Colonial Office assumed control over the area in 1924,[1] and continued the system of Direct Rule used by the British South Africa Company; there was little change as far as the Mambwe were concerned. The British South Africa Company retained some Mambwe territory, as part of the Tanganyika Estate. This Estate was purchased by the Government of Northern Rhodesia in 1938, and some of the alienated land restored to the Mambwe, to be used for the Citemene Control Scheme.[2] Although this alienated land was returned in part, the original alienation is an important factor in Mambwe affairs, for it taught them that the Europeans had the power to take their land from them.

In 1930 the Colonial Office implemented the policy of Indirect Rule. The Mambwe had lived for almost forty years under Direct Rule when the new system was introduced, and during this period the position and functions of the chief, the critical political position, had been clearly affected. The chief was no longer a leader in war, for war between African peoples had been abolished. The chief's control of economic enterprises had vanished. The slave trade organized by the Arabs had been suppressed, and ivory was much more difficult to obtain. The British had already begun to supervise the cycle of agricultural production, by limiting the times of burning for the ash-planting cultivators and the use of land among the fallow cultivators; and the chief's powers of direction were taken from him. The exchange, sale, and slaughter of animals was regulated.

The chief had lost some of his judicial authority. He had no rights to enforce judgements or to punish offenders; he had to send offenders who refused his conciliation to the Magistrate's Court set up in Abercorn by the Company. The use of the poison ordeal was forbidden.

The chief's close authority over the people was further weakened by their wider dispersion over the land. The large stockaded village state had been abandoned during the early years of British

---

[1] Northern Rhodesia Order in Council 1924.
[2] See *Annual Report for the Year 1938*, Department of Agriculture, *Northern Rhodesia*, p. 10.

rule, and smaller villages came into existence. The number of
headmen grew, and many of these were commoners.

In addition to these direct limitations on his secular powers,
the chief found his supernatural authority under attack from the
missionaries. Mission teaching of Christianity struck at the roots
of the chief's ritual authority over his people. Although the chief
continued to perform his ritual duties, these duties were not
recognized as part of his official position by the administrators,
who were sympathetic to the efforts of their fellow-Europeans,
the missionaries.

Most important of all, an authority now existed whose power
over the chief was apparently unassailable; the British were the
real masters, and both chiefs and people knew it. The chief's right
to employ force to carry out his orders was completely abolished:
he ruled by grace of the British. A new political dimension had
been added to Mambwe life; both princes and commoners could
now gain political power through the Administration, either by
working for it as policemen and clerks, or by attempting to
influence its decisions in their favour.

Finally, the British brought with them not only a supreme
political authority, but also a new economic system. The Mambwe
were involved in an unfamiliar set of relations, based on money.
Money and European goods percolated into the reserve. The
traders who followed the missionaries and administrators became
the most influential of the agencies which were transforming the
material conditions of Mambwe life. All Mambwe became to a
greater or lesser extent the consumers of manufactured goods:
they had been dragged into the world market.

It would not have been surprising, perhaps, if the cohesion of
Mambwe society had collapsed under these successive blows.
That Mambwe society did not collapse was due to two main
reasons. First, the British recognized the position of the chief.

They did not attempt to by-pass the chiefs and create a direct
administrative system of their own; they worked through the
chiefs. Even when the British upset the traditional balance of
power, they supported the office of chief. By acknowledging
Nsokolo as the senior chief, and the other chiefs as petty chiefs
and district headmen, they lent their authority to these positions.
When the British selected one person to be chief in favour of another, they always made their choice from among the claimants

thrown up by the indigenous system of inheritance. Implicitly they gave official value to the indigenous system of selecting heirs. The royal clan was confirmed in its hereditary position; a new validity was given to the claims of the ruling group to rule. Second, the British did not attempt to control the distribution of land within the reserve. Although they took over the whole area, and alienated some land for European settlement, they did not interfere with the land rights of individual Mambwe within the demarcated reserves. The traditional system of distributing the land for use was allowed to continue. In this system the chief's role was vital. All land rights sprang from the chief: any Mambwe could claim land for cultivation by submitting to the chief's authority. The British did not question the chief's position as 'owner of the land', and left intact his traditional relations with his people in this all-important sphere of Mambwe life. Officially divested of much of his judicial and administrative authority, the chief yet retained his traditional position in relation to the land. This left the chief with an authority over his people, which, in the future, was to determine his political role on a wider stage.

The policy of Indirect Rule brought about a radical change in the previous administrative system. The posts of petty chief and district headman were abolished, and Native Authorities and Native Courts with paid African officials were instituted.[1] The Mambwe were divided into three groups, ruled over by three salaried chiefs. Nsokolo was recognized as senior chief, and Mpande and Mwamba as chiefs. They were given considerable powers; each was given a Native Court, in which he sat with salaried assessors to judge civil and criminal cases; the court of Nsokolo acted as an appeal court to the other two, and appeals from his court went to that of the District Commissioner. In effect the salaried chiefs were incorporated into the government of Northern Rhodesia, and became agents of the Administration. The other Mambwe chiefs were reduced to the level of headmen,[2]

---

[1] Native Authorities Ordinance, 1929. Native Courts Ordinance, 1929. Amended by Native Authorities Ordinance, 1936, and Native Courts Ordinance, 1936.

[2] They are occasionally referred to as ex-chiefs in official notices and records. In 1943 the *General List of Chiefs*, p. 11, listed the following: *royal*—Kela, Chakonta, Chivuta, Fwambo, Luimbo, Penza, Tanzuka; *commoner*—Chileshya, Chindo, Koa.

which strengthened the relative importance of the three administrative chiefs.

This division into three had an approximate correspondence with
the division of authority within the Mambwe system. Nsokolo
had always been recognized as the senior chief. Chief Mpande's
area, which is entirely given over to ash-planting cultivation,
included all the chiefs of the Maswepa lineage, and other royal
chiefs whose titles were junior to Mpande's. The grassland cultivators were represented by Chief Mwamba, an elevation of his
status over Chiefs Kela and Fwambo.[1] Kela's district was incorporated into Nsokolo's administrative area, and Nsokolo now had
both forest and grassland people under his control. The subjection
of Kela to Nsokolo gave Nsokolo the largest chieftaincy by far,
but left Kela with a bitter grievance, for he was traditionally at
enmity with Nsokolo and resented being subordinate. Kela's
sense of grievance was exacerbated by the elevation of Mwamba,
to whom he was traditionally senior. Nsokolo several times attempted, but failed, to get Kela appointed as an administrative
chief.[2]

The decline in power and prestige affects the traditional chiefs
in many ways. They can no longer use force against their people,
and are dependent on supernatural sanctions to enforce their
wishes.[3] Chief Kela's suicide was, I believe, the consequence of his
inability to impose his authority, and a resort to supernatural
forces. Before his death I heard Kela deplore the loss of the former
status and dignity of his title, and fulminate against the Europeans
and the other chiefs. When Kela found that his young wife had
eloped to Tanganyika, he took two men with him and went to
Chief Muti, of the Tanganyika Mambwe, and demanded that
Muti should hand over the couple to him. Kela publicly threatened
to kill the lovers, which he could certainly have done in the old
days. Chief Muti sent a message to the couple to hide themselves,
and told Kela that he did not know where they were. Muti
was afraid of Kela's anger and of the consequences to himself if
Kela killed anyone. Muti told Kela that when he found the couple

---

[1] I have not been able to discover what lay behind the elevation of Mwamba.
The British may have chosen the first Mwamba because of his personal qualities.
[2] See p. 182 below.
[3] This may be the reason why none of the traditional chiefs are practising
Christians.

(*a*) Harrowing a Field with Cattle

This group comprises a husband and his two wives and his sons, assisted by two widows who are working for food (*ukupula*). They are driving the village herd over a flattened field in which millet seed has already been sown

(*b*) A Prince's Grave

The hut in the foreground is the grave of a prince (*anang'wa*), formerly the royal headman of the village. A group of Jehovah's Witnesses are holding a service, led by the standing man. This was the third service; the first was a pagan ceremony, and the second followed the practice of the London Missionary Society. After the Witnesses had finished, a European missionary conducted another meeting in the village.

PLATE III

he would send them back to Northern Rhodesia. The Mambwe say that Kela knew that Muti was concealing the lovers. Kela returned from Tanganyika to his own village, and the following night came to Kasunga village after dark, and entered a hut used by adolescent boys in which he was accustomed to sleep when he visited Kasunga village. This hut belonged to the divorced sister of Kela's runaway wife. Two boys were asleep in the hut, but did not hear Kela come in. During the night Kela hanged himself from the rafters with his scarf. One of the boys rose at dawn, and bumped into the dead man's feet; his screams aroused the village. Kela's intention was obvious: to bring supernatural sanctions on the father of his recalcitrant wife and on headman Kasunga whom Kela suspected of seducing her. The spirit of Kela dead had more power and authority to punish than Kela alive.

The Aisa Mambwe had always treated Kela with the greatest respect, as the senior chief of the Luwandi lineage, and after his death they buried his body under the floor of his hut and later deserted the village in the traditional manner. The drought that followed Kela's death was attributed to Kela's spirit, and by inference, to the Europeans who had driven him to such straits.[1] Strong feelings of hostility towards Europeans were current at this time, because of the proposals for Central African Federation, to which the majority of the Mambwe appeared to be opposed. These feelings were heatedly expressed at a meeting held by Chief Nsokolo on his return from the chiefs' meeting at Lusaka[2] a few weeks before Kela's death. Many prominent Mambwe were present, and Nsokolo was brusquely told that when he went to the forthcoming conference of chiefs and Provincial Commissioner at Kasama, he was to oppose some of the new agricultural regulations that the people did not favour. If Nsokolo did not oppose these regulations publicly, the people would know that the Europeans had bribed him. The death of Kela and the threatened drought appeared to strengthen this wave of tribal consciousness and opposition to Europeans. Nsokolo did speak against the disliked regulations, and subsequently refused to punish offenders against them brought before his court. Three months later he was deposed. To the Mambwe it appeared that Kela's supernatural authority was still strong and active, in striking contrast to the decrease in his secular powers.

[1] See p. 164 above.   [2] See p. 216 below.

The elevation of the three administrative chiefs over the other traditional chiefs is displayed today in the different appearance of their villages. The traditional chief's village is similar in all respects to that of any other Mambwe village, royal or commoner —a collection of wattle-and-daub huts with thatched roofs. There is nothing to indicate that a chief lives in it. The village of the administrative chief is quite different. It contains a number of public buildings built of brick: the courthouse, the dispensary, the school, sometimes a church, all of them solid symbols of the influences which dominate present-day Mambwe life. The demonstration plots maintained by the agricultural assistants and messengers are laid out in neat lines, and the crops labelled. Beside the plots are the brick houses of these African officials. Near the village is a brick house for the use of visiting European officials. The spatial distribution of buildings resembles the old stockaded village state; the chief's brick house, surrounded by the huts of his wives, is set apart, and is still called the palace (*isano*). The courthouse is isolated from the main body of buildings. Even when the inhabitants are out of the village at work in the fields, there is an air of bustle: strangers come to have their cases tried and to consult officials; there is always a queue of sick persons outside the dispensary; the schoolboys may be singing or playing football. The different uniforms of the African officials strike the eye. It is immediately evident that the village of the administrative chief is a capital.

The distinction between traditional and administrative chiefs is quite clear to all Mambwe. They recognize the Native Courts, for the justice dispensed there is based on their own traditional concepts, although many of the offences for which people are tried nowadays are consequences of British rule—failure to prepare the long mounds recommended by the Agricultural Department as a preventive against soil erosion, failure to dig proper latrines, failure to pay tax, failure to renew bicycle licences, failure to make a child attend school, etc. In all matters where European-inspired laws are concerned, the Mambwe take their cases to the Native Courts, but in other matters, such as disputes about marriage payments, divorce, assault, etc., they do not hesitate to seek justice from the traditional chiefs, although they are not supposed to do so. If the traditional chief does not satisfy the people, or finds that the case merits punishment, whether by fine or imprisonment, the matter is taken before a properly constituted Native Court. Village headmen have no power to try cases, but the traditional system of adjustment between conflicting parties is universally followed. I have already given an example of a dispute in Kasunga village about a marriage payment which was first taken to the head of the lineage segment.[1] If not settled by the lineage head, cases are then taken before the village headman, and he settles those disputes that he can. But if the case is important, involving damages or cattle and money in any quantity, it is taken before the Native Court. The headman has no legal power to enforce his decisions: the Court has. Thus a distinction is made between traditional matters and those which are the consequences of British rule.

The symbol of an administrative chief's authority is a pith helmet such as British Army officers once wore with tropical uniform. The traditional chiefs usually wear a kind of turban of coloured cloth. Chiefs Nsokolo and Mpande wear both. The administrative chiefs are adept at adapting their headgear to the demands of the situation. When they visit the headquarters of the administration at Abercorn, or when in the presence of British administrators, or when visiting villages on tours of inspection, they invariably wear their pith helmets. When they preside at ceremonials they leave the helmets behind and expose their turbans. They take their helmets into court, but place them on the table before them, a compromise which neatly symbolizes the dual nature of the court's function.

Chief Yasapa Mwamba was deposed in 1950 for failing to enforce agricultural regulations, and for dismissing offenders brought before his court for contravening these. His nephew, Tailosi, was appointed to his place. Tailosi presides over the court and deals with European officials; Yasapa presides over all ceremonial and ritual functions that demand the presence of the chief. The people do not recognize Tailosi as the 'true' chief: they say that he is only 'the chief of the British'. The division between traditional and administrative chiefs is exemplified in the existence of these two men in one village. In accordance with the distinction between them, Yasapa wears a turban, while Tailosi wears a pith helmet.

---

[1] See p. 140 above.

The Native Authority is responsible for a number of duties in connection with the administration of tribal affairs. The Native Authority keeps registers of tax-payers, collects the taxes when due, and punishes defaulters; it keeps the roads within the reserve in good repair, and pays the workmen for their labour. These duties have constantly been augmented. Today the Native Authority is responsible also for the issue of licences of all kinds: for firearms, bicycles, hunting, marriage; for the upkeep of schools and the employment of teachers; for the cleanliness and hygiene of villages; and for the maintenance of law and order within the reserve.

The Native Authority employs paid and unpaid officials to discharge these duties. A number of councillors are responsible for particular aspects of tribal administration: health and education, agriculture, finance, etc. Two of the councillors work full time at their administrative tasks, and three others work part time. This system is analogous to the situation in the former village states, where the chief was advised by the captains and councillors[1] drawn from the ranks of the commoner clans. The present councillors of the Native Authority are also selected from among the commoners.

Each councillor in charge of a department has technical advice from European specialists—the agricultural, veterinary, medical, and educational officers employed by the Government. In addition, assessors are appointed to assist the chiefs to try cases. Each court also has a clerk, who must be educated and able to read and write English, for he is responsible for keeping the court records and for balancing the accounts. Two constables (*kapasos*) are appointed to keep order in the courts, to serve summonses, to arrest individuals when necessary, and to act as messengers between chief and chief, chief and people, and chief and the Administration.[2] These men wear a uniform. There is also a schoolmaster and a dispenser in each administrative chief's village. The chiefs, salaried councillors, court clerks, constables, teachers, school

---

[1] Most of the original holders of traditional posts died out during the period of Direct Rule, and were not replaced. I found only two captains (*amusika*) still surviving. The captains' main function, to lead in war, had disappeared, and with it went the rank of captain, which is no longer used.

[2] The District Commissioner himself supervises the work of the Native Courts.

attendance officers, and dispensers are all paid from the Native Treasury.[1] The members of this African public service in effect form an African bureaucracy.

The officials of the Native Authority and Native Courts are in intimate contact with the officials employed directly by the Europeans. Uniformed agricultural and veterinary officials employed directly by the specialist European government officers live in the administrative chiefs' villages. The African clerks, messengers (a kind of uniformed but unarmed police employed directly by the District Commissioner), interpreters, and African policemen at headquarters, by the very nature of their duties, must constantly meet the African public servants employed by the Native Authority. The same individuals have often served on both sides. The present full-time councillors are middle-aged men with long records of service as Government clerks. There is an obvious advantage for the British in having such men appointed to these posts in the Native Authority. Their loyalty has been tested by many years of service with British officers; they can read and write; they understand the system of administration; they are known to be sensible men. Similarly, the Native Court clerks and assessors are often former Government employees. The existence of these two interlocking bureaucracies forms a local labour market that has more than a local significance, for together they form a field of political relations in which Africans can learn political techniques: graduates from these local schools of politics have already played an important part in a much wider political field. Politically, these bureaucracies are the agencies through which the conflicting interests of British and Mambwe are expressed.

The Native Authority is in a position of considerable power over the Mambwe as a whole, and positions within the Authority

---

[1] The establishment of Native Treasuries by Native Authorities was permitted by Ordinances 9, 10, and 25 of 1936. The court clerk of each administrative chief keeps a court record book giving details of the cases heard, collects fines and fees, and issues summonses. He also holds licence books and collects firearm, game, bicycle, and dog licence fees. He pays in these monies at intervals to the Native Treasury clerk who keeps the main books. The estimates are drawn up annually by the District Commissioner, after a meeting with the chiefs, at which the technical officers (agricultural, veterinary, etc.) may be present to advise. The estimates are approved (or otherwise) by the Provincial Commissioner. See Carey Jones, 'Native Treasuries in Northern Rhodesia'.

are eagerly sought. A great deal of lobbying goes on for appointments, and although the final selection is made by the British, the men put forward have already been the objects of considerable manœuvring. Accusations of bribery are frequent, but difficult to prove. Some posts, such as court clerk, require the appointment of an educated man; others, like that of assessor, can be filled by an illiterate, but only one who has a good knowledge of customary law. On the whole, the present officials of the Native Authority are educated men, and of the eight assessors at the three Native Courts, only two are illiterate. The struggle for these posts are part of present-day Mambwe local politics, and the object of most political intrigues is to bring the decisive power of the District Commissioner and the British authorities on one side or another of their internal divisions. The deposition of Chief Yasapa Mwamba provided an opportunity for a realignment of Mambwe internal political forces, and the moves that took place over the appointment of his successor illustrate how such matters are settled.

Nsokolo at first attempted to have Chief Kela promoted to an administrative chief, and thus take the salary away from the Mwamba title. This proposal was unacceptable to the Administration. A conference was called by the District Commissioner in Abercorn to determine Yasapa's successor, and the proceedings here displayed all the conflicting elements involved in the relations between the Mambwe themselves and between the Mambwe and the British. The District Commissioner presided. Chief Nsokolo and Chief Mpande attended, and also traditional Chiefs Kela, Mwamba, Fwambo, and Mpenza—all of the Luwandi lineage which held the Mwamba title. Traditional Chief Kowa was also present, the only commoner chief within Mwamba's administrative chieftaincy. The Native Authority was represented by the five councillors, the Treasury clerk, two constables, two court clerks (from Nsokolo and Mwamba), and two school attendance officers. The District Commissioner's interpreter, his head messenger, and a second messenger (all of them Mambwe), represented the official African civil service. Twelve headmen of the Mwamba chieftaincy and a large number of villagers represented the people.

There were two candidates: a son of Nsokolo, and a sickly brother of Yasapa, called Samson. This candidate was a poor one, for a sick man was unlikely to be appointed, particularly as Yasapa was still alive and active. Nsokolo's son therefore had a good chance. Traditional Chief Mpenza, acting as spokesman for the Luwandi lineage, during the course of the meeting suggested another candidate: Tailosi, a son of Yasapa's deceased elder brother, a young man of twenty-five with a good education, who had completed Standard IV at a mission school. Mpenza stated that the majority of the people in Mwamba's area were in favour of Tailosi. Tailosi was also supported by Chief Mpande, by two of the councillors, by the other candidate Samson, and by all the members of the Luwandi lineage, as well as the headmen. The messengers also supported Tailosi. Nsokolo was taken by surprise by Tailosi's nomination, and said that he was not satisfied, claiming that the deposed Yasapa and his brother Samson would make trouble in the future, and that Mwamba's people were 'bad and difficult to govern'. He said they spoiled their chiefs; when Yasapa was appointed to the title he was a good man, but his people had spoiled him. Nsokolo asked why Tailosi had not been mentioned before the present meeting, although several preliminary meetings had been held. Chief Mpenza said that Tailosi had not been suggested before because they had thought he was too young, but they now realized that his education gave him a great advantage, and Mpenza apologized for failing to tell Nsokolo about Tailosi before this meeting. One of the messengers then said that it was Mambwe custom for a father to be succeeded by his son; Tailosi was the rightful successor. It was not customary for Nsokolo to appoint his sons to the chieftainships of Mpande and Mwamba. This palpably false statement of Mambwe succession was at once contradicted by a councillor, who said that the correct order of succession was for younger brothers to inherit in order, then the sons of the brothers who had held the title. This councillor was an adherent of Nsokolo, and was permanently resident in Nsokolo's village. The District Commissioner said that he was satisfied that the people wanted Tailosi, and, in spite of his youth and small stature, he would make a good chief. Tailosi was thereupon declared to be the new Chief Mwamba.

This conference displayed all the divisions and conflicts in Mambwe politics. Nsokolo attempted to impose his own son on another area. The Luwandi lineage resisted this attempt: they

cleverly withdrew their doubtful candidate and brought forward
another acceptable to the British, for Tailosi was well-favoured
by the missionaries who had educated him. Mpenza's bland
explanation about Tailosi's education was eye-wash; the senior
men of the lineage believed that Tailosi would be a mere front
for his uncle, and that the real power would be left in what they
considered to be the proper hands. The councillors divided along
the lines of their personal loyalties to different members of the
royal family; the two who supported Tailosi both lived within
the Mwamba chieftaincy. Chief Mpande opposed Nsokolo; if
Nsokolo's son had been appointed, the principle of Nsokolo's
right to interfere in the succession of the territorial chiefs might
then be applied to his own. The District Commissioner brought
some of his own African staff, who are trusted men. One of them
tried to support the choice of Tailosi by giving the District
Commissioner a partial version of Mambwe rules of inheritance.
Nsokolo attempted to curry favour with the District Commissioner by slandering Mwamba's people, accusing them of encouraging Chief Yasapa in opposing agricultural regulations.
Nsokolo's condemnation here of the Aisa Mambwe was ironical,
for three years later he himself was deposed, and although the
issues were involved, the principal charge against him was one of
failing to enforce agricultural regulations.

The large attendance at this meeting was a tribute to the importance of the administrative chieftainship of Mwamba. The salary
that goes with this chieftainship, although small, is regular and
certain;[1] the money is important.

The commoner members of the Native Authority are in an
influential position, for they have easy access to the District
Commissioner. Most of them are former employees of the British,
and the Administration has the final decision in their appointment.
These men know who appointed them, and why, and that their
salaries depend not on the chief but on the British. They can
bring pressure on the chief by threatening to expose him to the
British when he condones failure to observe regulations, which
he is constantly forced to do to retain his people's confidence.
This ultimate responsibility of the Native Authority to the British
renders the Native Authority suspect to the Mambwe. They

---

[1] Mwamba and Mpande get six pounds a month and Nsokolo eight pounds.

regard the Native Authority as an institution brought about by the British, a direct agent of British rule, a mere channel through which unpleasant and unnecessary orders are directed from above. The policy of Indirect Rule implies that the Native Authority accepts responsibility for making regulations and ensuring that they are enforced within the tribal area: the people do not regard the matter in this light. They do not think of the Native Authority as a responsible group making necessary regulations in the interests of the people, but regard them as the agents of British rule. The orders of the Native Authority are considered to emanate directly from the British. Some regulations are bitterly resented, especially those controlling agriculture. These regulations are designed to benefit the people, but agricultural regulations are regarded with extreme suspicion, for any tampering with the land is thought to be a step towards alienation. The loyalty of the people to the chief is clearly distinguished from their obedience to the Native Authority. The Mambwe give their allegiance to the chief. They will obey the chief even if his orders contradict the regulations issued by the Native Authority, whom they regard in exactly the same light as the clerks, police, messengers, officials of the technical services, etc., who are employed directly by the British. I observed the following clear example of this. The deposed Chief Yasapa Mwamba sent a messenger round the villages appointing certain days for fishing parties. Seven villages were ordered to fish on one day, and ten others on a day in the following week. The people prepared the poison, and on the day appointed, set off with their baskets to the Saisi river. As they walked along towards the river, they were accosted by a uniformed African agricultural official. This man ordered the people to return at once to their villages and abandon the fishing, for the use of poison had been forbidden. He demanded the names of the people present and said they would be brought before the court. The people refused to give their names, and told the official that the chief had ordered them to fish, and only another order from him would stop them. They said they cared nothing for the regulation, and the official should go and see the chief about it. Finally they brushed him aside and continued on their way. This confidence in the chief was all the more striking in that he had been deposed, and they knew well that he had no standing with the Administration. Further, when the fishing was over, they gave the tribute fish

o

from the catch to Chief Yasapa, and not to his nephew Tailosi, the administrative chief.

If the Native Authority enforces unpopular regulations, the people expect the chief to realize that they are unpopular, and to exert his authority to rescind them. Naturally the Administration objects strongly to a chief conniving at the evasion of regulations. The chief is therefore in frequent conflict with the other members of the Native Authority, as well as with the British. This conflict emerges from the official reports. In 1952 the Annual Report stated:[1]

> . . . Chief Nsokolo is obviously jealous of the power and knowledge of the Councillors. However, they continue to work satisfactorily and there has been a general improvement in the area due to their influence. They are all elderly men, retired Government servants with a knowledge of their duties, and of an age that commands respect in the community. The junior chiefs, not men of forceful character like the senior Chief, have assisted the Councillors to the best of their ability and do not seem to be at all jealous of them. Time alone will prove that the educated Councillor is an asset and not a rival.

This rather sanguine estimate of the conflict between the chiefs and the members of the Native Authority was not upheld by events, for in 1953 not only was Nsokolo deposed, but some of the members of the Native Authority were discharged, and new men brought in, all of them, including the new Nsokolo, former Government servants. The Administration expects the commoner members of the Native Authority to be loyal to it, and not to the chief.

The headman cannot oppose the chief in the same way as the members of the Native Authority. The headman is not paid for his duties, and since the formation of the Native Authority there is no doubt that his authority has diminished. The headman cannot officially try cases, and cannot exercise the sanction of force to discipline his villagers. He must turn to the Native Authority to compel his villagers to dig latrines, keep the paths in good order, etc. The headman's position is purely one of prestige and social status. But the headman owes his position to the chief, and gives his loyalty directly to the chief, and not to the institution of the Native Authority nor to the British. The British identify the chief

---

[1] *Annual Report for the Northern Province, 1952*, p. 4.

with the Native Authority, and through him they hold the loyalty of the headman: the chief carries the loyalty of the headman upwards through the Native Authority to the British.

The institution of the Native Authority depends entirely on British support, and the commoner members of the Authority are aware of this. They have no roots in the traditional Mambwe social system, and the people have no say in their appointment to office. Although their salaries are really paid by the people, out of taxes, they recognize that the British enforce payment. They have all been trained in the British service, and owe their eminence to British influence: they have a strong interest in complying with the orders and wishes of the Administration. Nevertheless, they too have a conflict of loyalties: to the chief and to the British. They often take the same unco-operative view of agricultural regulations as the people, and their ambiguous attitude towards their own regulations is the main source of difficulty with the British authorities.[1]

In this complex of political and administrative relationships, the chief plays a vital role. His position is not simple. He is an agent of the British Administration and the main instrument for the implementation of British policy: at the same time he is the representative of his people to the British, and the guardian and spokesman of what they consider to be their interests.[2] When these dual functions of his office come into conflict, as they must, the chief is compelled either to find a compromise acceptable to both sides, or to identify himself with one of them. Complete identification with the British will deprive him of the respect of his people and thereby undermine his authority, and consequently, his usefulness as an agent to the British; identification with his people against the British will endanger his tenure of office. The personal qualities demanded of the person holding a chieftainship are therefore of primary importance. The chief must be sensitive not only to the traditional moral values rooted in the indigenous

---

[1] Two councillors and two court assessors were dismissed at the time of Nsokolo's deposition. See p. 218 below.

[2] Cf. Schapera, 'Present-Day Life in the Native Reserves', p. 58; Gluckman, *Custom and Conflict in Africa*, p. 154; Colson, 'Modern Political Organization of the Plateau Tonga'; Barnes, *Politics in a Changing Society*, pp. 136–139; Mitchell, 'The Political Organization of the Yao of Southern Nyasaland', p. 154; and Fallers, *Bantu Bureaucracy*, pp. 195–203.

system but also to those of the Europeans; he must be sensible of the political movements that influence the changes of British policy; and he must himself be capable of conducting political manœuvres. The British hold the final power: they can both appoint and depose a chief, as well as the incumbents of any office in both sets of bureaucracies.[1] The relations of chief and British administrators also have wider repercussions, for they influence, and are influenced by, the political movements that arose from African participation in the whole industrial economy of Northern Rhodesia. It is against this background that the relations of the chief with his people must be examined.

The potentially conflicting roles of the chief—agent of the British to his people, and people to the British—are becoming increasingly difficult to play. The chief is at the point of contact between two systems which are becoming increasingly hostile, and the strains and stresses of his office are augmented by the participation of the Mambwe in the industrial sector of the economy. The system of migrant labour is the basis of the present industrial economy in Northern Rhodesia, and the subsistence economy underwrites the wages earned by Mambwe. But the reserves must exist simultaneously with the mines if the present total economic structure is to continue to function in its present form. Indirect Rule is a policy adjusted to this situation. The Administration uses the chief as its agent in an attempt to retain the tribal integrity of unemployed casual workers, and to fulfil its fundamental task of maintaining peace and order. But, as Gluckman remarks of Natal, '. . . . the political task of Government is primarily to maintain and control the labour-flow'.[2] Although Read found it 'increasingly a matter of surprise' that the Nyasaland Administration should continue to go on supporting the old chiefs and at the same time encourage recruiting for the mines and industry,[3] there is no contradiction: this is exactly what might be expected. Tribal cohesion and migrant labour are essential to one another. But the Native Authority cannot work smoothly without the co-operation of the chief. The chief polarizes the

---

[1] Mambwe awareness of British power is an effective check against arbitrary acts by chiefs and councillors, for the people know that the District Commissioner will investigate such acts, if they are brought to his notice.

[2] 'Analysis of a Social Situation in Modern Zululand', p. 17.

[3] 'Migrant Labour in Africa and Its Effects on Tribal Life', p. 625.

loyalty of his people and gives a mantle of traditional authority to the bureaucrats of the Native Authority.

The capacity of the chief to co-operate with the Administration in view of these varying conflicts gives him a profound significance both to Mambwe and British. The chief represents the people in the complex and unfamiliar world brought about by British rule. The refusal of Nsokolo to co-operate in enforcing the regulations of the Native Authority withdraws from that Authority the sanction of his traditional powers, and is therefore tantamount to an act of revolt. Within the indigenous Mambwe political system, the struggles between chiefs and claimants to chieftainships are of a different nature. In Gluckman's words, the chiefs fear rivals, not revolutionaries. But Nsokolo's disobedience challenged the whole established system of authority. When the Administration suspended Nsokolo and later deposed him after this incident, the whole complex of political factors in Northern Rhodesia was involved. Nsokolo had taken part in political activities outside the reserve,[1] to which his disobedience within it was the corollary. Nsokolo's refusal to enforce regulations previously authorized by the Native Authority destroyed that body as an effective instrument of Indirect Rule. At the same time that Nsokolo was deposed, the Native Authority was suspended, and the District Commissioner himself assumed the powers of a Native Authority and ruled the Mambwe directly.[2]

---

[1] See p. 216 below.
[2] *Northern Rhodesia Government Gazette*, 25th June 1953.

CHAPTER VI

MAMBWE EXTERNAL POLITICS

INDUSTRIAL EXPERIENCE

COPPER-MINING by Europeans in Northern Rhodesia began on a small scale in 1906, and the first mine, Kansanshi, was delivering ore in quantity in the 1920s. Other and bigger mines were soon developed. This mining development coincided with the political change from the rule of the British South Africa Company to that of the Colonial Office. By the 1930s, when the policy of Indirect Rule was implemented, the Copperbelt had become an important factor in the raw materials market of the world.[1] Today, with its sister-area across the frontier of the Belgian Congo, the Copperbelt supplies about one-quarter of the Western world's supply of copper. As the copper mines grew in number, secondary industries also developed. Northern Rhodesia became a centre of intensive European industrial development.

This development multiplied the number of jobs available to the Mambwe and to other Central African peoples, and increased their wages. The scale and manner of labour migration changed from desultory and haphazard searches for work to organized and certain journeys to known markets. The organization of the copper industry in turn affected other European enterprises: the sisal planters of Tanganyika set up a centralized organization to collect and deliver men to work, that resembled the industrial enterprises in scale and efficiency. During this whole period of expansion, the number of Africans in employment grew steadily. The War gave an added boost to development, and the number of employed Africans again increased. I have shown the increase in number of Africans employed in Northern Rhodesia during this period in Table XIV.[2]

---

[1] See Gann, 'The Northern Rhodesian Copper Industry and the World of Copper: 1923–1952'.

[2] Figures supplied by the Commissioner for Local Government and African Housing, Government of Northern Rhodesia, Lusaka.

TABLE XIV

Number of Africans in employment in Northern Rhodesia at
various periods, according to official censuses

Year	Total employed, including juveniles and females	Adult males only
1946	140,776	126,529
1951	228,251	202,580

Thus the annual increase in the number of Africans in employment (10 per cent) was four times the estimated annual increase in population ($2\frac{1}{2}$ per cent). These large increases in the number of Africans in employment indicate the scale of development that has taken place. The Mambwe have played their part in this development. I have been unable to obtain comparable figures of the growth of employment among the Mambwe, but we may assume that they were affected by this development in a similar way to other African peoples. I have compared the numbers and percentages of taxable Mambwe males registered as being absent at work by the Administration Census for the three years from 1950 to 1952 with the total figures for Northern Rhodesia in 1951, in Table XV. The total number of Africans in paid employment shown by the official figures includes those Africans who are permanently urbanized. The Mambwe percentage is lower than the national, but this may be due to a number of causes,

TABLE XV

Number and percentage of adult Mambwe males working for
wages compared with the number and percentage of all Africans
working for wages in Northern Rhodesia, in the year 1951

Year	All Africans			Mambwe		
	Taxable males	Total in employment	Percentage	Taxable males	Total in employment	Percentage
1950	—	—	—	5,224	2,212	42
1951	441,921	202,580	46	5,783	2,169	38
1952	—	—	—	6,045	2,407	40

including the methods by which the different counts were made. This alone leaves room for some error. But the figures are sufficiently close to show that the Mambwe are fully involved in wage-labour.

It is important to remember that wage-labour is not a novel phenomenon for the Mambwe, although the intensity of participation in the industrial economy has increased, as the above figures show. The Mambwe have worked for Europeans for sixty years. The first wonder and bewilderment at European life and behaviour has worn off; they are more sophisticated now. The Native Authority schools have built on the work of the missionaries and are producing an ever-increasing number of Mambwe able to read and write English; and these schools have been operating for a generation. The Mambwe have learned by experience that the language of commerce and industry is English and that a man who cannot speak English is handicapped in the search for a well-paid job. To learn to speak and write English well is not only an economic asset, but also opens the door to a universe of new ideas. At work the Mambwe are exposed to the propaganda of African-controlled religious and political organizations. Many of them have been members of trade unions during their work periods, and others have taken part in political activities on behalf of Africans of all tribes. Some Mambwe have been stimulated to attempt to achieve material success by acquiring capital in the manner of the Europeans.

Mambwe participation in this large and growing system of industrial relations—an industrial revolution—cannot but affect their knowledge of the world outside their own tribal group and expose them to experiences of an order quite different from any possible in an isolated agricultural area. When two societies of such a different kind exist side by side in the same land, and both are dependent on the same supply of labour, no rule or regulation can prevent the passage of ideas as well as men and goods from one to the other. Besides learning how to work in an industrial system, the Mambwe labourer also learns about industrial and political organizations, strange sports and amusements, and the habits and manners of Europeans. The industrial complex of Northern Rhodesia is a great school, whose graduates return to their tribal areas filled with new knowledge: to labour is to learn. The Mambwe see that European industrial workers in the towns enjoy a standard of living that is more comfortable and secure than anything that they have experienced at home, and they notice that already some Africans have achieved a standard comparable with the Europeans. It would be astonishing if the Mambwe did not begin to question their own role and rewards in this system, and bring back to the reserve a new conception of themselves and their place in the world.

The material rewards of town life appear to be so great when compared with those of rural life, that it might be expected that more Mambwe would leave the reserve permanently, and settle in the towns.[1] The great majority in fact return to the tribal area. The reasons for this are rooted in the whole economic relationship between reserve and town in Northern Rhodesia, and the consequent conditions of employment within the industrial system. The Mambwe have two main reasons for returning to the reserve, one economic, and the other social; these affect one another.

Mambwe have no security of employment within the towns. This insecurity of employment is one of the general conditions of labour in all under-developed countries; the men are unskilled, work for short periods, and present themselves in large numbers for employment.[2] Because of their lack of skills, and the fact that they are considered to have land to provide for their subsistence, their labour is cheap; thus it is difficult for a man to settle in the towns. He can do this only when he is given a house and a wage that can keep his wife and family as well as himself, and provide his children with clothes, education, etc. Mambwe rights to the use of land are their final security; they may be expelled from any job in the towns, but not from the land. The land is always present in their minds as a place of refuge. I have given a case above where a man from Kasunga village was quite unsuccessful in the town, and applied to his father's brother for the fare to bring him home (cf. p. 119). Without this security he would have

---

[1] I found it impossible to arrive at any accurate estimate of the percentage of Mambwe who had become permanently stabilized in the towns, i.e. those men who had abandoned the tribal area for ever to live permanently in towns and bring up their children there. Permanent stabilization could be estimated only after the men had died. A man may live for ten to fifteen years in a town and even then return to the tribal area.

[2] Cf. Redford, op. cit., and Lewis, *The Theory of Economic Growth.*

been destitute. The possession of land gives the Mambwe a certain independence, and prevents the unrestricted exploitation of their labour. At the same time, the possession of land helps to keep their wages low, and militates against their developing quickly into workers entirely dependent on their wages to live. Low wages, lack of social insurance and pensions, competition for jobs, the fluctuations of industrial production, the unpredictability of Europeans in Mambwe eyes, the fear of strangers[1] —all these render the industrial situation one of insecurity and anxiety to the Mambwe, as well as a source of material goods and new experiences. In the tribal area a Mambwe can depend on a wide circle of kin to provide aid and subsistence in the event of illness, accident, or old age. The forms of personal dependence are an inseparable part of the subsistence economy. The Mambwe are aware of the dangers of the town; when a man is old or sick, he is discarded. If he has no relatives to help him, what can he do? In the town he is isolated. In Chief Mpande's village there was an old man without a family who had returned in 1952 from Southern Rhodesia, where he had lived since 1905, when he left the area with a European who had taken him away as his servant. He had no living brothers or sons to help him; all his immediate kin had died, and he was too old and sick to work alone in the fields. He appealed to the chief for aid, claiming a remote connection with the chief's mother, and was given an old kitchen to live in. People helped him with scraps of food to eke out the allowance that the chief made him. When I asked some young fellows returning to work on the Copperbelt after a holiday in the village if they intended to stay away, as they were so well-dressed and prosperous and had quite evidently done well there, they pointed to this old man. Their leader, a son of Chief Mpande, an intelligent man of thirty-five, a former sergeant who

---

[1] The Mambwe credit strangers with a special knowledge of sorcery; they are potentially dangerous, not only because they may do a man some immediate physical harm, but also because they may have magic which cannot be turned away. Strangers are always dangerous, and particularly so when a man is far from home and away from the supervision of his ancestors and his own protective medicines. Few Mambwe have foreign wives, apart from some Bemba wives among the people of Chief Mpande's district who have a border with the Bemba, and some from the Inamwanga and Lungu peoples, to whom the Mambwe consider themselves akin.

PLATE IV

An Administrative Chief

Royal Chief Mpande with his son. Chief Mpande is holding a pith helmet, the symbol of his authority as an administrative chief. Chief Mpande's son was on holiday from his job on the Copperbelt. Their relative prosperity is evident from their dress.

had fought against the Japanese, and at present an official in the
underground police of one of the copper mines, said: 'That is
what the Europeans do to you if you stay away too long in their
towns; the town is good, but the village is better.' The old man
was a living warning that real security for a Mambwe lay not
with the Europeans, but among his own people, in the network
of social relationships that we call the tribal system.

In addition to this economic uncertainty, there are psychological
reasons that make a man prefer to come home. In the town he is
an exile, parted from his relatives. He may be able to have his
wife with him for a time, and I have recorded cases where two
or three brothers working in the same town have brought their
widowed mother to live with them there; but this is done at the
expense of the goods which the money for their dependants'
upkeep would otherwise have bought. The atmosphere of the
towns is always alien. The whole group is isolated among
strangers, with different habits and morals, and though stimulating
for a time, this does not provide those spiritual satisfactions to
which they have been conditioned since childhood. When a
Mambwe goes to the towns he exchanges the accepted tribal
discipline of his chief and seniors for the arbitrary and, to him,
unpredictable restraints of police and officials. The familiar morality of his own people is replaced by the confused morality that
results from the conditions of native locations.[1] The unfamiliar
laws and edicts of the Europeans are a constant restraint on his
behaviour; tribal discipline is a harness which fits easily: to the
Mambwe it is freedom. In town, he suffers from the nostalgia
for home and familiar faces that troubles all exiles, whether Black
or White.

The Mambwe attempt to overcome the isolation and difficulties of town life by supporting one another in the industrial
situation, and by operating kinship ties. Brother follows brother
to the same place; members of the same village tend to group

---

[1] Social control in towns is not entirely a matter of police officials and European laws. Quite a substantial field of behaviour is governed by accepted norms
on the Copperbelt, and these are enforced by the Urban Courts. See Epstein,
Juridical Techniques and the Judicial Process. However, a Mambwe still finds the
situation in the towns perplexing, for he lacks an accepted means of defining
some social situations there, whereas in tribal society he knows quite clearly
what behaviour is expected from him in different situations.

together. In 1952 there were approximately 2,500 Mambwe work-ing out of the tribal area; a considerable proportion of these were said to be in one town, Mufulira.[1] Although the Europeans may regard all wage-earners indiscriminately as Africans, the Mambwe cling fiercely to their tribal identity, and refuse to lose it.[2] The tribal emphasis within the unstable industrial system is an implicit statement of a Mambwe's economic and social stability, an assertion of his unique rights and duties as a Mambwe. His work for wages has taught him that his most important security is the land: he has no insurance, pension, or other social security, apart from the land. The tribe and the chief are closely identified, and the increasing knowledge and experience of the Mambwe has given the chief a new value, as the symbol of their traditional collective rights in opposition to the Europeans. The Mambwe are beginning to grasp the methods and policies of the Europeans, formerly so mysterious and obscure, and to fear them. The history of South Africa and other countries where great areas of African land have been alienated, apparently for ever, is well known to them, and this knowledge is an important element in their enhanced loyalty to the chief.

The sporadic character of industrial development in Northern Rhodesia, its concentration on the Copperbelt and its rapid growth in production, the mobility of the population, the influ-ence of the large industrial centres—all these have brought about a profound change in the very character of Africans. The Mambwe are now industrial wage-earners with distant allotments. They bring back from work a new awareness of the tribe's significance in the world as a whole and a new set of ideas drawn from their industrial experiences.

---

[1] The Mambwe tribal representative informed Chief Nsokolo during his visit to the Copperbelt that there were 1,100 Mambwe in Mufulira. This number is probably exaggerated, and certainly includes wives and children. However, Mufulira is popular with Mambwe workers.

[2] Cf. Mitchell, *The Kalela Dance*, p. 29, 'The evidence seems to suggest that casual interaction among Africans on the Copperbelt is essentially determined by membership of a tribe'. This analysis of social relationships among urban Africans illuminates the whole question of the significance of tribal ties within the industrial system.

New Religious and Economic Groups

Of all the new ideas brought back to the tribal area, only one has so far seriously challenged the authority of the chief: the religious movement of the Watch Tower Bible and Tract Society, commonly known as Jehovah's Witnesses. This fundamentalist sect originated in the United States of America in the latter half of the nineteenth century, and from there spread all over the world.[1] It now has a considerable following throughout the whole of Africa. A White official from the headquarters of the organization in America came to a meeting in Kitwe in January 1953 which was attended by over 20,000 African delegates from both Northern and Southern Rhodesia.[2]

The Watch Tower Society is a millenarian movement which preaches that God's kingdom was born in 1914, that Armageddon is now actually in process, and that the earthly rule of princes and governments is drawing to a close, to be replaced by heavenly rule in the immediate future. The faithful are divided into two groups: the Heavenly, who number exactly 144,000, and whose ranks are now almost completely filled, and the believers. On the Day of Judgement that heralds the destruction of earthly kingdoms and the advent of the heavenly kingdom, only the Heavenly and believers will be spared; the remainder of mankind will be condemned. They believe that the Lord is guiding His people to a united work and faith, and that this can be brought about only by an international organization, teaching the scriptures, and performing the Lord's commands under His direction, this being made manifest by the Society, which He has appointed to supervise the work on earth in an executive capacity. Pastors are not appointed, but each company has a Chairman and a Secretary. The affairs of the Society in Northern Rhodesia are now conducted by a White American.

⁀The Society emphasizes the futility of earthly rulers in the face of the shortly-coming kingdom, and this belief has led them into clashes with established authority at different times in their history. During the 1939–45 War, Witnesses were gaoled in Britain, America, and Germany, for refusing to take up arms. After the 1914–18 War, the Society issued a tract, *Millions Now*

---

[1] Stroup, *The Jehovah's Witnesses*.
[2] Press report, *Central African Post*, January 1953.

Living Will Never Die, which had an enormous sale all over the world. This pamphlet stated that the 1914–18 War was Armageddon, that the end of the world was near, and that when it came, those believers who were lame, blind, or sick would be made whole, and that no person now living would see death if he believed, for the heavenly kingdom would come in their lifetimes. During the 1920s the Society, acting on this belief, was in a militant phase. Neither at that time, nor since, has it hesitated to claim an authority surpassing that of earthly rulers.

This movement was brought to the Mambwe by a labour migrant, Anok (Enoch) Simpungwe. Anok worked for a time at the Wankie Colliery in Southern Rhodesia during the 1914–18 War, and returned to the Mambwe Reserve in 1917. He had been converted to the Society's beliefs while working at the colliery. Anok was a man of parts, who had been educated at the London Missionary Society school, and for a time had been employed by the missionaries as an evangelist and teacher. He settled in his own village of Tukamolozya, in Chief Kela's area, and set about converting others to his new beliefs. He achieved some success, and was joined by other ex-labourers who also had become Witnesses while away. Tukamolozya village became known as 'Zion' to the Witnesses. The headman grew weary of Anok's increasing activities and complained to Chief Kela. Anok appealed to Chief Mwamba, who gave him permission to form his own village, which he and his followers built in Mwamba's area. The new village was called Galilee, and Anok was recognized as headman. Anok established a church organization within the village, with himself as pastor and other men as deacons and elders.[1] They did not drink beer or dance, and they forbade polygyny and divorce. If a man quarrelled with his wife, the case was heard by the other members of the community, who could suspend the errant party. Suspension implied exclusion from the company's meetings for a prescribed number of days. They cultivated

---

[1] The history of this movement among the Mambwe was obtained both from District records and from the files of the first and subsequent companies of the Society in the Mambwe area. The original company included many former evangelists and clerks, and they kept files in the manner of the Government offices, with copies of letters received and sent, etc. There is therefore a full written history of the movement among the Mambwe, in considerable detail. I also interviewed men who belonged to the original company.

their fields in the ordinary way. They refused to shake hands with people who were not members of the Society, although they greeted these by clapping hands. They also shaved their heads except for a tuft in front (*kasumpa*), as a mark of their conversion. The bans on dancing, drinking, and shaking hands are still maintained by present-day Witnesses. With Galilee as their centre, they attempted to convert the people of other nearby villages, and sent men to read the Bible and Society pamphlets to any who would listen. This they still do, and Witnesses are often to be seen reading out of their books to a little group of Mambwe.

Anok built up such a following that he finally alarmed both chiefs and Administration. The Witnesses did not refuse to pay taxes, but they did refuse to give tribute labour to the chief. When a British official visited their village, or called on them to attend his office, it was their habit to refuse to come at first, and wait until they had been ordered several times before obeying. They believed that earthly government was almost over and that the Kingdom was near. In 1922 several of the Witnesses were arrested, including Anok. The British Magistrate ordered them to cease their propaganda and threatened those who refused with three months in gaol. Some held fast to their faith and went to gaol. The backsliders were given a beating and released. This official action somewhat diminished Anok's authority, and on his release from gaol he was allowed to return to Galilee.

They lived in relative peace for some years after this, but in 1937 there was more trouble. This time the Witnesses were divided among themselves. Anok had broken the rules of the Society by announcing himself pastor and appointing others to be deacons and elders, all such appointments being anathema to the Society. He evidently based his organization on that of the London Missionary Society which had trained and employed him as an evangelist. Anok did not practise the beliefs of the Society; he had in fact founded a new sect, with himself in charge. A White official had arrived in Northern Rhodesia from America to put the Society in order. Anok quarrelled both with the American supervisor of the Society and with his own followers. Finally, an African came from headquarters to stay in Galilee for a month and report on Anok's conduct of affairs. This report was unfavourable to Anok. The inspector said that Anok had embezzled funds raised to purchase a bicycle to be used for collecting the Society's literature from the post office in Abercorn and a gramophone on which recorded sermons and talks were played to converts. He had also made unauthorized collections of money. While the investigator was on his way back to Lusaka, Anok forestalled his report by accusing him by letter of having committed adultery with a wife of a man in the company. This accusation was not accepted at headquarters, and the Society decided to expel Anok. The company broke into two groups, for and against Anok.

While the company dealt with these matters, the Administration once more moved against the Witnesses. The American supervisor had visited the Mambwe and Lungu the previous year, and had reported adversely on Anok to the Administration. The District Officer visited Galilee in 1939, and some of Anok's people complained about his rule, and said they were tired of his headmanship. The District Commissioner and Chief Nsokolo themselves visited the village, and ordered the people to disperse and the village to be burned. Anok knew of these moves against him: his father's brother was the head messenger. He approached Chief Mwamba for permission to build a brick house, and proposed to marry Linile, a woman of Mwamba's family. Permission was granted, and Anok built his brick house near a village of Chief Mwamba's brother, and married the royal woman. It is clear from these moves that Anok had decided that the Society was finished with him and that he wished to establish himself with Chief Mwamba. This polygynous marriage finally disrupted the company. Some of them followed Anok to his new village. Chief Mwamba brought pressure on a royal headman, Aron, to take in some of the genuine Witnesses who had broken their connection with Anok, and the remainder were allowed to form a new village, with a Witness of the royal clan as headman. This village is now the largest within the Mwamba chieftaincy.

The Watch Tower Society at that time provided a religious field within which Africans could feel responsible for both organization and conversions. Anok was converted by a fellow labourer in 1917 when the Society's affairs were conducted from an office in Cape Town. A White supervisor was not appointed to Northern Rhodesia until 1936. This period of twenty years was long enough to allow many of the local companies to develop their own idiosyncratic beliefs and organization. Converts often used the name of the Society without any real understanding of its beliefs and purposes. Nevertheless, the Society is a strongly centralized authoritarian movement, and both dogma and orders are dictated from above. When the White supervisor did arrive in Northern Rhodesia, he at once set about protecting the name of the Society by checking all the local companies who called themselves Witnesses. As a result of this inspection many companies seceded from the genuine Watch Tower Society but continued to call themselves Jehovah's Witnesses. Other companies, such as Anok's, were completely repudiated by the Society.

The Watch Tower movement in its initial phase in Central Africa, immediately after the 1914–18 War, was subversive of all constituted authority. Although the Society was not ostensibly a political movement, its denial of the validity of earthly rulers and its refusal to recognize their authority inevitably gave it a political role, for their beliefs struck at the very foundation of the concepts of all established authority. Both chief and Administration alike regarded the Society with dislike, and in this they were joined by the Christian churches, who challenged its claim to be the sole instrument of the Lord's work on earth. The opposition of Whites to the Society gave it a further value in African eyes.

The Witnesses challenged the chief's authority by refusing him tribute labour. They also tried their own cases as far as they could, another blow at the chief's prerogative. Witnesses did not absolutely refuse to obey the British, but were tardy and uncooperative. When the expected heavenly rule failed to materialize, and the Witnesses were subjected to prosecution by both chiefs and British, the movement degenerated into another dissident Christian sect.

The chiefs were quick to see that the Witnesses were undermining their authority, and did not hesitate to call in the British to break up the community. Chief Nsokolo himself came with the British officers to see that Galilee was burned down, although it was not in his own chieftaincy. Nsokolo had refused to allow Witnesses to teach in his area from the very beginning of the movement, and they were never able to gain a foothold there. Nsokolo was supported in this policy by the White Fathers, who also did not like the movement. The power of the chiefs was asserted when Galilee was burned down and the Witnesses forced

P

to seek other villages to accept them. Many headmen would not take them, fearing both the displeasure of the chiefs and the trouble that the Witnesses caused, and without the acceptance of a headman, no Mambwe can find land to cultivate. This was the real weakness of the Witness community. They could not live side-by-side with traditional communities and yet keep themselves wholly apart. In the last analysis they were dependent on the chief for rights to the use of land, and an attitude of disobedience to the chief would in the long run have resulted in the denial of the use of land.

By 1939, when Galilee was destroyed, the original subversive impulse was spent. The Society in Northern Rhodesia had been reorganized by the American supervisor in Lusaka, who brought the true Witnesses firmly under central control, regularized their dogma and services, and repudiated the dissidents.

Anok had called his company Jehovah's Witnesses although he had by no means obeyed the instructions of the Society. He had in fact founded a new church with himself at the head. Anok had status and authority as the leader of his group which he could never have achieved within an established European religious organization. As headman of a village he had political authority and presided over the courts within his village. Anok founded an organization that was independent of chiefs, Administration, and missionaries alike. He sought for personal prestige and power within a sphere of his own creation, by exploiting the ideas he had absorbed as a migrant labourer, whether through genuine conversion or not, and combining these with his knowledge of church organization. He clashed with the Administration first; later, when the number of his converts grew and his power increased, he clashed with the chiefs. In his attempt to set up a system outside the traditional political system Anok challenged the authority of the chief and the challenge failed. The chiefs won, and the new forces that Anok represented were diverted into the traditional political channels. Anok admitted his defeat when he accepted the authority of the headman of the royal clan and married the chief's sister. These actions at once broke the original company into two: Anok and his personal followers, and those others who agreed to adhere strictly to the Society but to accept the rule of royal headmen. The Witnesses remain strong in Mwamba's area, in which they first established themselves, and they now have four villages there, almost entirely populated by Witnesses. Three of these have headmen of the royal clan. These royal headmen depend for their positions on their kinship relationships with the chief; thus, the integration of these communities into the existing system, and their loyalty to the chief, is guaranteed.

The existence of separate communities outside the traditional Mambwe social organization demands that they should have land, to provide their subsistence.[1] Land cannot be acquired for either subsistence cultivation or cash farming other than through the chief, and this gives the chief a powerful weapon when combating the challenge of new classes of men who might emerge to threaten his authority. Apart from the Witnesses, the most important of these potential new classes are the traders and individual farmers.

In the old days the chief was the banker of the whole community and enjoyed a monopoly of trade: today commoners can acquire and use their own capital. Some men are able to earn higher wages than others, because they have acquired skills such as driving and repairing cars, carpentry, and reading and writing English well. Such men can save enough money from their higher wages to invest capital in small businesses, which, among the Mambwe, are almost wholly trading concerns. A licence to trade must be approved and paid for, and this entitles a man to stock up with goods and go into business. There are a large number of these small traders or peddlers among the Mambwe, ranging from a man with a few goods that he has brought back from the Copperbelt and wishes to sell, to proper shopkeepers. Every other village has such a trader, for the Mambwe see in trading the high road to wealth, although most of them go to the wall, and only a few manage to make money. I found nineteen men in Chief Mwamba's area, which had twenty-seven villages, who had taken out traders' licences, but only seven of these had invested a capital of more than ten pounds.[2] Many of them had a

---

[1] Sundkler, *Bantu Prophets in South Africa*, p. 33 et passim, stresses this point in his study of the Separatist Church Movements in South Africa.

[2] I was unable to make an exact inventory of the stocks held by these men. The Mambwe are normally secretive about money and property, and were particularly suspicious of questions about land and property throughout this

licence, but no stock, and only two of them had buildings used solely as stores. Nine of them had brick houses, and used a room in the house as a store. In Kasunga village the headman's sister's son, Adam Sikaombwe, carried on a trader's business from his brick house, but in a desultory way: his stock when I saw it consisted of a few rolls of cloth, some neckties and shirts, and a few pots and pans. Sikaombwe had brought back a stock of goods from the Copperbelt, bought out of his earnings as a carpenter, but this was almost dissipated and had not been replenished. Like many other petty village traders, Sikaombwe had a brick house, a plough, a gun, a bicycle, and several suits of clothes, and all these had absorbed part of his original capital.

There are no Indian traders within the reserves, and only one in Abercorn, so a Mambwe who sets up as a trader must compete with the established European concerns: few Mambwe can acquire sufficient capital to compete successfully on this scale. There are three large stores within the Mambwe reserves, one in each chieftaincy, which all stock a wide range of goods. Two of these are owned by a British trading concern which has branches all over Central Africa. The other is owned by a member of the royal clan, Adam Frog (Sichula), an exceptionally able and experienced man. Each of the three administrative chieftaincies has one of these large stores sited within it.[1] The two European stores serve the people of Chiefs Nsokolo and Mwamba, and Adam Frog's store serves the people of Chief Mpande. Chief Nsokolo's village, within which the European store is sited, is the furthest from Abercorn, and employs two African storekeepers. None of Chief Mwamba's villages is more than thirty-five miles from Abercorn, and the European store in his area is sited half-way between Mwamba's village and Abercorn. This store employs one storekeeper. Chief Mpande's village is fifty-seven miles from Abercorn, and the steep road to it is very bad. Many of the other villages in Mpande's area are even further away. Adam Frog built his store on the road to Mpande's village, about thirty-five miles from Abercorn, and this site saves Mpande's people from going either to the European store in Nsokolo's

period because of the general agitation about Federation. I considered it inadvisable to enquire too closely about money matters, as my purpose might have been misunderstood.

[1] Sites for stores are controlled by law. See p. 19.

village or to the European stores in Abercorn. He also keeps a subsidiary store in Chief Mpande's village, in which he employs an African storekeeper, thus strengthening his grasp on the trade in this area. Adam also acts as agent for a European trader in Abercorn. None of the other Mambwe traders have such a large stock as Adam Frog or the two European stores, and therefore cannot offer the same variety or choice to their customers.

Adam Frog's success is based on his own ability, his wide experience of European ways, and his status as a member of the royal clan. He spent twenty years on the Copperbelt, where he had an important post in the Municipal Location Superintendent's office, besides engaging in trade. There he was an African of some local eminence, a member of the Tribal Elders' domestic court,[1] and well known to Europeans as well as to his own tribesmen and other Africans. Adam retired to Chief Mpande's area, and built a brick house and store, and later built another store in Chief Mpande's village. He also employs men to work for him in his fields.

In competition with these enterprises, the small Mambwe traders have only one apparent advantage: they can give credit. None of the large stores—including that of Adam Frog, who thoroughly understands his business—give credit; they deal only in cash. The small trader gets no real advantage through giving credit, however, for he has many bad debts and often has to wait a long time for repayment of other debts. As he usually lives in a village among his kin, he finds difficulty in refusing their continual demands and eventually may dissipate his stock among a group of debtors who are in no position to pay him back when he needs cash, and who resent his pressing them. This was the situation of Adam Sikaombwe in Kasunga village. Adam had given goods on credit to many of the Kasunga villagers, and he told me that he was tired of the business and intended to give it up. The successful traders are generally those who move away from their own immediate kin and build brick houses in distant villages.[2]

All of the seven traders who operated on a small scale in Chief Mwamba's area had ploughs and cultivated fields for their

---

[1] See Epstein, *The Administration of Justice and the Urban African*, pp. 6 ff.

[2] Cf. the Tonga smallholders and farmers in Allan, et al., *Land Holding and Land Usage*, pp. 178 ff.

subsistence. Trading was an additional activity. But their capital and profits, small as they are, raise their standard of living above that of the ordinary villager. In addition, although they have debtors who take a long time to pay, this gives them followers, for the debtors are under an obligation. Thus, even when his stock is expended, the small trader always has a number of men attached to him by debt.

Mambwe cannot farm on a European scale, nor make substantial profits, even when they have ploughs, harrows, and carts. They cannot get land except through the chief; they require capital for the more elaborate productive tools—ploughs, oxen, carts, etc., and to employ men to labour for them; the soil itself is poor and needs fertilizers to improve yields. The distance of the Mambwe area from suitable markets is an almost insurmountable obstacle to successful cash farming, as the Europeans have found. A few specialized crops can be grown profitably, of which coffee is the most important. But coffee is a crop which requires skill and labour to produce profitably in this area, although the quality of the local variety is good.

Few Mambwe can enrich themselves, therefore, either by trading or farming. But by pursuing both occupations at the same time a Mambwe can make some money. The Administration buys grain to store in Abercorn against years of drought and to feed the permanent population. One European trader takes lorry-loads of grain to the Copperbelt: he buys this grain through Adam Frog. Again this market is limited, as the trader has only two lorries, with which he makes two runs a month. The trade in fish from Lake Tanganyika, which is very lucrative, is in the hands of the Lungu, who come round Mambwe villages on bicycles. All these factors have inhibited the development of a class of peasant farmers and traders within the Mambwe reserve, but nevertheless some exist. One thing that is quickly learned by all Mambwe in the towns is that labouring is the hardest way to earn money. Many men return from wage-labour with an ambition to engage in trade, but their lack of capital and the limitation of the local market combine to create a high casualty rate among them.

With a limited market and constant competition, the trader-farmer is obliged to seek every method of securing his position that is available to him. He must have the goodwill of the chief, and the wider his range of contacts with other Mambwe, the more likely is he to be successful. Most traders who have made any success at all are also involved in Mambwe politics, which gives them both power and prestige. Adam Frog, the most successful of all, knows many Mambwe well through his long period of service on the Copperbelt, where he was appointed by the chief to look after Mambwe interests. Adam is held in high respect and many Mambwe owe him obligations for help when they worked on the Copperbelt.

Four of the other seven relatively successful farmer-traders within Chief Mwamba's area were well known to me. One of them, Eliot Simusokwe, was a full-time councillor in the Native Authority, and engaged in trade on his necessary journeys through the area. Eliot also bought grain at harvest time for the Administration stocks. Many people spent the money he gave them for their grain on his goods. Eliot was in a powerful position to perform favours for people; his goodwill was valuable. He came originally from Tanganyika, and his brick house stands on its own, about two miles from the nearest village. He is an old man now, and limits his activities; but in addition to considerable interest among the Mambwe, he has acquired one of the largest herds of cattle in the area. Similarly, George Simukulwa, head-man of his own village,[1] was formerly an assessor at Chief Mwamba's court and married a sister of Mwamba. George made his career almost entirely within the Mambwe reserve. He is a man about sixty, and the missionaries trained him in his youth as a teacher and evangelist. George taught for a time in the mission school and thereafter lived in different villages to convert and encourage Christians, for which he received a salary. He began to trade as well and gradually built up some capital. He made only one trip out of the reserve to work, and found a job as a clerk. Eventually he became a court assessor, and built his brick house round which the village grew. By his energy, shrewd-ness, and political influence, George built up a good business as a trader, and educated two of his own sons at the school at Lunzuwa. One of these sons is now a Government clerk and the other a trader in the Abercorn Native Location. George supplied the capital for this business, and is therefore a sleeping partner.

---

[1] See p. 79 above.

George inherited three wives and their children from deceased brothers, and dissipated the remainder of his capital in providing marriage payments for his inherited sons. This was no loss, for he gained followers in return for the money. He lost his assessor's post through malpractices, so that today he is principally a headman who carries on a little trade on the side, and the main profit-making business is carried on in Abercorn by his son.

The other two traders whom I knew are Gibson Sinfukwe and Andrew Silupiya. Gibson is a former assessor at Chief Nsokolo's court, and was born in Nsokolo's area, but when he retired from the court he built his brick house near Chambanenje village in Chief Mwamba's area. This village moved its site, and hence Gibson's brick house now stands quite by itself, about four miles from the present village site. Gibson is a good farmer, one of the few Mambwe who use a plough and oxen: he learned to do this at the mission. He grows English potatoes and vegetables and sells them on the Abercorn market, and uses the money to buy cloth and beads and various other small articles to trade round the villages. His brick house and surrounding gardens are very well kept, and have a European appearance. Andrew Silupiya lived in Luembe village and I have already described his career (see p. 133). Andrew is a Lungu, but married two wives from the Mambwe royal clan, and resides in Chief Mwamba's area. He is ambitious to become the headman of Luembe village, and is likely to achieve this.

All of these successful traders, with the exception of Andrew Silupiya, have held political appointments; and all of them have wives of the royal clan. They are men of substance, able to perform favours for others. All of them have educated their sons. Eliot's eldest son is a Treasury clerk in Tanganyika; one son of George is a Government clerk and the other a trader in Abercorn; Gibson's son is in Standard V of the school at Lunzuwa; Andrew's sons are both clerks, one with the International Red Locust Control, the other with the Tanganyika Government at Mbeya. They are therefore attempting to perpetuate their own higher standards, for their sons earn higher wages than the average unskilled Mambwe, and will work for longer periods. They all read and write English well; they have all attended a mission school; they all live apart from their relatives or have tried to do so; they all have links with the royal clan; and three of them are either present or former officials of the Native Authority.

This group of successful farmer-traders is under considerable strain, for apart from the competition they face in a limited market they are suspected of being sorcerers. The Mambwe accuse all successful men of practising sorcery.[1] If one man's crops grow consistently better than those of his neighbours, the neighbours do not ascribe the better crops to better methods of cultivation but to sorcery. It is not ploughs, but medicines, that bring higher yields. All successful traders are said to 'know something'. They do not live like others: the spatial separation of their brick houses, which cannot be moved when the village moves, and their isolation from their relatives, besides their money, indicate their supernatural powers. They are not 'natural'. All of the above four men show signs of strain: they are touchy and quarrelsome, conscious of their power, and aware of the charges made against them. A certain aggressiveness of personality may be necessary for a man to emerge as a successful trader, but it may not be a coincidence that George Simukulwa had a mental breakdown and became violent in his village after a poisoning incident.[2] He was released after a month and sent home, but in March 1954 he was again admitted to the hospital in Abercorn and has been kept there. He appeared to be an intelligent but unstable individual.

The rivalry between members of this group of farmer-traders appeared in a most acute form in a conflict between George Simukulwa and Anok Simpungwe, the former leader of the Witnesses. The two men had known one another since the time when they both taught in the mission school. George resented Anok's spectacular success in making converts and winning adherents in the area in which he himself worked as an evangelist. Moreover, Anok too set up as a trader after his break with the Society, no doubt with the capital he acquired through his church, which caused the dispute between the company and the headquarters of the Society. Anok married Linile, a daughter of

---

[1] In this the Mambwe resemble their Bemba neighbours, for Richards, *Land, Labour, and Diet*, p. 215, reports of the Bemba: '. . . to be permanently much more prosperous than the rest of the village would almost certainly lead to accusations of sorcery.' Cf. also Krige, *The Realm of a Rain Queen*, p. 269; Hunter, *Reaction to Conquest*, p. 317; and Gluckman, 'Lozi Land Tenure', p. 37.

[2] I had to take him under restraint to hospital.

Chief Yasapa Mwamba's brother, and sister of Tailosi, the administrative chief, and began to trade in Mwamba's area. George was then an assessor at Chief Mwamba's court, and he seduced Linile, the royal wife of Anok. Anok brought an adultery suit against George and received eight pounds in damages. Anok divorced Linile; George married her, and paid one cow and £2 10s. in marriage payment to her parents. This happened in 1944, after the mission dismissed George for taking the wives of his deceased brothers. Anok complained to Linile's father after the divorce that he had paid two cows and £7 marriage payment for Linile, but had got only one daughter by the marriage. He demanded the return of part of the marriage payment. He proposed to leave the cash, but asked for one cow back, saying he would leave the other cow to 'nurse the child' (*caulezi*),[1] a recognized arrangement among the Mambwe.[2] When George heard of Anok's proposal, he told the woman's father to refuse to accept it, but to keep the marriage payment entire. George said that he would use his authority as an assessor to throw out Anok's case, if he sued in court for a return of part of the marriage payment. George reasoned that as Anok had one child by the marriage, a case could be made out that he was not entitled to the return of any part of the marriage payment. When the child grew up, George could then claim another beast for 'nursing'. The woman's father had agreed to Anok's proposal, which was reasonable and in accordance with Mambwe custom. But he allowed himself to be persuaded by George, knowing well that his argument was unsound, and trusting to George's power as assessor to bring everything about as George wished. Accordingly, the father told Anok that he would not return any of the marriage payment.

The case should have been heard in Chief Mwamba's court, as all the parties concerned lived within his chieftaincy. But Anok suspected that he would get little justice there, and said that when he brought the case, he would take it before Chief Nsokolo. George heard of this and wrote to Nsokolo. The contents of this

---

[1] From *ukulela*, to nurse.

[2] When this happens, the cow to 'nurse the child' is regarded as payment to the divorced woman's new husband for rearing the child, and ensures that when the girl grows up and is married that the genitor's rights to share in the marriage payment are recognized. If this animal is not given, the new husband can claim the father's share of the marriage payment for the girl.

letter are obscure, but there is good reason to suppose that bribery was involved; naturally none of the parties will admit this. Nsokolo returned George's letter with a few lines from himself saying that he had taken note of George's wishes. This letter fell into Anok's hands. He did nothing with it for a time, and went on a visit to some of his followers in Abercorn. When he returned to his brick house, he fell ill. Because of his religious activities, he feared the Whites, and would not go to the hospital in Abercorn. He went to stay in the village of the Lungu paramount chief, Tafuna, where some of his followers lived. He was three days there, but showed no improvement, and his followers persuaded him to leave, saying that his enemies were poisoning him. They took him to another Lungu village and there he died. He had been sick for only five days. As soon as he died, some men came at night to his brick house, broke in, and tore up all his books and papers, and strewed them over the surrounding fields.

The conflict between George and Anok was known to all, and people blamed George for killing Anok by sorcery. The struggle between the two men was personal, economic, and political. They competed in the same fields, both in trade and religion, and they competed for the same royal wife.

The cash-economy introduced by the Europeans, and the Mambwe belief that trade is the quickest way to wealth, has created a group of farmer-traders. But the growth in wealth of this group is inhibited by the distance of the Mambwe area from the large industrial markets and the poverty of the soil, both of which have hindered the development of a local market of any size. None of the traders is substantially wealthier than the three administrative chiefs, although relatively wealthier than many of the traditional chiefs. Indeed, the administrative chiefs themselves use their salaries to become farmers and traders, or have set up relatives as traders. Chief Nsokolo has a farm on which he employs five men; this farm is supervised by one of his sons. Another son manages a store in Nsokolo village, but it has to compete there with the European store, and did not appear to be thriving. None of the traders employ men in large numbers; even Adam Frog employs only one storekeeper regularly, and farm labourers occasionally. The economic activities of the traders have

not developed on a scale large enough to bring them into politics
as a separate class, seeking the protection and furtherance of their
specific interests. All the commoner traders have attempted to
find a place as individuals within the indigenous political system.

The traders are in economic competition with the European
stores, and their lack of capital would soon drive them out of
business if they depended solely on their trading. But they are
able to farm as well as trade, and their subsistence cultivation
in effect subsidizes their trading. They are only able to compete
as traders because they also have land to farm. And their rights
to the use of land—even to grow the small surplus that can be
sold on the limited local market—derive from their membership
of the tribe. They depend on the existence of the Mambwe social
system for their present rights to the use of land, and thus are
dependent on the chief. As long as the small profits they earn are
linked to the present system of land distribution, the farmer-
traders bolster up the system, and support the chief.

The system of migrant labour links reserve and town together,
and gives the Mambwe a dual interest in the whole economic
system of Northern Rhodesia. The Mambwe spend part of their
lives as wage-earners in the industrial system, and part as subsistence cultivators in the reserve. As wage-earners, the Mambwe
have an interest in industry, and as cultivators they have an
interest in land. In the country they work for themselves; in
the towns they work for employers. Their dual interests in the
economic system are not opposed, but complementary. In the
industrial sphere, the Mambwe join with other Africans in organizations such as the Mine Workers' Trade Union, designed to
protect and further their interests as wage-earners.[1] Such organizations are still developing, and the African industrial worker has
not yet achieved the industrial and political representation typical
of the permanent town-dwellers in the industrial societies of
Europe.

Nevertheless, the industrial experiences of the Mambwe are
broadly similar to those of industrial workers elsewhere. There is a
conflict of interest between employers and employed. But in
Central Africa this conflict is complicated by the social and

---

[1] There were eight trade unions in Northern Rhodesia in 1950 with a
membership of 27,332. See *Labour Administration in the Colonial Territories*,
p. 15.

economic divisions between Europeans and Africans, for although the management of all the large companies is White, the workers are drawn from both Black and White groups.

When a Mambwe goes to the Copperbelt, he is exposed to a ferment of ideas that do not arise simply from his employment, but involve many other considerations. He experiences the colour bar and the superior economic position of the Whites within the system, even though many are wage-earners like himself. He learns that in other parts of Africa similar struggles are taking place, and that Africans have been treated harshly by the Whites. He is educated not only in labour relations, but also in political theories. His labour is largely unskilled, and it is difficult for him to acquire and practise skills that will enhance his earnings, and hence his standard of living. His employment is temporary, his rights to social insurance and pensions rudimentary, and his whole position insecure. He learns that his only real security is his traditional rights to the use of tribal land, which guarantees his subsistence and protects him from the vagaries of the industrial system.

THE POSITION OF THE CHIEF

The growing opposition of the Mambwe to the Whites, nurtured by their wage-labour experiences, is expressed in many forms. Mambwe joined the trade unions and took part in demonstrations against the colour bar and other restrictions on their activities. Many of them became members of the African Congress, an organization that claims to represent the interests of all Africans in the territory. In the reserve, the chief became the symbol of their unity in opposition to any further alienation of their land, and the spokesman of their demand for more land. Their growing political development was crystallized in their opposition to Federation, which was so marked that it was called 'Federation Fever'.[1] They opposed the Whites at the most significant points of contact between the two groups: the industrial workers went on strike; the African Congress leaders appealed to

---

[1] This term is used in official reports. The *Annual Report on African Affairs for the Northern Province, 1952*, p. 3, states that: 'The political consciousness of the African population has increased during the year in the widespread discussion of the Federation proposals.'

public opinion in Britain and attempted to influence the decisions of the House of Commons; the tribesmen defied agricultural and fishing regulations. Their dual interests forced the chief to collaborate with other political organizations based on the industrial sector of the economy.

Gluckman has analysed the increasing opposition to Whites in South Africa of the Zulu of Natal, and found it expressed in four main ways:[1]

(1) White innovations have been resisted and traditional customs revived;

(2) Opposition is expressed through dissident Zulu Christian churches;

(3) Zulu have joined organizations with other Bantu urban workers, e.g. trade unions;

(4) A heightened allegiance has developed to the chief, and especially to the Zulu king.

This analysis helps us to understand the difference between Black-White relations in South Africa and Northern Rhodesia. The Zulu resemble the Mambwe in some ways. They are both patrilineal, cattle-keeping peoples, and both are involved in an industrial system. They have reacted to White dominance in much the same way. But one important difference between them is that the Mambwe have not expressed their opposition to the Whites through the proliferation of dissident churches. Apart from the Watch Tower movement, which is opposed to chiefs and trade unions and Whites, the Mambwe appear to be disinterested in such organizations. Part of the reason for this, I believe, is to be found in the nature of the channels of opposition to the Whites. The Mambwe have expressed their opposition in three main ways.

First, they have striven to further their economic interests in the industrial sector by supporting the flourishing trade union movement.

Second, they have defended their interests in the land, the basis of their subsistence, through an enhanced loyalty to the senior chief, Nsokolo, and forced him into the political field in opposition to White interests.

---

[1] 'Analysis of a Social Situation in Modern Zululand', p. 165.

Third, they have further expressed their dual interest in the total economy of the Territory by supporting such urban organizations as the African Congress, and the African representatives on the Legislative Council.

Because of the different conditions in Northern Rhodesia, the Mambwe have been able to engage in an attempt to achieve direct political representation. The Zulu have been prevented from expressing their opposition to the Whites in the political field because of the attitude of Whites towards African political aspirations in South Africa. The Zulu came into armed conflict with the Whites generations ago and were defeated; the Mambwe have never had a trial of strength with the Whites. Many energetic Zulu find it difficult to play any active part in the political field, and turn to the dissident churches in which they can organize their followers and create positions of authority denied to them elsewhere.[1]

The Mambwe reached the peak of their overt opposition to the Whites in their resistance to the proposed Federal Constitution. They did not oppose Federation as such; but they demanded that they should be included in the new political structure. Their agitation was aimed at achieving political representation. The District Commissioner informed the Mambwe of the reasons that were held to necessitate the new political organization, and sought to allay their fears. The Governor of Northern Rhodesia toured the country and took every opportunity of explaining the proposed Federation to the Africans.[2] During this tour he visited Abercorn, and addressed the Mambwe chiefs. These assurances did not alleviate the Mambwe suspicion that the new Federation would be inimical to their interests unless they had a direct voice in the political deliberations. Many conferences were

---

[1] I am not here suggesting that there is a simple relationship between political repression and the proliferation of dissident sects. Deprived groups in many societies have tended to be attracted towards religious movements, and the connection between religious and political movements is complex. Cf. Sundkler, *Bantu Prophets in South Africa;* Gluckman, 'Analysis of a Social Situation in Modern Zululand'; Kuper, *The Uniform of Colour,* pp. 121 ff.; Hunter, *Reaction to Conquest,* pp. 560 ff.; Shepperson, 'The Politics of African Church Separatist Movements in British Central Africa, 1892–1916'.

[2] The Government issued a booklet to be used by Europeans in contact with Africans, setting out assurances that their land would not be touched under the new Federation.

held with African leaders, in London and elsewhere. The Africans were united across tribal rivalries in their opposition to the Whites, and the Mambwe followed the various discussions and conferences with great attention. In the reserve they gathered round wireless sets to hear the news, and discussed the articles in the newspapers. The subject was continually discussed, even in the most remote villages. The discussion and agitation concentrated all the feelings of distrust and animosity that the Mambwe felt for Whites, and gave their whole opposition to the Whites a political cast. They supported the African Congress, which acted as spokesman for African interests, and in 1952 the Mambwe subscribed the sum of £150 for Congress funds. This money was collected in small sums from villagers, and is a material illustration of the strength of their interest and feelings.

Chief Nsokolo took the money to a meeting called by Congress in Lusaka in September 1952, which was attended by the majority of the Northern Rhodesian chiefs. All of them had brought a subscription for the Congress funds. At this meeting the chiefs publicly stated their opposition to the Federation proposals. A committee of chiefs was formed to support Congress in its activities against Federation, and Chief Nsokolo was elected to this committee. Mr. (later Earl) Attlee, the leader of the British Labour Party, then in Opposition, interviewed this committee, and heard their reasons for opposing Federation. Thus, for the first time, the Mambwe were brought into direct contact with the politics of the British Commonwealth as a whole.

The co-operation of chiefs and Congress represented the collaboration of the leaders of the Africans' dual interests in industry and land. Chief Nsokolo was exercising a new political role as representative of tribal interests in a wider political sphere.

When Nsokolo returned to the reserve he reported to a meeting of chiefs and elders. He gave an account of the money spent and the proceedings of the Lusaka conference. The Mambwe hoped that this opposition would put off Federation. The widespread discussion had educated the Mambwe, and they were now aware, in however confused a way, of their place in the economic and political sphere of Central Africa. They saw themselves and other tribes in opposition to the Whites as a group; they had acquired a new political consciousness.

These events coincided with the imposition of new agricultural regulations enforcing the digging of anti-erosion ditches in the Mambwe area. The Mambwe have never liked any interference with their agricultural practices, and now many refused to comply with these regulations. The Native Authority had approved and issued the regulations, but the Mambwe considered that these emanated directly from the Administration. Every action of the Administration at this time was regarded with the utmost suspicion. The Mambwe expressed their political opposition to Federation, which they considered was being foisted on them, by resisting these regulations. It is significant that these regulations concerned the land. The mood of the chiefs and elders at this meeting was angry and aggressive, and it was here that Nsokolo was told that he must oppose the new regulations.[1]

In February 1953, a son of Chief Nsokolo and one other man were arrested. They were charged with conspiring to incite the people to disobey the anti-erosion regulations issued by the Native Authority, and with telling the people that they would not be punished in the Native Courts if charged by the agricultural kapasos for refusing to dig ditches. The trial was held in Abercorn, and both men were found guilty and sentenced to eighteen months' imprisonment. Both were members of Congress. I attended the trial and the evidence was clear that Nsokolo's son had indeed gone round the villages instructing the people to defy the regulations.

Chief Nsokolo was suspended from his office for three months, because 'for the past five or six months, he has been openly encouraging his people to disregard Native Authority orders designed to promote agricultural and veterinary progress'.[2] Two

---

[1] See p. 177 above.

[2] Statement on the suspensions of three chiefs and the arrest of one, made to the Legislative Council of Northern Rhodesia by the Chief Secretary. See press report, *Central African Post*, 24th February 1953. Chief Kambwali was suspended for ordering his people to fish in defiance of the closed season regulations. Chief Milambo, an Aushi chief, disregarded certain laws concerning the Game Ordinance establishing a game reserve in his area, and told his people that the agricultural, forest, fish, and game staff would be turned out. Chief Kasoma followed Milambo's lead and was arrested on a charge of threatening Government servants with violence if they continued to perform their duties. The Chief Secretary stated that the chiefs had been making 'bombastic declarations', and that the Government would not tolerate any flouting of the law. He made an oblique reference to political purposes

councillors of the Native Authority and two assessors at Nsokolo's court were dismissed from their posts, and the functions of a Native Authority assumed by the District Commissioner. When the three months period of suspension had elapsed, Nsokolo was deposed, ordered to leave his village, and told to live in a village on the border of Chief Mpande's area. The wheel had gone full cycle; the Mambwe were now again under Direct Rule.[1]

Indirect Rule had augmented the power of Chief Nsokolo, for the appointment of three salaried administrative chiefs, with Nsokolo as the senior, had given him considerably more power and authority over the Mambwe than he had known in the past. This administrative system centralized authority among the Mambwe, and at the same time this authority had been given a new significance from beneath, as the Mambwe demanded that Chief Nsokolo should act as their representative in the total political field brought about by industrialization.

We have already seen that Nsokolo's position in the administrative structure was ambiguous: the agent of the Administration to the people, and the representative of the people to the Administration. He operated at the intersection of two different systems of interests and values, and, if he was to retain his post, he should have found some compromise acceptable to both sides.

The delicate poise of Nsokolo's position between his people and the Administration was disturbed by his new role as representative of the people in the wider political field that developed with the Federation proposals. Nsokolo attempted to represent his people in a conflict that embraced all the different political interests in the Territory—the industrial employers, the African and European trade unions and political parties, the White settlers, and the Administration itself. He made direct contact with political forces that formerly would have dealt with him and

---

in these disturbances: 'The misguided men who have been suspended, and any other persons who may have been influenced by them, will realize now, I trust, that the Government will not tolerate flouting of the law and will deal firmly with any contravention of it.'

[1] After a period of direct rule by the District Commissioner, a son of a previous Nsokolo was appointed to the position, and the Native Authority reformed and restored. This man was the logical successor to the title, for he was a son of a previous Nsokolo, born after his father had succeeded. He was an agricultural assistant employed by the Administration.

his people only through the Administration.[1] This new political role was not in opposition to those of the trade union and Congress leaders, but was complementary; Nsokolo represented Mambwe land interests, while the others represented industrial and urban interests. But this new role was incompatible with his function as an agent of the Administration. As a political representative demanding a new political structure, Nsokolo operated on a political level denied to the District Commissioner. The senior members of the Government of Northern Rhodesia are its political representatives: the District Commissioner is not in direct contact with the representatives of Black and White political interests. The Governor is; and it is through him that the District Commissioner expresses his official views. Nsokolo's political activities outside the reserve explicitly supported the strike action taken by Africans in the industrial field as a protest against Federation. The defiance of agricultural regulations within the reserve was complementary to the strike action, and Nsokolo, encouraged by his people, supported this too. Industrial strikes and agricultural defiance were the two final sanctions that Africans could employ against the Whites, and both were political actions. The people forced Nsokolo to take action, as their representative. These activities outside the reserve by-passed Nsokolo's administrative superior, and if these activities had had a successful outcome, he would have been able to bring pressure on the District Commissioner. His activities were not successful, and he was deposed. This struggle is not yet ended, for the conflicts have not been resolved, and it is more than likely that the deposed Nsokolo, who is still chief in Mambwe eyes, will remain as the rallying-point for Mambwe tribalism in the future.

---

[1] He was not the only chief to do so. Citimukulu, the Bemba paramount chief, with other Northern Rhodesian and Nyasaland chiefs flew to England in an attempt to influence opinion there against the Federation proposals.

CHAPTER VII

CONCLUSION

BRITISH rule incorporated the Mambwe into a world-wide economic and political system, and changed their traditional mode of life. But the Mambwe were not entirely isolated before the British came; the natural highway between East and Central Africa passed through their country and thus exposed them to outside influence. They had defended themselves against the Lunda and Bemba, fought with and against the Ngoni, and traded with the Arabs. The Mambwe had adopted both goods and customs from the strangers who came their way, and from the moment that the British arrived, were willing to sell their labour in return for European goods and money.

Property had always played an important part in Mambwe life. In the old days they had flocks of sheep and goats as well as cattle. They were accustomed to the use of goods that could not be produced locally, and traded ivory, iron, and slaves to the Arabs, in exchange for cloth, beads, and guns. Thus British rule has not been the only agency of change; the process of Mambwe social life has been continuously modified from without. In recent times the missionaries arrived before the administrators, and deliberately set out to change Mambwe life and beliefs. Traders and farmers followed the missionaries, and were followed in turn by the industrial and mining companies. All these influenced Mambwe life, but perhaps the cash-economy itself has been the most important agency of change. As the Mambwe acquired money and substituted money for traditional media of exchange, almost every aspect of Mambwe life was affected. Money seems likely to affect them even more in the future. Before the Europeans came, rank and wealth were correlated: the chief acted as banker for his people, monopolized trade, and exacted tribute labour from his subjects. Today skilled men can earn money outside the subsistence economy and independently of the chief's influence. They invest this money in clothing and household goods, and, now that wages have risen, in better houses, ploughs, agricultural implements, and cattle. This increasing prosperity is relative to the former condition of their lives, for there are no wealthy Mambwe, as wealth is judged by Europeans. No Mambwe, chief or commoner, has yet managed to buy a motor-car, for example.[1] The money economy has certainly improved their material conditions, and the Mambwe are anxious that this improvement should continue. Their engagement in a system of industrial relations has added a new dimension to their lives. They take part in economic activities with the Whites, and they desire to take more part in political activities, for they are consciously working to free themselves from their poverty and backwardness, and to achieve social and political equality with Europeans.

However, the widespread use of items of European material culture has so far brought only superficial changes to tribal life. Although the Mambwe wear European clothes, read books, ride bicycles, and listen to the wireless, these changes have not yet seriously affected their kinship and political relationships. The bonds of kinship are still effective, even within the industrial sector, where kinsmen can assist one another in many ways. They tend to congregate in the same labour markets, and to take up similar work, and this association keeps their social ties in constant use.[2] They value the money and goods that they get from wage-labour, but realize that at present there is no final security for them in urban employment, and that real security lies only within the tribe. They have a very shrewd appreciation of the relative importance to themselves of town and country. The kinship ties continue to function within the new economic system because they are related to the land rights, and these are more important to the Mambwe than casual employment for wages. They do not divorce their land rights and obligations from other social rights

---

[1] This was written in 1954. Since then the successful trader Adam Frog has acquired a second-hand car. Citimukulu, the Bemba chief, bought a car in 1952.

[2] As a consequence, social and economic class differences between urban Africans tend to coincide with tribal differences. Thus Mitchell, *The Kalela Dance*, p. 16, states: '. . . the evidence from Northern Rhodesian towns suggests that frequently tribal and class categories coincide.' This observation is confirmed by McCulloch, *A Social Survey of the African Population of Livingstone*, p. 67: 'There were marked indications that the most skilled and better paid jobs were being done by members of specific tribes or groups of tribes. There was a tendency, in other words, for economic class to correspond with tribal group.'

and obligations, for land rights are part of their general status as tribesmen.[1]

Thus the money economy has not disrupted Mambwe subsistence production, although industrialization has brought so much money into the reserves;[2] indeed, at the present level of industrial wages, material gains from wage-labour depend on the support of the subsistence economy. The possession of tribal land is likely to retard any attempts to change the Mambwe from cultivators into full-time industrial workers. Such attempts may soon be made, for the system of migrant labour has been criticized as 'wasteful' of man-power. The Chairman of one of the largest mining trusts in Northern Rhodesia states that 'The old concept of rural inhabitants coming to the towns to work for shorter or longer periods and returning home for comparatively long intervals is a waste of man-power and an anachronism.'[3] However, the alternative to migrant labour is the creation of a settled African labour force in the urban areas, and this may take a long time, and will depend not only on events within Northern Rhodesia but also on events far outside its borders. For instance, the rate of economic development and the pace of European immigration are both factors which will affect the size and character of any permanent African proletariat. Furthermore, the present political relations between Africans and Europeans help to determine African attitudes towards permanent industrial employment. As long as the Mambwe have rights to the use of

---

[1] On this whole theme see Gluckman, 'Lozi Land Tenure', where he demonstrates that this holds true for all Bantu societies in southern Africa, and states, p. 39: 'In Bantu society, the rights of a subject to land are part of his political status.'

[2] I found it impossible to assess exactly how much the Mambwe are earning from wage-labour. If the average monthly earnings of absent labourers is estimated at £2, exclusive of free food and housing, the total earned in 1952 would be £4,814 a month. Not all of this comes back to the reserves; much of it is spent in the towns, but often on clothes and durable goods that are eventually brought back to the reserve. Between £5 and £20 is the usual sum brought home from the Copperbelt, although some bring more nowadays, for wages are constantly rising. The amounts brought back from Tanganyika are not so great. In 1953 the Native Treasury balance sheet showed a revenue of £3,004 1s. 1d., of which £1,169 7s. 3d. was income in the form of tax. Money is circulating in the reserves, therefore, and is more and more dominating social relations.

[3] Prain, 'The Stabilization of Labour in the Rhodesian Copper Belt', p. 308.

tribal land, they will cling to the land and their tribalism, for it offers a security they understand. Even in England, peasants who owned land outright were the last to be involved in the industrial system.[1] Chambers states that the cottage-owning population in England seems to have increased after enclosure, and that even the proletarianized labourers continued to remain on the soil in increasing numbers until late in the 1830s. The real flight from the countryside only began when improved farming techniques and railway transport caught up with farming practices and turned the former peasants into pure proletarians.[2] Similarly, only some radical change in the agricultural methods used by the Mambwe will alter their present attachment to the tribal system. The Mambwe have neither the capital nor the techniques to change their customary methods of cultivation, even if they wished to do so: and without these no great increase in production is possible. The customary methods of cultivation ensure at the moment that each family can sustain itself by subsistence production, but at the same time limit the possibility of increasing production. So far even the Europeans have failed to discover how to turn the poor Mambwe soils to greater economic advantage. If a suitable cash crop were introduced, communications improved, and capital for tools, fertilizers, seeds, etc., made available, the possibility of a more intensive use of the available soil would be created. Such specialized development of Mambwe land is not incompatible with the tribal system of land tenure,[3] and would probably be acceptable to the Mambwe, but so far no suitable cash crop has been discovered.[4] If, on the other hand, large-scale farming were introduced, to take advantage of modern

---

[1] Chambers, 'Enclosure and Labour Supply', p. 339, states that the peasant community of the Isle of Axholme, which did not suffer from enclosures, lasted for two generations after 1840, when the landlord villages began to show a steady decline. Chambers quotes a contemporary as describing these people as living worse than the occupants of the poor house, and that they worked like negroes, but 'all is made amends for by *possessing* land'.

[2] Ibid., p. 341 et passim.

[3] In Kenya, Tanganyika, and Uganda, some tribes have profitably cultivated cash crops on peasant small holdings, held under tribal systems of land tenure. For example, the Soga of Uganda have successfully adopted cotton as a cash crop, but their soil is sufficiently fertile to support populations of several hundreds per square mile. See Fallers, *Bantu Bureaucracy*, p. 51 et passim.

[4] The development of cattle ranching remains a possibility.

methods and equipment, the number of holdings would inevitably have to be reduced, thus disturbing the tribal system of land tenure. A few men, as we have seen, already use ploughs to cultivate land they hold under the tribal system of tenure. But the larger holdings that these men work are already resented by others, for the Mambwe population is increasing, and pressure on the available land is constantly growing.[1] Some of the younger Mambwe already discuss the need to acquire land by purchase, so that they can farm on a larger scale with more advanced European-type methods. But the Mambwe recognize that if land could be bought and sold the majority would be at a great disadvantage compared with those few men who had adequate capital. Moreover, they suspect that once land became a saleable commodity it would rapidly pass out of the hands of Africans into those of Europeans. Large-scale farming of Mambwe land would also require the simultaneous development of opportunities for the surplus population to settle permanently in the towns, and to earn wages large enough to support them there. But at the moment in the industrial labour markets the Africans experience discrimination and unequal treatment in comparison with White workers,[2] and their general attitude to Europeans is one of distrust.

---

[1] The pressure on land is not yet so great as to force the Mambwe authorities to limit the area that an individual may cultivate. However, the Citemene Control Scheme determines the number of blocks and size of each village area according to the type of woodland. But if the population continues to grow, some further control may be necessary in the near future. Such controls have already been introduced by tribal authorities in several places. In the Lundazi District, to the south-east of the Mambwe, one Angoni chief, according to Trapnell, *Soils, Vegetation and Agriculture of North-Eastern Rhodesia*, p. 101, has forbidden cultivation of coppice of under eight years growth, and has attempted to restrict the acreage of new gardens. In South Africa some tribes have introduced restrictions on the use and retention of land (Cf. Schapera, *Native Land Tenure in Bechuanaland Protectorate*, and Sheddick, *Land Tenure in Basutoland*). The Basuto have restricted a married man to three fields. Gluckman discusses the development of laws to restrict the size of holdings among the Lozi, Zulu, Tswana, and others, in *Essays on Lozi Land and Royal Property*.

[2] An African underground worker in the copper mines earns from £4 10s. to £20 5s. a month, while a White worker earns £108 a month, and in addition gets a bonus based on the selling price of copper (*Annual Report, Northern Rhodesia*, 1952, p. 14). It is significant of the different scale of earnings that in this report, as in other official documents, African wages are expressed in shillings and European wages in pounds. While it is true that Africans are employed on different work, many of the White unskilled workers earn very high wages.

This insecurity in the urban areas has made their land even more significant to them, and any attempt to replace the tribal system of land tenure, however beneficial to production and to individual Mambwe farmers working for a profit, would be regarded with hostility by the Mambwe as a whole. They would certainly resist any policy aimed at compelling people to leave the land for the towns, and a permanent exodus would depend on an improvement in the status and opportunity offered to Africans in the industrial sector of the economy.

Apart from these purely economic factors, the Mambwe have other reasons for clinging to their land. They are peasants, brought up to country life, and they seem at the moment to prefer village life to town life. They would prefer to work locally for wages, if the labour market was large enough, and a policy that brought industry to the neighbourhood of Mambwe country would undoubtedly gain their support, and cut the rate of migration to the mining towns.

Mambwe participation in industry has not led to a breakdown in tribal life. Even the absence of large numbers of men has not meant less food for those left at home, owing to the lack of specialization in the work of men and women. Even when the proportion of women to men in a village is high, they are able to provide their own subsistence, although there is a limit to this disproportion. A connection undoubtedly exists between the number of women in a village and the maintenance of subsistence production; when the men are too few the women cannot carry on by themselves. Although few Mambwe women go out to work, most village women can claim the services of some man, either father, brother, son, or husband. Many of the younger men take their wives with them to their place of work for at least part of the time they are away, and many of the men who have retired from work have more than one wife. As we have seen, 28 per cent of the married men in the eight villages of my census were polygynists, and these were almost all over thirty years of age and retired from wage-labour or else working locally. These factors, together with high marriage payments and virilocal residence in marriage, have worked favourably to preserve Mambwe marriage and maintain the stability of village groups. The Mambwe say that the number of divorces has increased since men started to go out to work, but there are no comparative figures with the past. Whether divorce is on the increase or not, Mambwe village life is flourishing, and the number of villages increasing.

Whether industrialism will cause a tribal society to continue to cohere or to collapse depends on the interplay of a large number of factors: the internal system of organization and the solution of conflicts that arise within the tribe, the pressures of outside influences on these, the degree of participation in the industrial system, the political activities of the Whites, etc. The Mambwe have retained their cohesion and appear to be gaining materially from migrant labour, while the Bemba, on similar soils and with a lower population density, seem not to have gained, although they too have adhered to their tribal loyalties. Many of the Bemba villages already show signs of deterioration. In one Bemba district in 1952, 80 per cent of the male taxpayers were absent wage-earners, with consequent deterioration in the living conditions of the people left behind. Such a loss of men makes development of the reserves impossible, and even threatens the maintenance of subsistence production: 'Officers can exhort . . . but those listening are mostly the aged and women and children, and even these are joining their men away at work in increasing numbers.'[1]

The striking stability of Mambwe villages, which are the residential units of their society, raises the question whether patrilineal societies are better fitted than matrilineal societies to survive in conditions of rapid economic and social change. Read and Richards have both suggested that patrilineal peoples adjust themselves more readily than matrilineal peoples to the absence of large numbers of men. Read compares the patrilineal Nyasaland Ngoni with the matrilineal Cewa, and comes to the conclusion that the Ngoni show a far greater stability in family and village life and more care for the upbringing of children. Groups of brothers, or sons under a father, are more likely to hold together, in her opinion, than maternal uncles and sisters' sons.[2] The patrilineal Mambwe certainly show greater stability than the matrilineal Bemba, who are also equally engaged in wage-labour. The Bemba practise uxorilocal marriage, so that a man has no kin in his wife's village, and his interests lie in other

---

[1] *Annual Report, Northern Province, 1952*, p. 9.
[2] *Migrant Labour in Africa*, p. 625.

villages. Thus a Bemba polygynist with two wives experiences difficulty in keeping them both in the same village, unless they are sisters. One wife is bound through kinship to another village, and as these natal kinship bonds among the Bemba appear to be stronger than the marriage bond, the situation of the polygynist is one of tension and insecurity. Richards states that 'the Bemba woman relies very largely on the support of her family for her very strong position in married life.' The Bemba village is organized round a core of women, and men move from village to village.[1] This lack of residential stability of the Bemba male population, the high divorce rate, and their methods of shifting cultivation, were all suited to their former parasitic economy, for they found the food they did not grow themselves by raiding surrounding tribes. Bemba villages lack the permanence that has always marked Mambwe villages, and this has militated against them in the present situation. Many Mambwe men live and die in their natal villages, and the attachment of villages to definite estates encourages material investment in the village and thus enables the Mambwe to improve their condition. This Mambwe residential stability, based on traditional methods of land-holding and -usage, rather than their method of tracing descent, probably accounts for their present material prosperity. Profitable participation in the money economy depends on the mode of subsistence production, and its capacity to produce enough food in the absence of men. Even in matrilineal societies a father who acquires money and property increases his control over his sons, as opposed to the control exercised by his wife's brother. This change in authority was already evident in 1933 when Richards studied the Bemba,[2] and is even more marked today.[3] Property acquired through wage-labour tends to pass to sons, and not to other relatives, no matter how related, as we have seen among the Mambwe. Recent research in Central Africa seems to indicate that this development occurs within a number of matrilineal peoples in Northern Rhodesia, but exact comparison must await publication of other studies.[4]

---

[1] *Bemba Marriage and Present Economic Conditions*, p. 75 et passim.

[2] *Land, Labour, and Diet*, p. 116.

[3] Communication from Dr. A. L. Epstein.

[4] Communications from Dr. V. W. Turner and Miss E. M. Richardson, Research Officers of the Rhodes-Livingstone Institute, who studied the effects

Mambwe wage-earners keep in touch with their villages while they are away, and return to tribal life when they have earned the money they need. Young people soon settle down to village life, and resume their cultivation. With increasing years, a man's ambitions change. When he is young and newly-married, he seeks money, clothes, experience; when his children have grown up, he turns towards village life and the traditional methods of achieving status and prestige. These ambitions are bounded by the tribal system. Traditional leaders have not been replaced by new men, and indeed the Mambwe show a new and firm allegiance to the senior chief, Nsokolo. The Administration has encouraged this tribal cohesion by the system of Indirect Rule, described by one critic as 'government of illiterates, by illiterates, for illiterates'; he added that it is doubtful whether the 'effete and decadent chiefs could long maintain their traditional hold upon the people without the continued support of the British Power'.[1] This interpretation of the chief's role completely misrepresents the situation. The chief does not retain his traditional hold on the people only through a sentimental attachment, for it is related to a very real economic and social interest in the land. The chief expresses tribal solidarity in opposition to the Administration, and not in co-operation with it. The chief has been forced to become politically conscious in the wider field of Black-White relationships and to play a political role as representative of his people within this field. In Northern Rhodesia, industrialism has taught the Africans to place a high value on their land, and they look to the chief, who symbolizes their traditional social relationships, of which rights to the use of land are an integral part, to act for them and protect their interests.

The effects of industrialism and wage-labour on the Mambwe suggest that in the process of social change, a society will always tend to adjust to new conditions through its existing social institutions. These institutions will survive, but with new values, in a changed social system.

---

of wage-labour on various peoples: Dr. Epstein among the Bemba of Kasama District, Miss Richardson among the same people in Mpika District, and Dr. Turner among the Mwinilunga Lunda.

[1] Padmore, *Africa: Britain's Third Empire*, p. 128.

BIBLIOGRAPHY

A. *Works cited*

ALLAN, W., *Studies in African Land Usage in Northern Rhodesia* (Rhodes-Livingstone Papers No. 15). Cape Town: Oxford University Press, 1949.

—— (With GLUCKMAN, M., PETERS, D. U., and TRAPNELL, C. G.), *Land Holding and Land Usage Among the Plateau Tonga of Mazabuka District* (Rhodes-Livingstone Papers No. 14). Cape Town: Oxford University Press, 1948.

BARNES, J. A., *Marriage in a Changing Society* (Rhodes-Livingstone Papers No. 20). Cape Town: Oxford University Press, 1951.

—— *Politics in a Changing Society*. Cape Town: Oxford University Press, 1954. Transferred to Manchester University Press, 1958.

—— 'The Fort Jameson Ngoni', in *Seven Tribes of British Central Africa*, Colson, E., and Gluckman, M., eds. London: Oxford University Press, 1951.

—— (With GLUCKMAN, M., and MITCHELL, J. C.), 'The Village Headman in British Central Africa', *Africa*, xix (1949).

—— (With MITCHELL, J. C.), *The Lamba Village: Report of a Social Survey* (Communications from the School of African Studies, New Series No. 24). University of Cape Town, 1950.

BRELSFORD, W. V., *The Succession of Bemba Chiefs*. Lusaka: Government Printer, 1944.

CHAMBERS, J. D., 'Enclosure and Labour Supply in the Industrial Revolution', *Economic History Review*, v (1953).

COLONIAL OFFICE:
Labour Administration in the Colonial Territories 1944–50. London: H.M.S.O., 1951.

COLSON, E., 'The Role of Cattle Among the Plateau Tonga', Rhodes-Livingstone Journal No. xi (1951).

—— 'Possible Repercussions of the Right to Make Wills Upon the Plateau Tonga of Northern Rhodesia', *Journal of African Administration*, ii (1950).

—— 'Modern Political Organization of the Plateau Tonga', *African Studies*, vii (1948).

COXHEAD, J. C. C., *The Native Tribes of North-Eastern Rhodesia: Their Laws and Customs* (Occasional Papers, No. 5). London: Royal Anthropological Institute, 1914.

CUNNISON, I. G., *Kinship and Local Organization on the Luapula* (Rhodes-Livingstone Communication No. 5). Livingstone: Rhodes-Livingstone Institute, 1950.

—— *History on the Luapula* (Rhodes-Livingstone Papers No. 21). Cape Town: Oxford University Press, 1951.

—— 'Perpetual Kinship: A Political Institution of the Luapula Peoples', Rhodes-Livingstone Journal No. xx (1956).

CUNNISON, I. G., 'History and Genealogies in a Conquest State', *American Anthropologist*, xli (1957).

DECLE, L., *Three Years in Savage Africa*. London: Methuen, 1898.

DE KIEWIET, C. W., 'South Africa, Rhodesia, and the Protectorates', *Cambridge History of the British Empire*. Cambridge: Cambridge University Press, 1936.

DOKE, C. M., *Bantu—Modern Grammatical, Phonetical, and Lexicographical Studies since 1860*. London: Lund Humphries, 1945.

EPSTEIN, A. L., *The Administration of Justice and the Urban African: A Study of Urban Native Courts in Northern Rhodesia*. London: H.M.S.O., 1953.

—— *Juridical Techniques and the Judicial Process* (Rhodes-Livingstone Papers No. 23). Manchester: Manchester University Press, 1954.

—— *Politics in an Urban African Community*. Manchester: Manchester University Press, 1958.

EVANS-PRITCHARD, E. E., *The Nuer*. Oxford: Clarendon Press, 1940.

FALLERS, L. A., *Bantu Bureaucracy*. Cambridge: Heffer, 1956.

FORTES, M., *The Dynamics of Clanship Among the Tallensi*. London: Oxford University Press, 1945.

—— 'Culture Contact as a Dynamic Process', *Methods of Study of Culture Contact in Africa* (Memorandum XV). London: International African Institute, 1938.

FORTES, M., and EVANS-PRITCHARD, E. E., eds. *African Political Systems*. London: Oxford University Press, 1940.

GANN, L. H., 'The Northern Rhodesian Copper Industry and the World of Copper: 1923–1952, *Human Problems in British Central Africa*, Rhodes-Livingstone Journal No. xviii (1955).

GLUCKMAN, M., 'Analysis of a Social Situation in Modern Zululand', *Bantu Studies*, xiv (1940).

—— 'Lozi Land Tenure', *Essays on Lozi Land and Royal Property* (Rhodes-Livingstone Papers No. 10). Cape Town: Oxford University Press, 1943.

—— (With ALLAN, W., PETERS, D. U., and TRAPNELL, C. G.), *Land Holding and Land Usage Among the Plateau Tonga of Mazabuka District* (Rhodes-Livingstone Papers No. 14). Cape Town: Oxford University Press, 1948.

—— (With BARNES, J. A., and MITCHELL, J. C.), 'The Village Headman in British Central Africa, *Africa*, xix (1949).

—— 'The Lozi of Barotseland in North-Western Rhodesia', in *Seven Tribes of British Central Africa*, Colson, E., and Gluckman, M., eds. London: Oxford University Press, 1951.

—— *Rituals of Rebellion in South-East Africa*. Manchester: Manchester University Press, 1954.

—— *The Judicial Process Among the Barotse of Northern Rhodesia*. Manchester: Manchester University Press, 1955.

—— *Custom and Conflict in Africa*. Oxford: Blackwell, 1955.

—— 'Anthropology in Central Africa', *Journal of the Royal Society of Arts*, ciii (1955), and *Human Problems in British Central Africa*, Rhodes-Livingstone Journal No. xx (1956).

GOULDSBURY, C., and SHEANE, H., *The Great Plateau of Northern Rhodesia.* London: Edward Arnold, 1911.

GRAY, R. F., 'Positional Succession Among the Wambugwe', *Africa*, xxiii (1953).

GUTHRIE, M., *The Classification of the Bantu Languages.* London: Oxford University Press, 1948.

HAILEY, LORD, *An African Survey.* London: Oxford University Press, 1938.

HELLMANN, E., *Rooiyard: A Sociological Survey of an Urban Native Slum Yard* (Rhodes-Livingstone Papers No. 13). Cape Town: Oxford University Press, 1948.

—— *Handbook on Race Relations in South Africa* (ed). London: Oxford University Press, 1949.

HUNTER, M., *Reaction to Conquest: Effects of Contact with Europeans on the Pondo of South Africa.* London: Oxford University Press, 1936.

INTERNATIONAL LABOUR OFFICE:
   The Recruitment of Labour in the Colonies. Report of the International Labour Conference, Geneva, 1935.

JOHNSTON, H. H., *George Grenfell and the Congo.* London: Hutchinson, 1908.

JONES, N. S. CAREY, 'Native Treasuries in Northern Rhodesia', *Human Problems in British Central Africa*, Rhodes-Livingstone Journal No. ii (1944).

JONES, D. PICTON, *Outline of Ki-Mambwe Grammar, 1893.* Out of print.

KRIGE, E. J. and J. D., *The Realm of a Rain-Queen: A Study of the Pattern of Lovedu Society.* London: Oxford University Press, 1943.

KUPER, H., *The Uniform of Colour: A Study of Black-White Relationships in Swaziland.* Johannesburg: Witwatersrand University Press, 1947.

LEWIS, W. ARTHUR, *The Theory of Economic Growth.* London: Allen and Unwin, 1955.

MACDONALD, R. A. S., *Memorandum on the Economics of the Cattle Industry in Northern Rhodesia, with Special Reference to the Native Cattle Industry.* Lusaka: Government Printer, 1937.

MITCHELL, J. C., 'The Political Organization of the Yao of Southern Nyasaland', *African Studies*, viii (1949).

—— 'Preliminary Notes on Land Tenure and Agriculture Among the Machinga Yao', *Human Problems in British Central Africa*, Rhodes-Livingstone Journal No. x (1950).

—— 'The Yao of Southern Nyasaland', in *Seven Tribes of British Central Africa*, Colson, E., and Gluckman, M., eds. London: Oxford University Press, 1951.

—— *The Yao Village: A Study in the Social Structure of a Nyasaland Tribe.* Manchester: Manchester University Press, 1956.

—— *The Kalela Dance: Aspects of Social Relationships Among Urban Africans in Northern Rhodesia* (Rhodes-Livingstone Papers No. 27). Manchester: Manchester University Press, 1956.

—— (with BARNES, J. A.), *The Lamba Village: Report of a Social Survey* (Communication from the School of African Studies, New Series No. 24). Cape Town: University of Cape Town, 1950.

MOFFAT, U. J., 'Native Agriculture in the Abercorn District', *Second Annual Bulletin of the Department of Agriculture, Northern Rhodesia.* Livingstone: Government Printer, 1932.

McCulloch, M., *A Social Survey of the African Population of Livingstone* (Rhodes-Livingstone Papers No. 26). Manchester: Manchester University Press, 1956.

Niddrie, D., 'The Road to Work: A Survey of the Influence of Transport on Migrant Labour in Central Africa', *Human Problems in British Central Africa*, Rhodes-Livingstone Journal No. xv (1954).

Northern Rhodesia, Government of:

Annual Report, Department of Agriculture. Lusaka: Government Printer, 1938–52.

Colonial Annual Report, Northern Rhodesia. Lusaka: Government Printer, 1946, 1952.

Census of Population, 1921. Lusaka: Government Printer.

Northern Rhodesia Government Gazette. Lusaka: Government Printer, June 1952.

General List of Chiefs. Lusaka: Government Printer, 1943.

Annual Report of African Affairs for the Northern Province, 1952. Kasama.

Order in Council (Crown Lands and Native Reserves) 1928.

Native Authorities Ordinance (1929 and 1936).

Native Courts Ordinance (1929 and 1936).

Cattle (Slaughter) Control Ordinance 1949.

Employment of Women, Young Persons and Children Ordinance 1949.

Padmore, G., *Africa: Britain's Third Empire*. London: Dennis Dobson, 1949.

Peters, D. U., *Land Usage in Serenje District* (Rhodes-Livingstone Papers No. 19). London: Oxford University Press, 1950.

Prain, R. L., 'The Stabilization of Labour in the Rhodesian Copper Belt', *African Affairs*, lv (1956).

Read, M., *Native Standards of Living and African Culture Change*. London: International African Institute, 1938.

—— 'Migrant Labour in Africa and Its Effects on Tribal Life', *International Labour Review*, xlv (1942).

Redford, A., *Labour Migration in England, 1800–1850*. Manchester: Manchester University Press, 1926.

Richards, A. I., 'Mother-Right among the Central Bantu', in *Essays Presented to C. G. Seligman*, E. E. Evans-Pritchard and others, eds. London: Kegan Paul, 1934.

—— 'Tribal Government in Transition', *Journal of the Royal African Society*, xxxiv (1935).

—— *Land, Labour, and Diet in Northern Rhodesia*. London: Oxford University Press, 1939.

—— *Bemba Marriage and Present Economic Conditions* (Rhodes-Livingstone Papers No. 4). Lovedale Press, 1940.

—— 'Some Types of Family Structure among the Central Bantu', in *African Systems of Kinship and Marriage*, A. R. Radcliffe-Brown, C. Daryll Forde, eds. London: Oxford University Press, 1950.

Schapera, I., 'Present-Day Life in the Native Reserves' in *Western Civilization and the Natives of South Africa*, Schapera, I., ed. London: Routledge, 1934.

—— *Native Land Tenure in the Bechuanaland Protectorate*. Alice: Lovedale Press, 1943.

SCHAPERA, I., *Migrant Labour and Tribal Life: A study of conditions in the Bechuanaland Protectorate*. London: Oxford University Press, 1947.

SHEDDICK, V., *Land Tenure in Basutoland*. London: H.M.S.O., 1954.

SHEPPERSON, G., 'The Politics of African Church Separatist Movements in British Central Africa, 1892–1916', *Africa*, xxiv (1954).

STEWART, J., 'Lake Nyasa and the Water Route to the Lake Region of Africa', *Proceedings of the Royal Geographical Society*, iii (1881).

STROUP, H. H., *The Jehovah's Witnesses*. New York: Columbia University Press, 1945.

SUNDKLER, B. G. M., *Bantu Prophets in South Africa*. London: Lutterworth Press, 1948.

THOMSON, J. MOFFAT, *Memorandum on the Native Tribes and Tribal Areas of Northern Rhodesia*. Livingstone: Government Printer, 1934.

TRAPNELL, C. G., *The Soils, Vegetation and Agriculture of North-Eastern Rhodesia*. Lusaka: Government Printer, 1943.

WALLER, H., *The Last Journals of David Livingstone in Central Africa from 1865 to his Death*. London: John Murray, 1874.

WATSON, W., 'The Kaonde Village', *Human Problems in British Central Africa*, Rhodes-Livingstone Journal No. xv (1954).

WHITE FATHERS, *Bemba-English Dictionary*. Chilubula, 1947.

B. *Additional works which give some information concerning the Mambwe and their country*

ELTON, J. F., *Travel and Researches among the Lakes and Mountains of Eastern and Central Africa*. London: Murray, 1897.

FRAZER, SIR JAMES (ed. Downie, R. A.), *The Native Races of Africa and Madagascar*. London: Lund Humphries, 1932.

GIRAUD, V., *Les Lacs de L'Afrique Equatoriale*. Paris: Librairie Hachette, 1890.

GOULDSBURY, C., *An African Year*. London: Edward Arnold, 1912.

MOIR, F. L. H., *After Livingstone*. London: Hodder and Stoughton, 1923.

MORS, O., 'Some Notes on Marriage among the Mambwe', *Anthropos*, xli–xliv (1946–1949).

SWANN, A. J., *Fighting the Slavehunters in Central Africa*. London: Seeley, Service & Co., 1910.

THOMSON, J., *To the Central African Lakes and Back*. London: Sampson Low, 1881.

INDEX